CELEBRATE!
Holidays, Puppets and Creative Drama

Tamara Hunt and Nancy Renfro

Illustrations by L.D. Sears

TAMARA ROBIN HUNT, PH.D. is a professor of Drama at The University of Hawaii where she teaches a course in Children's Theatre, Creative Drama, and Puppetry and supervises the graduate program. As a director of plays for young audiences, Dr. Hunt specializes in programming for preschoolers and originated *Mo'olelo Ki'i Lima* ("to tell the stories with the hands"), a puppet show that annually tours the State of Hawaii. Dr. Hunt resides in Honolulu with her husband John, a professor of Genetics at The University of Hawaii Medical School, and their son Ian and daughter Tara.

NANCY RENFRO lives in Austin, Texas, with her architect husband, Robert Terry Renfro and menagerie of animals. She started the firm, Nancy Renfro Studios, in which creative concepts are adapted to classroom and library use. Her primary interest is to see education and creativity merge; she believes in the individual as a creative entity and incorporates this premise in her unique puppetry products, books and lectures.

DEDICATION

For

My sister Jody and my brother Kip
with whom
I shared so many joyful holidays

Tamara Hunt

For my brothers Bobby and Paul
and their families

Nancy Renfro

ACKNOWLEDGEMENTS

I would like to express my appreciation to the people who helped create this book. I am indebted to Naomi Okuma at Kahala Elementary school for making me feel so welcome in her library. Also to Janet Look and Valerie Carvalho at Aina Haina Elementary School for opening their classrooms for me to test ideas and photograph the children.

My deepest appreciation must go to my mother and father, Max and Jeannette Miller, for giving me a home where holidays always happened in warmth and splendor. And to my sister Jody and brother Kip for without them I couldn't have shared the crazy times of eating too much, giggling 'til goofy, and peeking at our presents.

Now that I am an adult with my own home, I see the joyful traditions anew with my own Hawaiian family. My husband John, son Ian and daughter Tara have all helped to keep the fun and frolic of holiday times so alive that I couldn't help but want to participate in writing this book.

In closing I thank my collaborator Nancy Renfro who shares my enthusiasm for celebrating life as if everyday were a holiday!

Dr. Tamara Hunt
University of Hawaii

To Tammy Hunt, who presented me with my first Lei and introduced me to Hawaii's (and her own special) celebrated spirit.

Nancy Renfro

With special thanks to:

- *Ann Weiss Schwalb* for serving as chief editor and consultant over the years for our many books, including this one. Also for contributing material for the Jewish holidays.
- *Marilyn Jorgenson,* for gathering data for the International holidays.
- *Laurie Stephens* for helping us compile and organize the bibliographies.
- *Georgia Bori* and *Solomon Schoekler Day School* for assisting with data for the Jewish holidays.

See back for other books published by Nancy Renfro Studios

Copyright© 1987 Tamara Hunt and Nancy Renfro
all rights reserved

photographs by Tamara Hunt

The author, however, grants permission for patterns, drawings and scripts shown in this book to be reproduced by the individual teacher for use in **non-profit** puppet activities in the classroom, church, library, theater or recreational areas. No part of this publication may be reproduced or transmitted in any form or means in quantity (electronic mechanical, photocopying, recording or by an information storage or retrieval system) for any other purpose without the written permission from Nancy Renfro Studios. Individuals desiring to use excerpts from this book may request permission for quantity type distribution for instructional type workshops or other similar, non profit purposes.

ISBN 0-931044-09-X

Published in the United States of America by
Nancy Renfro Studios
1117 W. 9th Street, Austin, Texas 78703
Tel: (512)472-2140

TABLE OF CONTENTS

SECTION I—TECHNIQUES

SECTION II—GENERAL HOLIDAYS

SECTION III—INTERNATIONAL HOLIDAYS

SECTION IV—BIBLIOGRAPHIES & RESOURCES

A Halloween Bag Habitat makes a happy home for a witch and ghost

INTRODUCTION

Everyone carries with them special memories of holidays past. Most of these memories begin in childhood. How many Halloween costumes can you remember? What favorite food did you eat every July 4th picnic? Perhaps your memories are of Easter egg hunts or the annual May Day celebrations at school? Whatever they are, holidays are impressionable events in the lives of young children. Traditional treats, surprise gifts, family gatherings all make their seasonal calendar meaningful. In fact, everyone, young and old alike, loves a holiday.

Dancing through the cycle of the year's holidays and celebrations, the authors have used puppetry and creative dramatics to host and help celebrate these special red-letter days. The book's focus is on holidays celebrated in the United States, mainly national and some religious, with an eye toward how *all* children can enjoy them, regardless of national origin or ethnic group. New Year's and May Day can help create a sense of the passage of time over a calendar year, as well as awareness of seasonal change. What better way to find out about spring than from Mr. Groundhog or the Passover Seder. Such events as Presidents Day and Martin Luther King's Birthday can serve as springboards for learning about values, such as honor and courage, as well as historical events. Through puppets, other cultures and folk legends of other coun-

tries can be highlighted as children follow the antics of St. Patrick outwitting a snake on St. Patrick's Day or participate in a snapping dragon dance during Chinese New Year.

A mixed bag of International Holidays is also included in the book's finale. The author's initial vision of the book was to include a holiday example from every major country in the world. However, upon setting to task, it was quickly discovered that the plan was an overly ambitious one. Instead, it was decided to settle on a random cross section, mainly to show possibilities with the hope that the teacher will adapt and customize ideas to fit specific holiday needs of other cultures. For instance, many countries celebrate similar holidays as those indicated in this chapter—harvest time, cycles of the moon, coming of spring, or the New Year.

We have also tried to keep in mind a variety of individual needs and group situations to allow flexibility with respect to time, budget, resources, space, and other considerations. Both simple and complex activities have been included to accommodate the interest and abilities of children between the ages from preschool through age ten.

So, put a puppet in your pocket and create a holiday glow that will spark your children all year long—and add memories that will last them a lifetime.

HOW TO USE THIS BOOK

The activities presented in this book are designed to celebrate the holidays, customs and traditions of America's people and to enrich children's knowledge of these holidays through artistic and dramatic curricular experiences. Several types of puppetry activities have been included. Some are quick and simple, taking an hour or so to complete. Others are more complicated and take several periods or longer. A great many patterns are included throughout the book. These are provided mainly to serve as teachers' visuals when presenting stories and poems for children, or instances when time is a limited factor. The authors, however, feel that children in general should be encouraged to create their own designs and spin-offs as much as possible, to stretch their creative potentials.

Each holiday presentation includes a variety of ideas and activities from which to choose that can be tailored into schedule and objectives. Activities may fall under the following categories:

Scene Setters include ideas for murals and mood enhancers to generate excitement about the holiday. Puppets created in conjunction with scene setters can be used for display as well as incorporated into later activities. Murals can also serve as backdrops for puppet shows.

Story Starters are a challenging way to encourage creative thinking and let the imagination run free. These activities fall comfortably under the language arts umbrella and can offer a new way to teach plot and character. Children especially enjoy putting on puppet shows based upon their stories.

Puppet Projects are quick, easy to make activities which can be incorporated into a busy school schedule. Most of the projects have accompanying dramatic activities. Others may serve as art projects where children simply construct the puppets and take them home. Ideas run the gamut from story aprons to full body puppets; mini-theaters with finger puppets to overhead shadow stories.

Feature Story Presentations are means of bringing literature to life by casting puppet characters and dramatizing the story, either informally or as a formal, scripted, puppet show.

When possible, stimulate interest in the activity and how it relates to the holiday. Discussing the holiday symbols and their meanings or asking children what their families do to celebrate a special day are some general ways to begin. For a special project, focus on the specific poem, story or song to help clarify events or create interest. You might ask: "Who can tell me what a groundhog looks like?" A photograph of a green, grassy Ireland might help children understand why green is the color of Saint Patrick's Day. A discussion of the colors of the American Flag might generate curiosity and interest in the symbols behind Independence Day.

Additional Book Ideas

There are innumerable, excellent holiday books which adapt well to puppetry. A selected list has been included in each holiday section to enlarge choice of activities. Each book includes a story synopsis and an idea for activity development. It is hoped the teacher will experiment and take liberties to adapt, expand or interchange ideas with other book selections.

SHARING HOLIDAYS

Exhibits

One way of sharing your puppetry activities is through exhibits in the principal's office or through the school and community library. You might even suggest an exchange exhibit with a school library other than your own. Puppets can be hung on clotheslines dangled from the ceiling or perched over weighted plastic bottles on shelves. Exhibits work especially well with small self-contained box style puppet theaters, accompanied by a short story or plot synopsis. Scene setters such as murals can be easily hung in hallways to set a holiday mood.

School Assembly

Holidays are usually a time for school assemblies and the sharing of holiday songs. Why not fashion puppets from song characters like Rudolph, Peter Cottontail and the like? Large body puppets as found under the President's Day section, can be used to read a speech, or dramatize a Hanukkah story. Consider presenting Overhead Shadow Shows as found in the Halloween section. The overhead projector is a bonus for the auditorium for it lends itself well to large audiences.

Share a Show

Give a holiday gift to the school by inviting other classes to your room to see a puppet show. The entire presentation, if limited to fifteen minutes, should not be too difficult for other teachers to fit into their daily schedules, and still short enough to maintain the interest of the guest audiences. This shared presentation can also be an excellent means of introducing children to some lesser known ethnic holidays.

Tour a Show

Small groups of selected children or special classes may find it rewarding to take their puppet shows into the community to perform at day care or senior citizen centers, together with neighboring district schools. A touring program requires considerable administrative support, as well as cooperation from other teachers who must be willing to dismiss students from regular classroom activities in order for them to participate. In addition, parents, may need to be tapped to provide car transportation and safety supervision. Despite the logistical problems, a touring show can be very beneficial to the participants themselves, as well as the audiences, and exemplify creative education at its best.

Involve the Family

Many parents, grandparents and older siblings may have talents which can be mobilized during holiday seasons. Parents with typing skills could be asked to type scripts; carpenters build holiday stages, which painters then decorate; seamstresses sew stage curtains and costumes; knitters knit yarn wigs; musicians record background music. Most parents would be delighted to make a small time contribution to a classroom project. However, the success of your requests will depend upon how an approach to the family is made. The traditional "check off sheet" carried home by the child is simply not enough. First, ask the children what special talents their family members have which might be helpful to a puppet show. Then call the parents, grandparents, siblings, etc. with your list of requests and special needs. Although it is more time consuming than a generalized memo, your personal approach will not only elicit more postive results, but it will also afford you an opportunity to speak to the family members about what you are doing in the class. They might have some other suggestions or talents which you never would have known to tap.

Share the Secret of Your Success

Once you have had a successful experience in puppetry, share your insights with other teachers. Offer to do an in-service workshop to demonstrate your puppet making techniques. Every school and every situation is unique. If you have been successful in your own teaching environment, then you have the knowledge and skills to contribute to your own faculty which an outsider, no matter how famous or talented, cannot offer in quite the same way. Share what you've learned and encourage other teachers to get involved. Who knows? You may turn your school into a lively, thriving, creative puppet center.

Invite the Press

Puppets and children are a magical combination. They provide perfect subjects for newspaper photographs and irresistible, lively segments for television cameras. The press can be alerted to good media possibilities by first mailing them a press release and then, several days later, following up with a phone call to clarify details and answer questions—theirs or your own. Your press release should give the date, school address, brief description of what's happening, as well as the name and phone number of who to contact for further information. The children will love seeing themselves on television, the administrators will feel proud to read in the paper about innovative programs taking place in their schools, and you will get a well-deserved boost for your accomplishments.

PUPPET MAKING

Amidst the ongoing necessities of lesson plans, grading assignments, attending meetings, serving on committees, contacting parents, writing reports and other miscellaneous tasks, you may wonder how to squeeze in time to make puppets. Holidays are the perfect place to start. As holidays approach, schedules become more relaxed, with diversions from regular routines benefiting all. Set aside some special time in celebration of a custom, tradition, or religious belief. The benefit (not to mention the charm) of introducing puppets at this time will eventually win over those who doubt the value of this effort in classroom time and energy.

The Construction Center

Making puppets requires the same kind of organization as does involvement in any art project—a space, tools, supplies. If a school is large enough to have an art room, then you may be able to unsurp a special corner for puppetry supplies. Generally speaking, however, it is easier to keep the construction materials in your own classroom where tools can be left and are then easily obtainable. Puppet construction can occur on the children's desk tops or on special tables set aside where small groups can work during free time. Individual boxes can be prepared for each major holiday containing special supplies for that holiday, such as green and red fabric scraps for Christmas and black and orange yarn, paper and trims for Halloween. Ask children to contribute to these boxes long before holiday time, by sending home a photocopy of a Wish List, specific to the holiday needs.

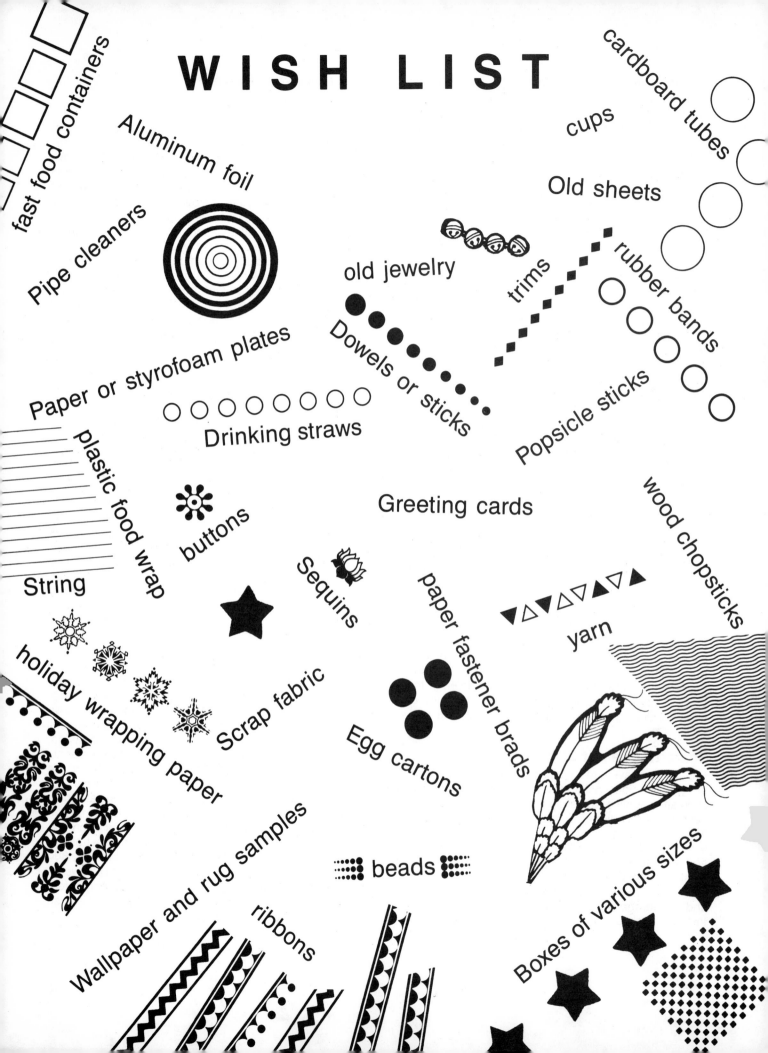

Every puppetmaking activity in this book includes a special list of key materials required to do that particular project. These vary from activity to activity. Have on hand some of the following basic materials for puppetmaking activities:

Tape—masking cellophane
Glue—white glue, glue sticks, rubber cement, paste
Tape—masking cellophane
Construction Paper—assorted colors
Cardboard—posterboard, oak-tag
Coloring Media—pencils, crayons, felt-tipped marker pens, tempera paint
Brushes—small, medium, large sizes
Fabrics and Felt—assosorted textures and types

PRESENTATION IDEAS

You might wish to add some of the following ideas to enhance holiday presentation.

All Year Round Puppet

A basic puppet can be improvised for year round use, with the addition of seasonal costumes and hats. Cut out and color the Basic S/he Puppet pattern that follow. This versatile puppet can be used with a fashionable holiday wardrobe for adapting to year round activities. Some hats and basic costumes are included also, to be attached paper doll fashions.

Story Apron

An apron with oversized pockets is perfect for concealing puppets, props and other surprises. Children will delight in seeing tails, dangling feet and eyes peering out of the tops of pockets. The Story Apron also signals to them that a story session is about to begin. Although any type of apron will suffice, as long as pockets are provided, a chef or carpenter-style apron is especially suitable for the poems in this book. The Scenic Panel can be attached to the bib section of the apron by means of buttons or Velcro pieces. Consider purchasing a ready-made chef or carpenter style apron. Restaurant suppliers, hardware stores, mail order catalogs or the kitchenware section in department stores offer intriguing varieties. Or, you might wish to purchase a ready-made colorful apron from Nancy Renfro Studios, tailor made for puppet telling. If you decide to make an apron of your own, instructions and pattern are included below. Experiment with a thematic holiday apron to enhance a specific application such as a foliage print for Arbor Day or red, white and blue for Independence Day. Or design an all purpose apron with five thematic pockets of favorite holidays, plus a sixth with a question mark for presenting other holidays, year round.

The addition of a lapboard can be used in conjunctins with the apron. This simple board is used primarily as a "stage" for your lap, upon which to rest a book or stand up puppets or props. Simply cover a rectangle of 12 inch by 18 inch cardboard with a piece of felt or contact paper, and you're ready to go!

Some apron guidelines follow:

Basic Butcher Apron—To make a basic butcher apron use denim, muslin or other heavyweight cotton fabric. Tape two large sheets of newspaper together and fold in half. Draw a shape as shown, following measurements indicated. Cut shape out and open up pattern. Cut a fabric apron and hem a 1/4″ hem around all edges.

Attach a neck ribbon (grosgrain or other) to neck; also ribbon ties to apron sides as shown.

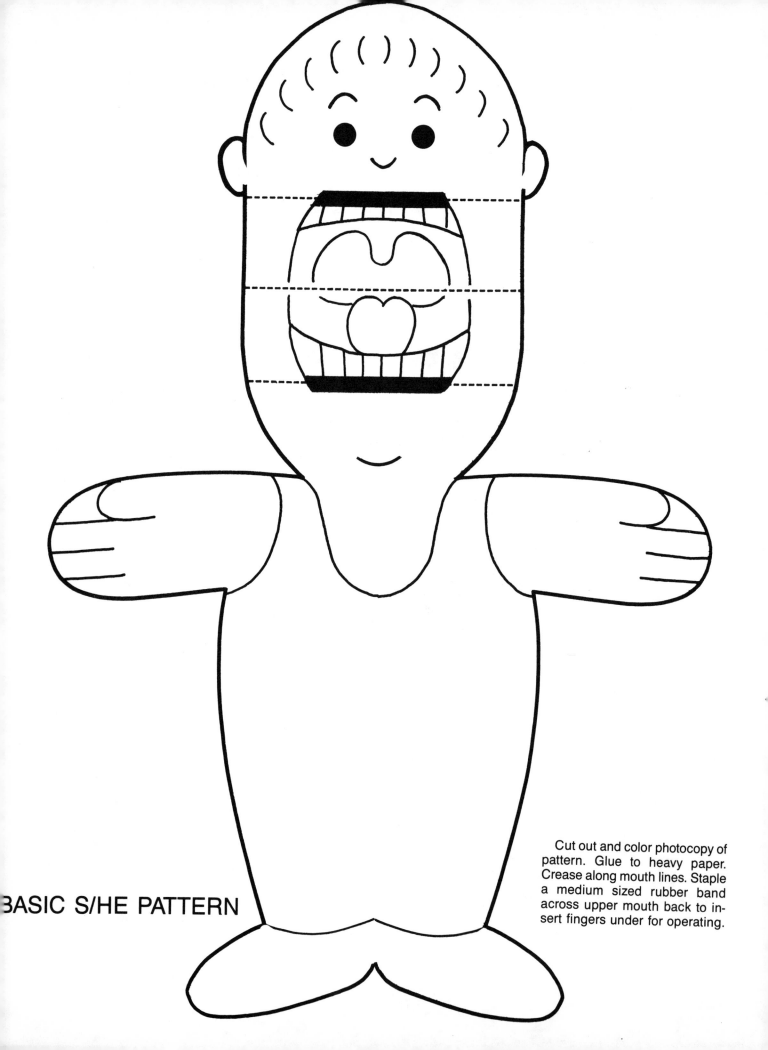

Cut out and color photocopy of
pattern. Glue to heavy paper.
Crease along mouth lines. Staple
a medium sized rubber band
across upper mouth back to insert fingers under for operating.

BASIC S/HE PATTERN

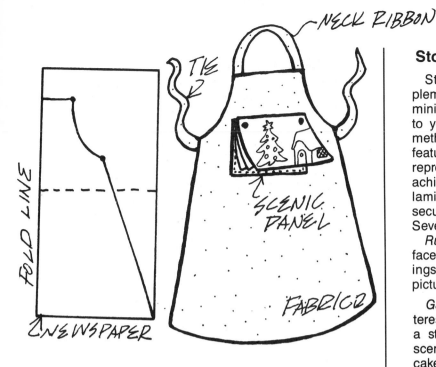

Apron with Changing Scenery—Interchangeable, colored 11″ by 11″ Pellon scenery panels can be arranged in sequential order and buttoned in place onto the upper edge of a 12″ × 12″ pocket, sewn to apron front. As each scene is finished, simply flip it up and back and tuck it into the pocket.

Poncho Apron—This unusual apron adapts well to all holidays since it easily represents the four seasons. It is a large circular segmented piece of fabric with a head hole located in center. Paint (with fabric pens) or applique designs, as shown, or create your own seasonal backgrounds.

Story Gloves

Story Gloves and finger puppets make ideal complements for poems, stories or other narratives. The miniaturization of the characters particularly appeals to young children and gives the leader a flexible method of presentation. A number of presentations feature paper finger puppet patterns, which can be reproduced, colored and cut out. Permanency can be achieved by covering with clear contact paper or laminating with plastic. Once complete, they can be secured to a glove or fingertips with double stick tape. Several glove possibilities are:

Rubber Household Glove—Provides a smooth surface for adhering small format images, such as drawings, photographs, greeting cards, or magazine pictures.

Garden Glove—Garden gloves come in an interesting variety of designs and colors, while making a sturdy glove for all around use. Changing felt scenery (such as a menorah, pumpkin or birthday cake) can be easily attached to the palm area of glove by means of velcro or a button.

Pellon Glove—Make a basic glove from heavyweight Pellon (interlining fabric). Use marker pens to color a scenic background, such as a winter wonderland or spring garden. Paper images can be attached to the glove tips by means of paper clips. Open up the paper clip slightly, and glue or tape clip to back of image. Cut a crosswise slit on each glove tip about 1/3 inch down to insert the paper clip through.

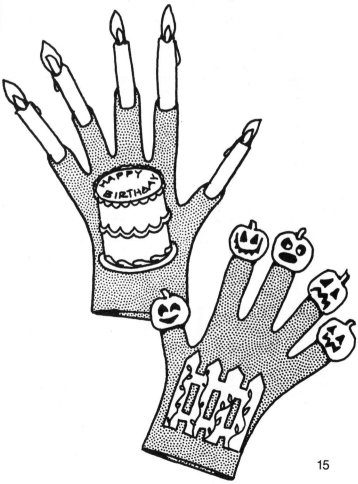

15

Cup and Container Theaters

Individualized theaters made from paper cups or cut down food boxes are intriguing visuals to depict holiday themes. Children can make their own mobile theater. Once completed, theaters can be brought home as a memory of the puppet experience. Tape a small drawing or picture (magazine, greeting card, or other) to end of a drinking straw; slip other end of straw through hole punctured in bottom of container. Attach scenic suggestions to edge of container and decorate exterior to match story theme.

SEDER PLATE

Paper Bag Holiday Habits

This habitat is quick to make and is suitable for matching with puppet characters. Small bags can be used with finger puppets while large bags serve hand puppets well. A large grocery bag provides an excellent surface for painting and pasting activities. The bag can easily be transformed into a bat's cave or witch's house (Halloween), tree (Arbor Day) or mailbox (Valentine's Day). The children can make envelope, paper plate or other type puppets to accompany the habitats, using basic construction techniques described elsewhere in this book.

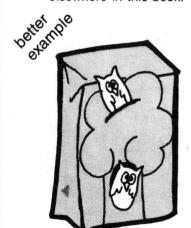

better example

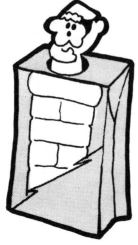

Peek-A-Boo Theater

Peek-a-Boo Theaters are especially appropriate for young children who revel in peek-a-boo games and hide 'n seek. Christopher Columbus peeking out a ship's porthole, ghost out of a haunted house or chick out of an egg are intriguing ideas to explore with young children. Make a design on a panel cut from poster board or other stiff cardboard. Choose appealing locations in the panel from which to cut out holes, such as under the water, in the sky, or inside a tree. The panels can be covered with clear contact paper or laminated in plastic for permanency. Finger puppets are ideally suited to this technique. You may wish to improvise some additional finger puppet characters of your own, as previously described, to suit the specific holiday applications.

Greeting Card Puppets

Save used holiday greeting cards. The marketplace abounds with holiday cards, making available instant images for puppet use. Ask children to bring in cards from home to augment the classroom supply.

Cut out pictures from favorite cards and attach them to drinking straws or other rods for simple puppet plays around holiday themes. Pictures may be laminated with clear plastic for durability. Pictures also can be easily adhered to rubber household gloves by means of double-stick tape.

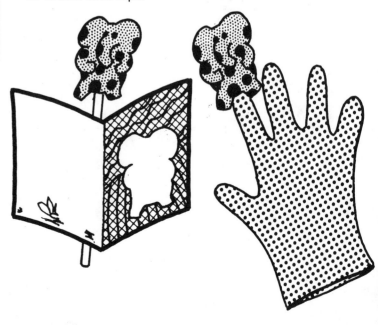

Box Theaters

A small theater can be easily constructed from a grocery carton. This theater can be made available for children to use in their free time with Paper Rod Puppets, maneuvered in front of the box's opening. The box can be placed on a table top or the lap for presentation.

Cut off the entire back and top, upper front and side sections of a carton as shown. Cover walls of carton with contact paper and decorate with drapery trim or other items. Peel away backing of carpeting tape (or other double-stick tape) and secure a strip across top, inside edge of box.

To make puppets, cut out and color imagery from stiff paper. Attach to end of drinking straws. Stick straws onto carpeting tape to make puppets stand in place. When not in use, protect tape by putting backing back in place.

Book Theaters

A storybook itself may provide a natural theater with the front and back covers, as well as interior illustrations furnishing background scenery for presentations. Place the book on a table with the outside covers facing the children. This positioning will allow the storyteller to read the inside text while gliding the Paper Rod Puppets along the top edge of the book.

Puppets can be made from paper cut-outs glued to drinking straws or popsicle sticks. Scenery and props, attached to spring clothespins, may be secured to the top of the book. If you are familiar enough with the story so that the text does not have to be read, then turn the pages of the book toward the children, thus allowing each page to create a different scene. Finger puppets are excellent for use with Book Theaters.

FRONT

CARPETING TAPE

STICK OR STRAW

PERFORMING WITH PUPPETS

The activities in this book are designed for group participation with minimal emphasis placed on the audience. However, there are occasions when a more formal means of presentation may be desirable, where one or several children rehearse and present a puppet show for an audience. The puppet show may be very short, as in a simple presentation of a poem, or longer to encompass a multi-scene story that the children develop based on a special theme or holiday idea. Certain theater conventions should be observed: puppeteers should speak loudly to be heard, and puppets should be both visible and believable.

The audience may consist of peer groups, younger children, or even parents. In a regular classroom situation, presentations can be spread over a week with five or six short segments performed daily. The younger children will usually enjoy several shorter presentations, rather than one very long one.

If you plan to involve the children in performing, there are several guidelines which, when followed, make the experience more successful. Before asking children to perform individually in front of a class, it is advisable to spend several sessions in group activities. In this way, children will be comfortable creating dialogue and will have group opportunities learning to speak loudly and manipulating various puppet types. Since beginning puppeteers sometimes have trouble making effective presentations, it is a good idea for children initially to work in teams so that they may focus on one skill at a time. While one child manipulates the puppets and provides the actions, another can recite the poem or provide narration.

Small groups of older children can be asked to improvise their own poems or stories, developing dialogue and presenting plays to each other or to younger groups. In preparing for this activity, it will be valuable for them to understand theatrical terms such as play, scene, conflict, resolution, dialogue, costumes, sets rehearsal, and performance. For clarity and planning, it is good protocol for them to write out their stories beforehand. However, it is not recommended that they memorize the scripts, line by line. This memorization approach often results in stifled performances since the children become more concerned about forgetting a line than projecting character, voice and action. What is most important is that they have a clear sense of the story line and can follow it, but that they improvise when it will benefit the story, as long as they remain consistent with the agreed upon story line. An excellent book to guide the teacher with puppet shows is *Puppet Shows Made Easy!* by Nancy Renfro Studios.

Staging the Show

Stages for a presentation can be as simple as a turned over table or a piece of fabric attached to a stick extended between two chairs. A more elaborate stage can be made from a large cardboard appliance box (refrigerator, TV, or other). Even though scenery is not necessary, children usually enjoy creating an atmosphere with scenery and are effective when painted on rolls of butcher or mural paper.

Props can be made by the children or brought from home. Assign sound effects to a child in the group who is not otherwise involved during the performance. No matter how simple or elaborate the production, performing with puppets allows children to practice many skills and to participate in a rewarding group venture.

GENERAL HOLIDAYS

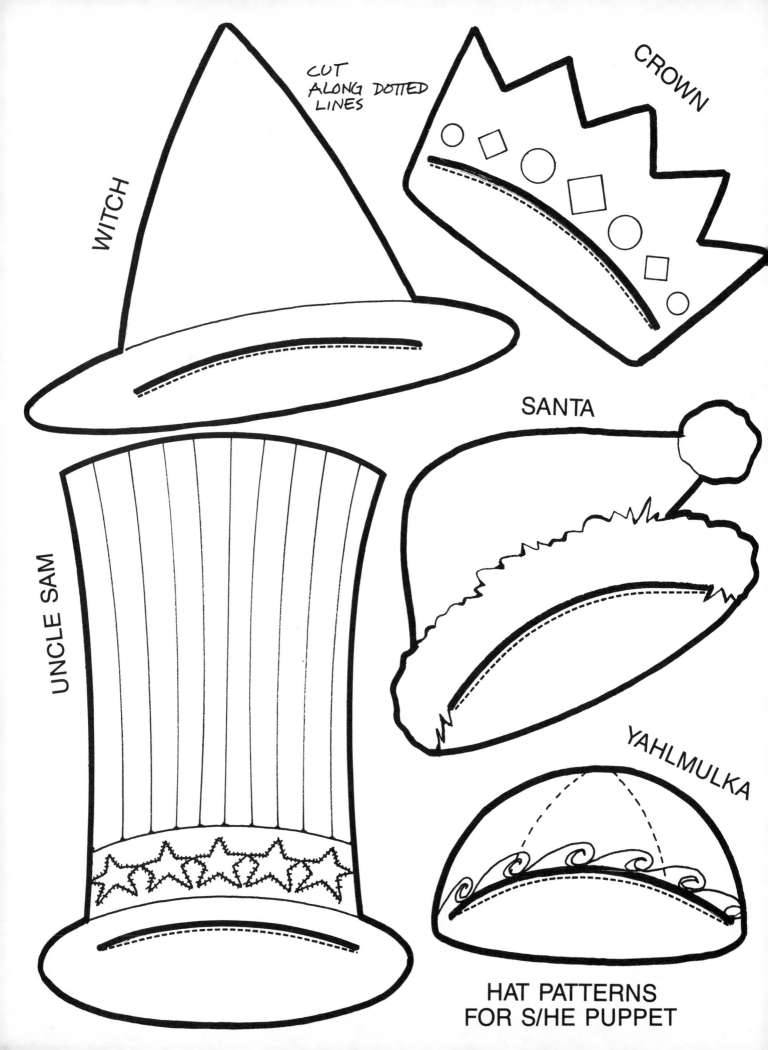

CUT ALONG DOTTED LINES

WITCH

CROWN

SANTA

UNCLE SAM

YAHLMULKA

HAT PATTERNS
FOR S/HE PUPPET

GOODBYE OLD YEAR, HELLO NEW YEAR!

Good-bye old year, hello New Year! Thus begins the rite of passage in which twelve months—or twelve moons for the Chinese—complete their cycle. The endless passage of endless time continues as one cycle is complete at the very moment that the next cycle begins.

A year to a child can seem to be very long, or very short, but the first day of any year is special because it sallies forth with new optimism, unlike optimism possible the rest of the year when reality is factored into the equation of what is possible and what is not. This New Year is an ideal time to have the children share the things of importance that happened to them in the previous year as well as the new resolutions they will pursue in the year to come.

TINY TINA CLOCK PATTERN

TINY TINA TIME TRAVELLER

Tiny Tina is a teeny, tiny person (only three inches tall!), but she is a giant when it comes to thinking big. She has magic powers and can travel through time whenever she wishes. She loves best to travel through an exciting twenty-four hour day. Some days twenty-four lucky things seem to happen to her, while on other days, twenty-four unlucky things happen. Of course she likes the lucky days far better than she does the unlucky ones. But then, as she knows—and we together with her—not all days can be good ones. Using the Tiny Tina puppet pattern that follows, have the group create a lucky or unlucky day in the life of Tiny Tina.

Give each child a sheet of construction paper to write an assigned clock number in the lower right hand corner. If there are under twenty-four children, then some children may be assigned two or more numbers in sequence. Ask each child in the group to draw a lucky or unlucky scene on the rest of the sheet of paper, above the clock number, for Tiny Tina to experience. For example, a lucky scene could show: money scattered on the ground, a race being won, or a super duper ice cream sundae. An unlucky scene might be: a black cat crossing a path, a toy being crushed, or even the TV set going haywire.

When the drawings are completed, they can be tacked to a wall or combined to form a "time sequence" mural. Each child can then take a turn operating a Tiny Tina puppet (refer to instructions that follow) and explaining what lucky or unlucky event is taking place in the drawing s/he created.

TO MAKE A TINY TINA PUPPET

Materials: Photo copy of pattern, heavy paper, paper brad.

Construction: Glue photocopy to heavy paper. Cut out clock and puppet's arms. Attach arms to the center of the clock with a brad, then attach a rod to the back of the clock. Turn the arms to the appropriate time as the child's story is told.

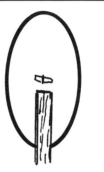 

OLD FATHER TIME'S MARCH

Marching and beating to the rhythm of syncopated sounds is the pacing rhythm of the activity. Divide the class into two groups. One group plays the inner circle of clocks, keeping the rhythm of the tick tock with marching, clapping and/or vocal sounds. The outer group wears Father Time Bodi-Puppets and marches around in an outer and larger circle. Read the poem and use a cymbal or gong to chime the final twelve strokes of midnight. After the line "See my surprise," let the puppeteers surprise everyone by revealing the Baby side of the puppets.

Repeat the poem as children switch roles.

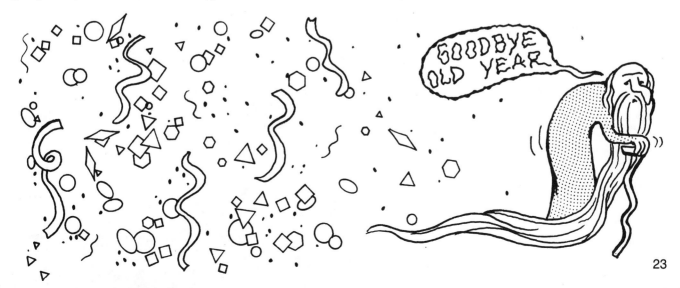

23

OLD FATHER TIME'S MARCH

I'm Old Father Time at the end of the year,
Listen carefully, what do you hear?
  Tick, tock, tick, tock.
  Tick, tock, tick, tock.
I'm marching along to the tune that I play,
Knowing that this is my very last day.
  Tick, tock, tick, tock.
  Tick, tock, tick, tock.
I'm watching the hands on the face of the clock,
Slowly they're moving both to the top.
  Tick, tock, tick, tock.
  Tick, tock, tick, GONG. (Beat 12 on a gong)
It's New Year's Eve ☆ Midnight ☆ First day of the year ☆
See my surprise. The baby is here.
(Repeat poem to lengthen march)

by Tamara Hunt

TO MAKE A
OLD FATHER TIME/BABY PUPPET

Materials: 2 paper plates, cardboard, white paper, newspaper or cotton, coloring media, string, scissors.

Construction: Attach two paper plates together as shown. Add arms. On one side draw a baby, on the other side draw an up-side-down old man. Use white paper for diaper and fringed newspaper or cotton for old man's flowing beard. Attach string to puppet arms and tie around child's neck. The length of the string should allow the puppet to rest on child's chest.

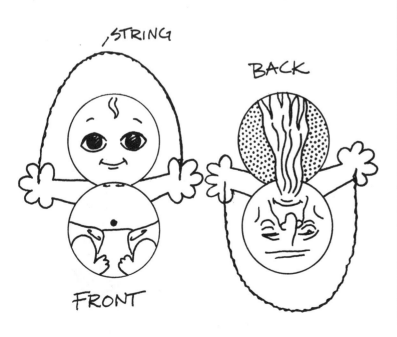

24   Old Father Time Paper-Plate Puppet

OLD MRS. WEATHER

Old Mrs. Weather is a very strange woman,
She changes her costume whenever she can,
She likes to be sneaky, just look at the sky,
You cannot predict her, even if you try.

I've seen her in autumn. She's dressed as the wind,
Blowing cool breezes and making leaves spin.

I've seen her in winter. She wears silver white,
Dancing with snowflakes in frosty delight.

I've seen her in springtime. She comes as raindrops,
Sprinkling on flowers and umbrella tops.

I've seen her in summer. She's gold as the sun,
Sending down sunshine to warm everyone.

Old Mrs. Weather is a very tricky woman.
She brings me surprises whenever she can.

By Tamara Hunt

A seasonal poem and Old Mrs. Weather paper puppet can be used to discuss how weather changes with each season and its effect on us. Use the basic paper puppet pattern found in chapter one to create an old woman (add cotton hair). This particular old woman has a collection of very "mod" and flashy dresses (one for each season) that can be attached, paper doll fashion, to the puppet's body. Change the dresses to match seasons as the poem is recited.

TO MAKE DRESSES FOR OLD MRS. WEATHER

Materials: Photocopy of S/he Basic Puppet (see section one), photocopies of 4 dresses.

Construction: Cut out along bold lines of patterns and color. Fold tabs back to attach to Old Mrs. Weather. Decorate each dress with motifs to match its season. For example: winter—snowflakes, spring—flowers, summer—suns and butterflies, fall—golden leaves.

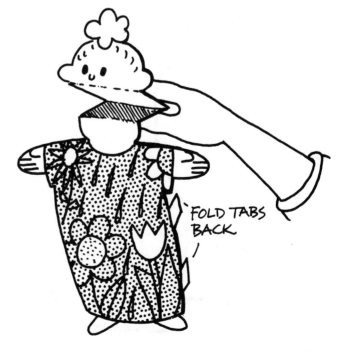

FOLD TABS BACK

25

DRESS PATTERNS

ALL YEAR LONG NEW YEAR'S THEATER

This mini, off Broadway theater presents shows all year long. It features changing seasonal scenery in which children star in their own mini reviews. Each child can create a theater from a pudding box and make a "self" puppet. The scenic strip designating four seasons makes easily changeable background to facilitate children's acting out or verbalizing whatever they wish, particularly the things the child enjoys doing each season.

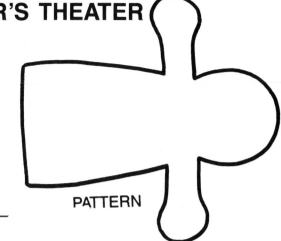

PATTERN

TO MAKE A MINI-THEATER AND SELF-PUPPET

Materials: 4-1/2 oz. pudding box, photocopy of Self-Puppet pattern, ice cream stick, one sheet 12″ × 18″ colored construction paper.

Construction: Cut away entire front side of box for stage opening. Cut slits along each end and bottom of box as shown. Cut four 3″ strips of paper from four different seasonal colored papers (fall—gold, winter—white, spring—green, summer—yellow) and draw appropriate details of each season on each strip. Glue or tape sequential seasons together and insert through slits at ends of the box. Glue or tape ends together to make a continuous loop. Cut out and color details on self-puppet and attach to the ice cream stick. Insert stick into a slit cut along "stage floor" area of box. Slide puppet back and forth for movement.

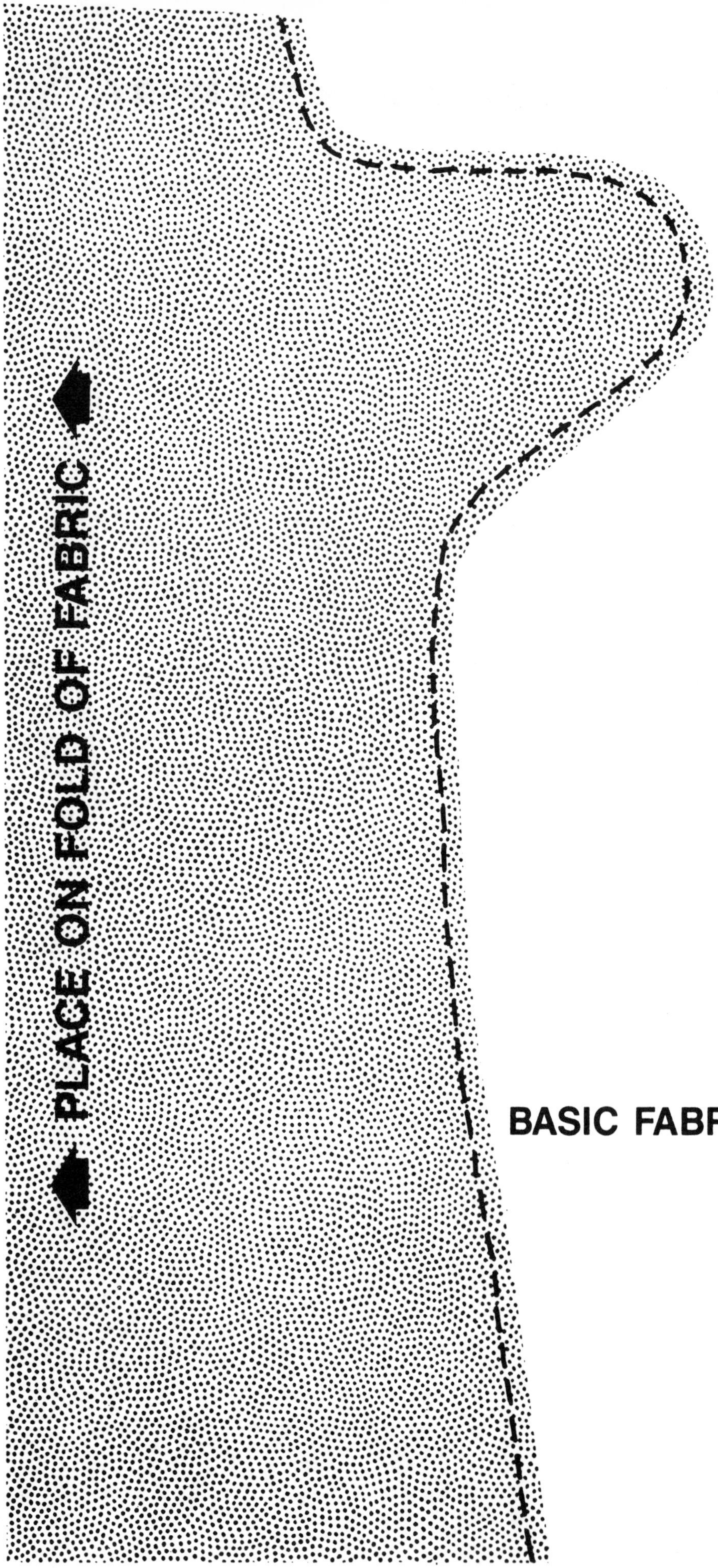

PLACE ON FOLD OF FABRIC

BASIC FABRIC BODY PATTERN

THE PEACEFUL WARRIOR

"I say to you today, my friends, that in spite of the difficult times and frustrations of the moment, I still have a dream. It is a dream deeply rooted in the American dream.

I have a dream that my four little children will one day live in a nation where they will not be judged by the color of their skin, but by the content of their characters.

I have a dream today."[1]

Martin Luther King, Jr. was often, appropriately termed, the Peaceful Warrior. He was a man of many dreams. His ancestry goes back through a history of slavery and sharecropping.

But he was fortunate in that his father, Martin Luther King, Sr. had already paved a better life and environment for young Martin to grow up in. Both senior and junior became pastors and wanted to help better the lives of their people.

Martin Luther King, Jr. born on January 15, 1929.[2], showed early promise as a studious student and possessed a superb choir voice as well as he often sang, with pride, many solos in various churches. He grew up with a personality that reflected a peaceable, loving and non-violent nature, even in an environment that may have encouraged violence. He became an inspiration to his people as he recognized that Black Americans were still not free and lived a lonely island of poverty. He helped them fight peacefully for equality, asking them to "march ahead," and not to turn back. With this philosophy came the many civil rights marches that symbolized his teachings at the time.

[1] Excerpt from speech, "I Have a Dream," by Martin Luther King, Jr.
[2] Martin Luther King, Jr. was born January 15, 1929. The official national holiday date, however, is set for the third Monday of January.

29

I HAVE A DREAM

Share with the group the life, work and beliefs of Martin Luther King, Jr. and what it means to help other people. For older children, read parts of his original famed speech "I Have a Dream" and discuss various points of interest. Ask the children to imagine something great that they would do to help the world be a better place. Have them write a short "Dream" speech for a Stuffed Bag Puppet to present to the group.

"I have a dream" topic suggestions:

Save the whales
Help endangered species
End war
Make all people friends
End world hunger

The addition of cardboard or real props (such as a whale for save the whales, or smoke stack for prevent pollution) may be used to emphasize a point.

TO MAKE A STUFFED BAG PUPPET

Materials: Small or medium sized paper bag, newspaper, short cardboard tube, construction paper, fabric, yarn and trim.

Construction: Tightly stuff a paper bag with crumpled newspaper until nearly full. Insert and glue a cardboard tube up neck of bag. Tightly gather the opening of bag and wrap masking tape around it to secure. Add paper features, egg carton eyes, yarn hair and other details.

Add a fabric body. Using pattern provided, cut out two pieces. Sew side seams, right sides together; turn right sides out. Hem bottom. Glue neck opening to tube neck.

NO NUKES

—TAPE

REFER TO PAGE 28 FOR BODY PATTERN

TREE-WORLD

Weeping willow, sweet-smelling pine, billowing apple, mighty oak—the tree world in all its diversity and mignificence surrounds us in our daily lives, yet we often take it for granted. To a child, however, a tree is something special, a friendly embracing creature to climb and hide, finding repose in its shade. The rich variety of trees around the nation and around the globe is a marvelous pivot upon which to rotate a puppet project. More than ever, this is the time in which a respect and appreciation for trees, especially in view of the trees' rapidly declining numbers and critical need for future nature preservation.

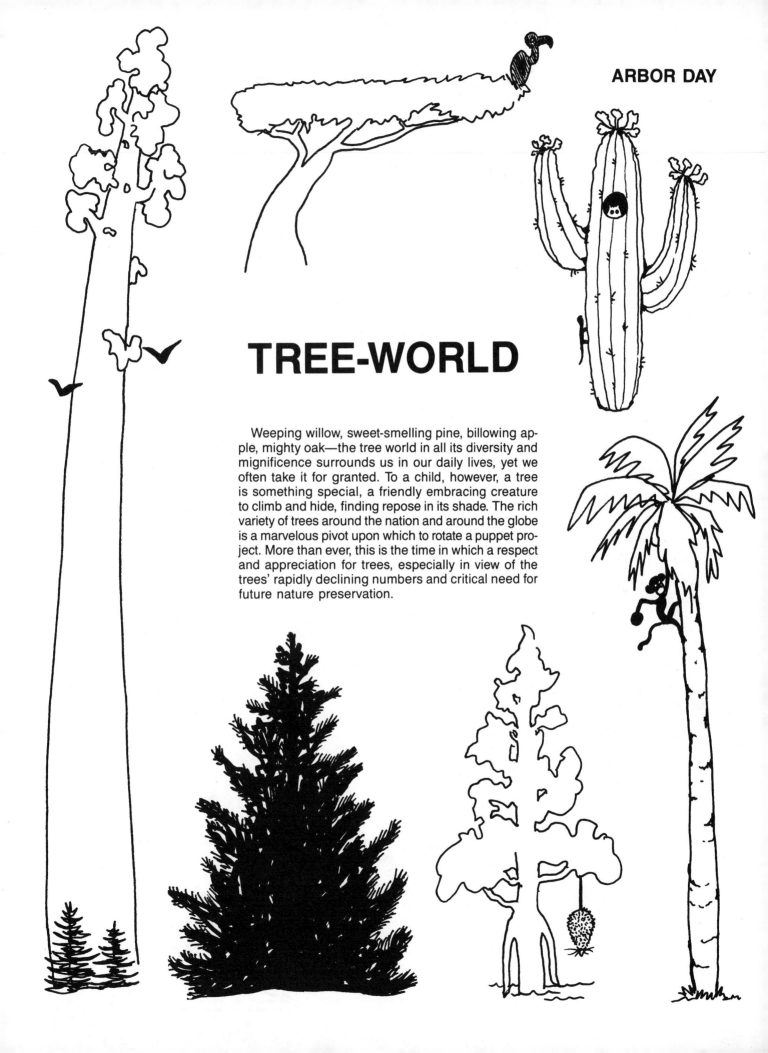

TREES GROW EVERYWHERE

Trees can be a fitting introduction for studying diverse geographical areas around the world. Divide the group into teams and ask teams to research the trees that grow in different areas such as the mountains, meadows, deserts, jungles, rain forests or islands. Cover the walls of the classroom with colored construction paper and group teams into geographical sections to paste the trees of their region. Paper puppet creatures of wildlife that live in these trees can be cut out and glued to a craft stick and then slipped into little slits in the trees. A chattering monkey or parrot in a South American jungle, sluggish sloth in an Australian forest or fierce tiger on an African plain's scrub will add lively focus to the project.

Upon completion, certain grade levels can celebrate Tree-Worlds by visiting "Open House" classrooms and hearing talks or viewing skits of each classroom's Trees.

WHO LIVES IN A TREE

Who lives in a tree?
Owl! Winks at me.

Who lives in a hive?
Bees! Buzz, buzz alive.

Who lives in a nest?
Birds! They coo and rest.

Who lives in the hole?
Funny little mole.

by Tamara Hunt

A tree makes a welcoming resting place for an assortment of companionable woodsy animal tenants. The Tree Home Puppet shown here is a fine novelty item with action parts to enhance the poem's contents. It also makes a suitable visual for discussing trees and wildlife with children, or to accompany woods theme stories.

TO MAKE A TREE HOME PUPPET

Materials: Photocopy of patterns, heavy paper.

Construction: Cut out and color photocopies of pattern parts. Glue to heavy paper to reinforce. Crease mouth along dotted lines as shown. Slit dotted lines elsewhere to insert birds in head nest and eyes on owl.

RUBBER BAND
DETAIL - BACK OF
MOUTH

ATTACH RUBBER
BAND

CUT ALONG LINE AT ↑ EYEBROW FOR BIRDS

A ↑ ATTACH TO BIRDS

OWL'S EYES:

BACK OF PUPPET

ON PUPPET'S FRONT CUT SLITS AS INDICATED BY DOTTED LINES. INSERT STRIP FROM THE BACK AS SHOWN ABOVE.

TREE PATTERN

↖ OWL'S EYES

cut out   cut out

PARK TREE, PARK PEOPLE

by Yvonne Winer

A tender note highlights this story that evolves around a central Big Tree in the park which is decorated by the thoughtful Park People. The children, playing the roles of the Park People, will enjoy witnessing the transformation of the Tree as each new decorative element is added to its branches. In the end, the Birds punctuate the story's actions and give the children an added sense of appreciation toward the park's wildlife. This is a sensitive story that can be replayed many times over with input by different people as well as variations on the Tree's decorations.

Ask the chilren to think of the different types of things that grow on trees (apples, nuts, oranges, flowers, etc.). Then ask them what they would like to see grow on a tree if they could grow anything in the world they wished (for example, candy, computers, gold coins, pictures, twinkling stars, etc.).

Pretend that the classroom is a lovely park that many people like to visit and take a stroll.

You will need the following:

Characters

Park People	Children with an array
Balloon Seller	of strolling clothes
Musician	such as hats, scarves,
Lollipop-Maker	umbrellas, walking
Birdman	sticks, etc.
Tree	Children with Bodi-Bag
Wind	Puppets
Rain	
Birds	Children with Paper
	Bird Puppets

Props

Colored Balloons	Real items
Jingle Bells	Real items
Assorted Candies	Candy canes, popcorn strings, licorice, etc.
Bird Feeding Trays	Made from food boxes

Note: The number of each item to be hung on the Tree can be determined by the number of children playing the Park People. Tie a two-foot length of string, looped together at the ends, to each item to be slipped over the Tree's out-stretched arm-branches.

If time is limited, the balloons and bird feeders can be prepared prior to the story rather than during the story as suggested in the text's actions.

Assign one child to play the part of the Big Tree with the Bodi-Puppet, standing in the center of the playing space with arms outstretched as if they were thin bare tree branches.

Assign a group of children to play the Park People and don the various strolling clothes. Arrange the Park People to one side of the playing space.

Assign five children to play the parts of the Balloon Seller, Wind, Musician, Lollipop-Maker, Rain, and Birdman. Arrange them to the opposite side of the playing space.

Distribute the props to the appropriate characters; the balloons to the Balloon Seller, bells to the Musician, candy to the Lollipop-Maker and feeders to the Birdman.

Assign a last group of children to play the Birds, or if the class is small, let the Park People double up and play the Bird parts. Arrange the Birds at random around the park.

Place the bird feeder trays with string ties near the Park People.

Cue the children on the story's actions, and begin the story.

PARK TREE, PARK PEOPLE

NARRATION	ACTION
In summer time, the Park People were happy because the weather was warm, the flowers gay, and the Big Tree was covered in leaves. So when they went for walks in the park, they were sheltered from the wind, the rain and the sun. But, in the winter, the Tree had lost its leaves and looked cold and bleak—and there was nothing to protect the Park People from the Wind and the Rain, and nothing to make the park look colorful.	*Tree looks cold and shivers as People stroll around it.*
The Park People then decided to have a meeting; a meeting to gather ideas to make the Tree more cheerful. "We could tie balloons on the Tree," said the Balloon Seller. "That will make it colorful."	*Park People gather together in the park to meet. The Balloon Seller gives the Park People the balloons.*

NARRATION	ACTION
So all that day they blew and blew and tied balloons to the Tree—red ones, yellow ones, blue ones and green ones. Then they stood back and looked at the cheerful, colorful Tree and clapped their hands with delight.	*Park People blow up the balloons, tie them on string loops and hang them on the Tree. They step back to admire the decorated Tree and clap their hands in delight.*
That night they went to bed and slept peacefully—"Snore...snore...snore."	*Park People lay down around the perimeter of the playing circle and pretend to go to sleep while the Wind "blows" through the park. It twirls around and removes all of the balloons off of the Tree.*
Early the next morning when the Park People reached the Tree, they looked at the Tree and couldn't believe their eyes. During the night, the Wind had come and blown away every single balloon. All the red ones, all the yellow ones, all the blue ones and all the green ones.	*Park People wake up and sadly inspect the barren Tree.*
"Cheer up, cheer up," said the Musician. "Why don't we hang bells on the Tree, jolly jingle bells that will tinkle when the wind blows!"	*Musician cheers up the Park People and passes out the bells to hang on the Tree. They stand back to admire the decorated Tree and clap their hands in delight.*
So all that day, the Park People hung the jingle bells on the Tree. They then stood back and looked at the tinkly Tree and listened and clapped their hands with delight.	
That night they went to bed feeling very pleased with the new idea—"Snore...snore...snore."	*Park People go to sleep while the Wind comes along and blows at the bells.* *The Tree shakes its branches to rattle the bells which interrupts the Park People's sleep.*
However, that night the Wind came again and blew and shook and rattled the Tree; the bells jingled so loudly that all the People in the village woke up and couldn't get to sleep again.	
So, the next morning they took down every single bell.	*Park People sadly take down the bells.*
"Cheer up, cheer up," said the Lollipop-Maker. "We could hang candles in the Tree. They won't blow away, and they won't jingle all night, and they could make the Tree look very cheerful!"	*Lollipop-Maker cheers up the Park People and gives them candy to hang on the Tree.*
"Yes, yes, let's do that," said the Park People! (The Park Children thought it to be an especially wonderful idea.)	
So, all that day the Park People hung candies on the Tree. They hung striped candy sticks, long licorice twists, jelly snakes, popcorn strings, and jolly chocolate shapes. When they had finished, they cheered and clapped their hands.	*Park People hang the candy up on the Tree. They step back to admire the decorated Tree and clap their hands in delight.*
That night they went to bed feeling very pleased with the new idea—"Snore...snore...snore."	*Park People go to sleep and snore.*
However, that night the Rain came...sshhh...shhh ...and melted down every single candy! At the bottom of the Tree was a slippery, sticky, gooey river of chocolate, licorice, popcorn and jelly! What a mess!	*Rain comes and "melts" the candy by removing each piece and laying it on the ground.*
The Park People stared in amazement! "Cheer up, cheer up," said the Bird Man. "I have a wonderful idea. We could put out bird feeders and attract all the colorful Birds in the park. Then we need never again be worried about the Tree being weary, because the Birds could live in it. The Birds won't be blown away by the Wind, won't make too much noise at night, and won't melt in the Rain!"	*Park People wake and stare at the Tree in amazement.*
So, all that day the Park People set about making bird trays, and hung bird feeders on the Tree, and put bird baths in safe places. When they had finished, they stood back and cheered and cheered, and clapped their hands.	*Bird Man passes out the materials for the bird trays which the Park People construct (see note under props) and hang on the decorated Tree. They stand back and admire the Tree, cheer and clap their hands in delight.*
So, that night they all went to bed feeling very tired and very happy! "Snore...snore...snore."	*Park People go to sleep and snore.*

35

NARRATION

Early the next morning as the sun rose, the Birds saw the bird feeders of honey, and the bird trays of seeds and crumbs, and the bird baths! They chirped and sang and came down to the park. When the Park People got there, they couldn't believe their eyes!

There were Robin Redbreasts, and Purple Finches, Yellow Orioles and Red Cardinals, and Bouncey Bluebirds and colorful Honey Birds. The whole Tree was alive with bright chirpy Birds waiting for a turn at the bird feeders.

Those Park People now believe they have the most chirpy, colorful, cheery Tree in the whole, whole world—do you think they have?

ACTION

Birds begin to gather around the Tree, singing and chirping joyfully.

Birds flit and chirp merrily around the Tree.

Park People clap their hands and show their happiness as the Birds chirp even louder in unison.

THE END

TO MAKE TREE, WIND, OR RAIN BODI-BAG PUPPETS

Materials: One large grocery bag, two medium-sized rubber bands, two 3″ wide fabric strips (length of child's arms), a 2½ foot long fabric strip or ribbon for securing around neck.

Construction: To construct arms, fold over the end of each fabric-strip and slip a rubber band in each hem; staple hems to secure rubber bands in place. Staple other end of arm strip to paper bag, just below flap.

Staple center of neck ribbon to top center of bag.

Use a rich assortment of materials and coloring medium to add character, pattern, and texture to the bag.

To wear, tie neck ribbon around the child's neck and slip rubber bands over wrists. The child then "becomes" the puppet and can pantomime actions using her own legs and the fabric strip arms.

RAIN

TREE

WIND

TO MAKE BIRD FINGER PUPPETS

Materials: Multiple photocopies of the Bird pattern.

Construction: Cut out and color them in an array of lovely colors with colored marker pens or crayons. Slit each Bird along the tab lines and curve the tab into a tube-shape to fit a child's finger.

TO MAKE A BIRDFEEDER

Materials: Food box, such as cereal, pudding, small milk cartons, and other types of box.

Construction: Cut out a large hole on one side of the box and tie a two foot long string, looped over, to the top for hanging on the Tree's arm-branches. Children may wish to decorate the outside of the boxes, or place real bird food inside their feeders.

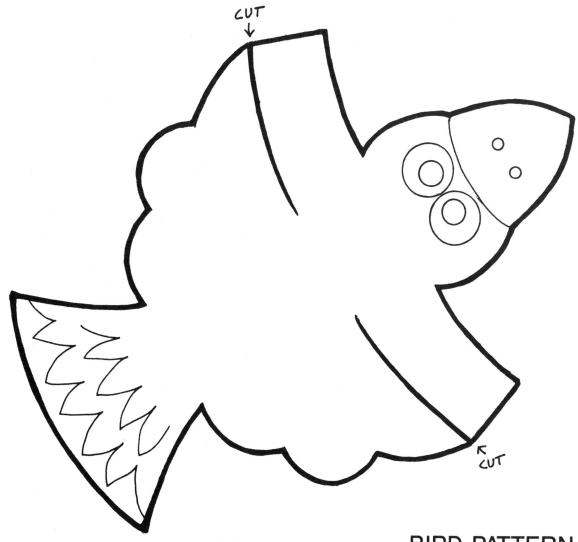

BIRD PATTERN   37

WHO'S AFRAID OF A SILLY OLD SHADOW

Who's afraid of a silly old shadow? A groundhog, of course! This prudent little creature is careful to check the weather first before coming out of its long and cozy winter hibernation on February second. Legend says that the groundhog, upon coming out of its hole and seeing its own shadow (if the sun is shining) becomes frightened and sulkily crawls back into its hideaway and six more weeks of cold, blustery winter follow. However, if the skies are gray and overcast and the groundhog does not have a shadow, it will come out of hibernation and begin activity. This was considered an indication, the early settlers believed, that there would be a sunny early spring coming soon.

A GROUNDHOG'S HIDEAWAY

A network of tunnels in an underground setting makes a beguiling display and backdrop for a groundhog in which to dwell. With a little imagination, the tunnels can be structured into an elaborate maze, which, in turn, becomes a puzzle for the children to solve, as they wind their way in and out of tunnels aided by curious Finger Puppets.

To make a hideaway, an "entrance" at one point and an "exit" at an opposite point. Then create an interlocking network of paper strips or tunnel drawings on a mural backdrop.

Or, the children can work together in approaching the maze hideaway and design it as a game. Have one

volunteer begin by writing "start" or "enter" at some point on the paper, then follow this up with one tunnel path for the groundhog. A second child adds a second tunnel path to first one. Let every child repeat this process, taking turns adding tunnels, until an entire maze is formed. Have some of the tunnels detour into dead end rooms with no exits. Children may wish to decorate these rooms with furnishings and appropriate items to make a groundhog happy (bed, chair, rug, swing set, refrigerator, books, toys, etc.) Finger puppets (see construction in next activity) can be tacked up on the display when not in use.

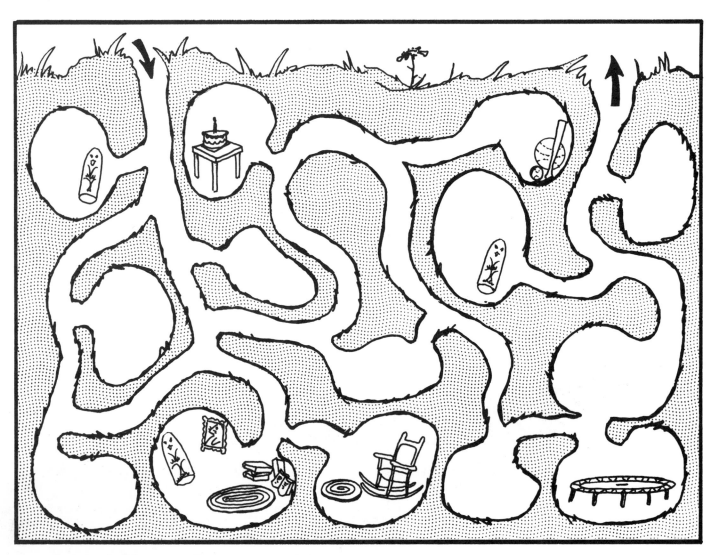

A maze mural for a groundhog to wander through

THE GROUNDHOG SLEEPS

The groundhog sleeps beneath the ground,
In a tunnel round and brown,
zzzzzz . . . .
On February's second day,
He wakens and without delay,
Runs quickly to the tunnel top,
And out his head comes, with a pop!

If skies are balmy, cloudy gray,
He hops outside to run and play.
But if the sun casts shadows black,
He scurries in and won't come back,
For it's his shadow that he fears,
And Spring will be delayed this year!

In six weeks time he'll peek again
Here he comes! LET SPRING BEGIN!

by Tamara Hunt

Groundhogs, (or woodchucks), and their relatives (marmots) make interesting topics for conversation. If possible, show pictures of these animals to the group and talk about the peculiar traits of each, especially the groundhog as described in the poem.

Using the Groundhog Finger Puppet and Peek-A-Boo Theater, recite the poem while peeking the groundhog's head out at appropriate time. Afterward, each child may wish to make a Peek-A-Boo Theater and Groundhog Finger Puppet to bring home.

TO MAKE A PEEK-A-BOO THEATER

Materials: Photocopy of pattern.

Construction: Color pattern and glue to heavy paper. Cut along dotted lines indicated for groundhog's doors. Crease doors along thin line and fold out for peeking through groundhog.

TO MAKE A GROUNDHOG FINGER PUPPET

Materials: Photocopy of pattern, heavy paper.

Construction: Cut out and color groundhog pattern. Tape ends into a tube shape to fit finger.

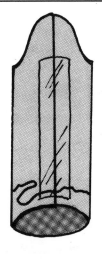

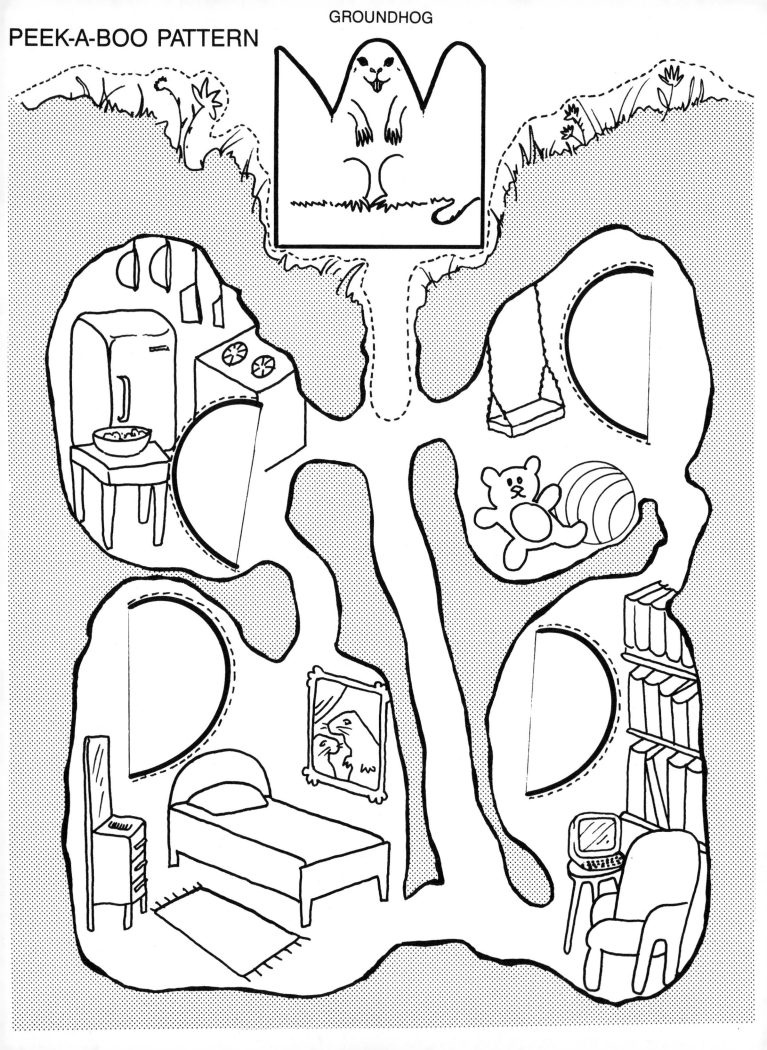

PEEK-A-BOO PATTERN

GROUNDHOG

FROM YOUR VALENTINE

Red is the Valentine color, hearts are the romantic symbol and Cupid makes mischief with his gold tipped arrows. All are evidential signs that Valentine's Day has arrived.

This popular holiday began many centuries ago when a priest named St. Valentine was put into prison because of religious conflicts.

According to one legend, he was a good man who grew beautiful flowers in his lovely garden, and gave many of them away to the children who lived nearby. He also befriended a white pigeon who carried messages back and forth between the children and himself when he was in prison. In return, the children sent St. Valentine notes that said they loved him. After his death on February 14th, the townsfolks wanted to celebrate his kindnesses and now send messages to one another just as St. Valentine and his children did—"From Your Valentine."

FIVE LITTLE VALENTINES

Five red valentines I take from my drawer,
I'll give one to (child's name), now there are four.
Four red valentines, pretty as can be,
I'll give one to _____, now there are three.
Three red valentines, can you guess for who?
I'll give one to _____, now there are two.
Two red valentines, sharing them is fun.
I'll give one to _____, now there is one.
One red valentine, lonely as can be,
I'm going to keep it for me, me, me!

by Tamara Hunt

Let the children make Valentine Rings to wear and distribute to other children while the group recites the poem.

Inquire of the children "What is Valentine's Day?" "What do you give on Valentine's Day and why?" Help the children understand that Valentines offer a means to tell others we care about them. Emphasize the concept of friendship. Wear a cupid Scenic Panel if desired.

Using the red valentine rings, recite the poem below. Remove the rings one-by-one and give to the children. Let them replace the rings when you are finished. Repeat until everyone has had a turn to receive a valentine.

TO MAKE VALENTINE RINGS

Materials: Red construction paper, 5 soda pop tabs or pipe cleaners.

Construction: Cut out five small hearts from red paper. Tape to top of soda pop tab (be sure there are no sharp edges by covering with tape), or a ring made from pipe cleaners.

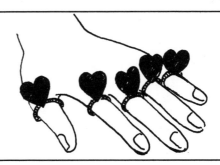

I'M A LITTLE MAILBOX

(Sung to the tune of "I'm A Little Teapot")

I'm a little mailbox short and stout.
Here is my face and here is my mouth.
You can put your Valentine Cards in me
And Zip! They'll get there speedily.

by Tamara Hunt

Dropping letters into a singing mailbox provides a novel experience for young children. A mailbox that has the appetite for letters of a Cookie Monster and a see-through stomach as well will have double appeal. A large supermarket bag is just the thing to convert such a servicable creature. Have children create valentines cards beforehand to use with the mailbox. You may wish to take advantage of the moment by helping the children learn about the postal system.

TO MAKE A SINGING MAILBOX

Materials: Supermarket bag, blue construction paper, photocopy of eagle emblem, acetate book report cover (obtained at stationery store).

Construction: Cut out eagle emblem and attach to flap of bag. Cut out a hole in the front of bag and tape acetate to inside of hole. Staple bottom edges together. Cut a big slit under flap of bag to insert letters. Cut another slit on one side of bag for easy removal of letters from stomach area. Cut a hole in back of bag, directly behind flap, to insert hand through and operate flap. Staple entire bottom of bag together so letters do not drop out. Cover bag with blue construction paper.

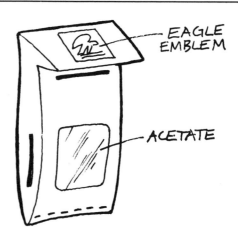

EAGLE EMBLEM PATTERN

MAIL

VALENTINE CLOWN

A frown is an upside down smile.
A frown is a grin down my chin.
So whenever I frown
Turn the Valentine down
And I'll smile, smile, smile
I'm a clown
I will smile, smile, smile.

by Tamara Hunt

Clowns are tricksters. Sometimes they make us laugh; sometimes they make us cry. This novel Valentine Clown Puppet is just the right vehicle for sharing friendship and similar values with children.

Let each child create a Clown Puppet from the pattern that follows. Once completed, have children hold the puppet so all the clowns' frowns face the group and recite the poem while they turn them around. Then ask each child, one by one, to state one special thing about a friendship that could make a sad clown feel happy, while turning the Clown Puppet upside-down to reveal a smile.

CUT OUT AND COLOR
CLOWN PATTERN.

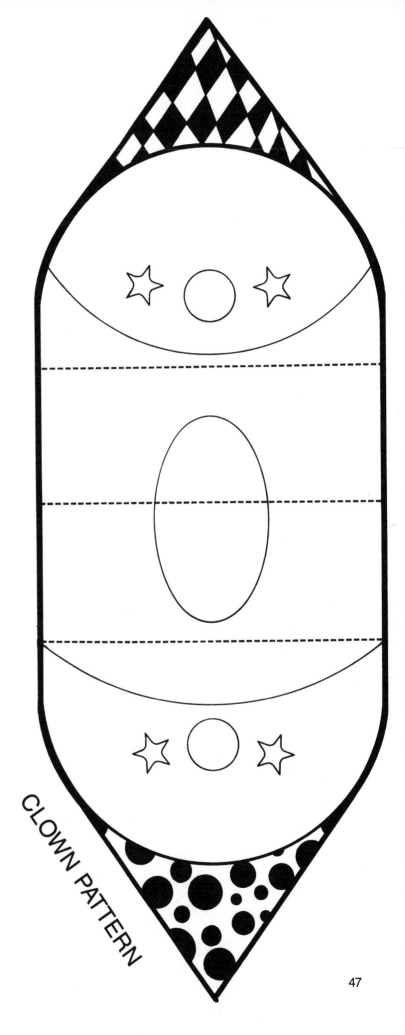

CLOWN PATTERN

47

HEART ROCK CONCERT

Stringing hearts together to create a Heart Throb Puppet that dances to heart "beats" is a good project to introduce to good-hearted children. When puppets are complete, select some rock music or other tunes to accompany the puppet's dancing. Or, if you wish, have a "Heart Rock Concert" and let each puppet perform its own song, poem or dance number.

TO MAKE A HEART THROB PUPPET

Materials: Red construction paper, string, yarn, trim and scrap fabric, two cardboard tubes, paper fastener brads.

Construction: Cut out a number of hearts of varying sizes. Use a hole punch (or make holes with pointed end of scissors) and punch holes in hearts so that they may be linked together with string or paper fastener brads. Cut four paper strips for arms and legs, fold like an accordian. Feet and hands can be weighted with small metal washers or coins. Tie strings to head and hand areas and link other ends of strings to separate cardboard tubes as shown.

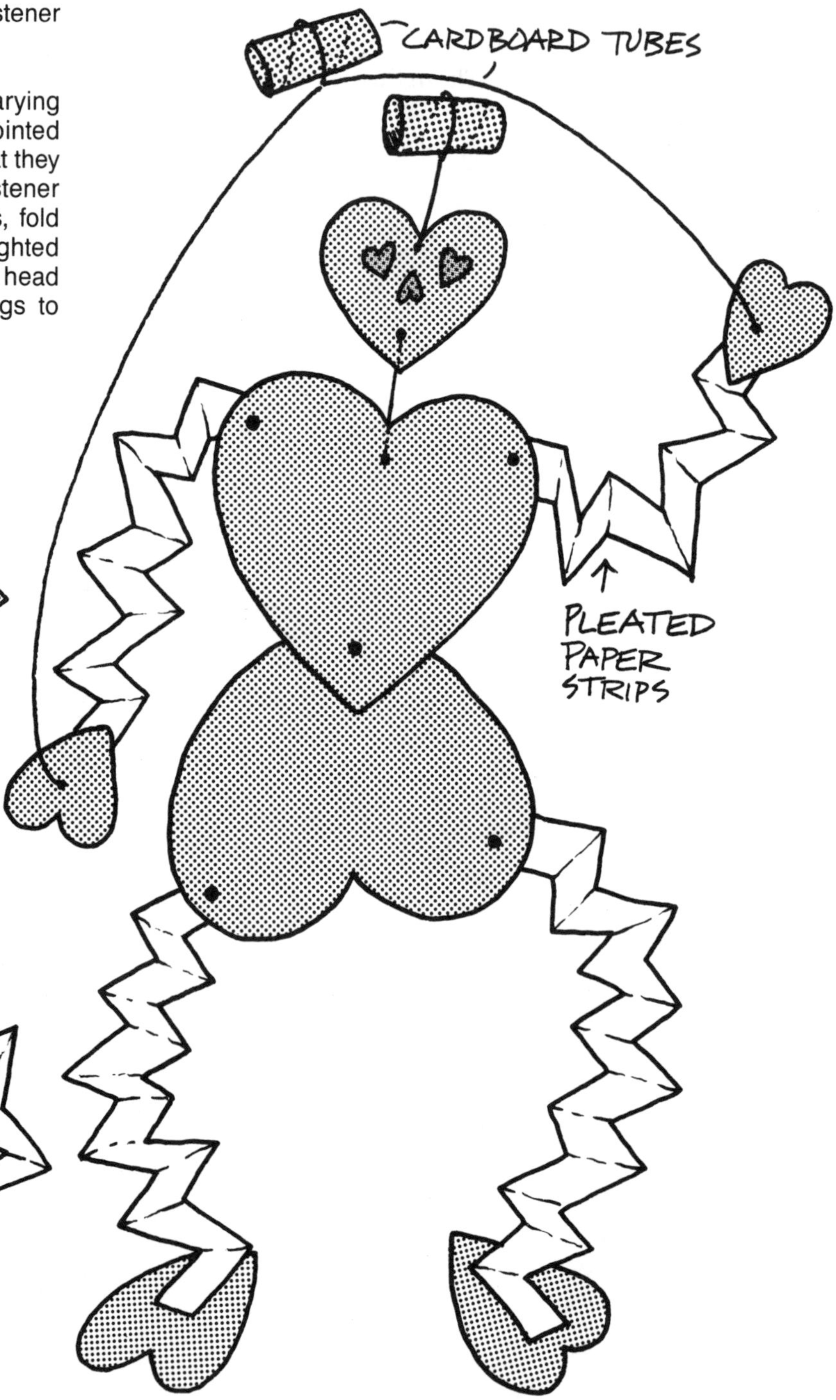

CARDBOARD TUBES

PLEATED PAPER STRIPS

DON'T BREAK MY HEART!

A broken heart might be just the thing to inspire a sob story, but it can end on a happy note. Divide the group into teams of two and give each team a large heart shape cut out from red construction paper. Ask each team to draw a quick, irregular line across the heart to divide it in any direction. Then have them cut along the line to produce two shapes. Each team should study their shapes to visualize a character or object. The shapes can be decorated with coloring medium, scrap paper or fabric. Each team of two will integrate the shapes into a story or short skit to present to the group. Shapes can be attached to sticks and operated behind a puppet stage or used in an open area instead.

Since friendship is an important aspect of celebrating Valentine's Day, it may be suggested that each story includes friendship as its theme.

Story Example: *Turtle and a Letter "3"*

A turtle who knew only how to count to the letter 2 went on a search around the world to find the big letter "3." In dismay, she discovers everything comes in pairs until one day...

Story Example: *A Quiet Person and a Noisy Person*

The quiet person wants to sleep but the noisy person won't let him. So the quiet person thinks of a drastic solution to stop the noisy person, and this is what he does...

LETTER "3"

TURTLE

NOISY PERSON   QUIET PERSON

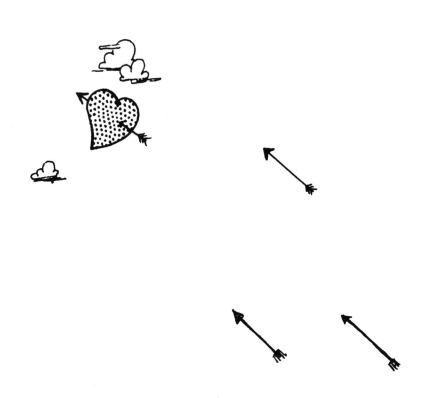

HAPPY BIRTHDAY MR. PRESIDENT

What does it take to be a great president? Perseverance, commitment, vision? All of these qualities help to make a president good and are worthy virtues to instill in children. When George Washington was fifty years old on February 22nd, years ago, a great banquet was held in his honor by eminent dignitaries and statesmen, in appreciation of his devotion to his country. Although President's Day was originally an occasion to honor this thundering man, and Father of our Country, it has since been set aside as a day to pay homage to all presidents. It also gives a fitting opportunity to take pride in and salute other famous Americans, such as inventors, explorers, artists, humanitarians and scientists, who have contributed to our country's greatness.

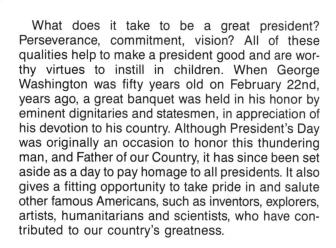

A stern Washington punders over policy (Bodi-Bag Puppet)

THE SHAPING OF AMERICA SHOW OF STARS

"Ladies and gentlemen, step right up, we have a treat in store for you! Today Abe Lincoln will honor us by reciting his acclaimed "Gettysburg Address," followed up with a lively act featuring Benjamin Franklin demonstrating his kite flying tricks and Mary Cassatt demonstrating painting techniques. Sharing the limelight on stage is Martin Luther King giving a talk about a dream he had and Mark Twain telling a tale about Tom Sawyer whitewashing the fence.

The shaping of America is fun to explore using a variety show format, with a "show of stars" style. Ask each child to research a president, hero or heroine in American history, literature or science—of their choice—and to create a Bodi-Bag Puppet for use in presenting a brief skit to the class. Prior to the activity, the children may share their research in written format, enabling the teacher to "preview" the variety show stars and scenarios, and enabling positive adult input for offering suggestions that will make the show both interesting and instructive for the class to watch.

In the process of the activity, share with the children the concept "greatness" and ask the students to specify how (and if) this term can be applied to the specific person selected. Develop a meaningful word list for them to review—trusting, courage, kindness, giving, important, honorable, and apply to their heroes and heroines, as appropriate, originating many of the words from the students' own suggestions.

TO MAKE AN AMERICAN STAR BODI-BAG PUPPET

Materials: Large supermarket bag, four medium-sized rubber bands, four 3″ wide fabric strips (length of child's arms and legs), 2-1/2 foot long fabric strip or ribbon, construction paper, assorted yarn, trim and scrap fabric.

Construction: For arms and legs fold over the end of each fabric-strip and slip a rubber band in each hem; staple hems to secure. Staple opposite ends of strips to body for arms and legs, as shown.

Staple center of neck ribbon to top of bag. Add yarn or fringed paper hair and paper or painted features. Create a costume from paper or fabric.

To Wear— Tie neck ribbon to puppeteer's neck and insert hands and feet through rubber bands.

THOMAS EDISON

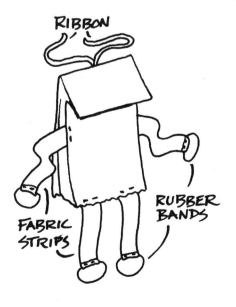

GEORGE AND MARTHA WASHINGTON

PERHAPS YOU'LL BE FAMOUS

Who are these people and what did they do?
Why are they famous? I'll give you a clue.

This woman had courage and space was her dream.
"America's first," she was part of the team.
(Spaceship-Sally Ride)

This man was an artist, cartoons told his tales
Of Mickey and Donald and cute Chip 'n Dale.
(Mickey Mouse—Walt Disney)

This man had ideas and used them that's true
To discover electricity, guess what he flew?
(Kite—Ben Franklin)

This man had great wisdom and so he believed
Regardless of race, everyone should be freed.
(Flag-Abe Lincoln)

This man sought adventure where no one had roamed.
He walked on the moon before he came home.
(Moon—Neil Armstrong)

Who are these people and what did they do?
Perhaps they'll be famous. Perhaps they'll be you!

by Tamara Hunt

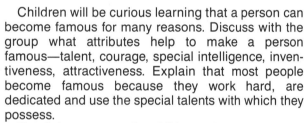

SYMBOL PATTERNS

Children will be curious learning that a person can become famous for many reasons. Discuss with the group what attributes help to make a person famous—talent, courage, special intelligence, inventiveness, attractiveness. Explain that most people become famous because they work hard, are dedicated and use the special talents with which they possess.

Read the poem to the children. Have them listen carefully and think about the answers that correspond with each Finger Puppet Symbol as it is held up. Repeat the poem and stop between couplets to have children guess the famous person's name. Ask the children to define what key qualities made each of the Finger Puppet symbolized characters outstanding citizens.

Afterwards, challenge each child to choose a famous (real or fictitious) person and give clues about that person, through pantomine or action, for the group to guess. For example: Columbus sailing and spotting land, Thomas Edison inventing the light bulb, George Washington Carver experimenting with peanut technology.

TO MAKE FINGER PUPPET SYMBOLS

Materials: Photocopy of patterns, rubber household glove, doublestick tape.

Construction: Cut out and color photocopy of Finger Puppet Symbols. To reinforce, glue symbols to stiff paper. Attach to glove by means of double-stick tape.

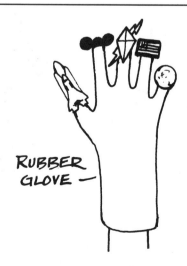

RUBBER GLOVE —

LOTS O'LUCK!

Of course everyone knows that St. Patrick's Day is for the fun-loving Irish, but it is also a day for everyone—since EVERYONE is Irish on St. Patrick's Day! This green holiday is the stomping grounds of elf-like leprechauns, who gleefully spend their time counting leaves on clover (hoping to find four leafed ones!) or coins of gold in pots at the end of the rainbow. However, not everyone knows of the marvelous legends surrounding this holiday or how St. Patrick drove away all the snakes of Ireland through his cunning and wit. We might just want to ask the folks of Killarney...

So say the folks of Killarney:

St. Patrick is known for having driven all of the snakes out of Ireland. That is, all but one, claim the folks of Killarney. And this one snake lives at the bottom of black Lake in the Gap of Dunloe in southwest Ireland. St. Patrick has been pursuing this snake for years, but still the serpent manages to elude him. So one day St. Patrick built a very small, but strong box, with nine brass bolts. He then approached the snake as it was lazily sunning himself beside the quiet waters of Black Lake and offered the box to the serpent. "It will make a superb home for you to snuggle up during the cold winter months, but I doubt if you will fit into it," challenged St. Patrick.

"Ah, Patrick," the snake laughed, "You've been trying to catch me for years and know how very clever I am. You surely must know I can twist myself into that box!"

"Oh, snake, I don't know about that, you're a sly old fang all right, but perhaps you're not as slippery as you used to be." Then Patrick wagered a gallon of porter on whether or not the snake could fit in the box.

On hearing that, the snake threw a loop with his body into one corner of the box and continued to twist and turn, tucking one coil, after the other inside until it fit perfectly in the box.

"There's just the tiniest bit of tail sticking out," observed Patrick. "I'll take care of that," said the serpent, and he did. When the serpent's body was out of sight, Patrick slammed the lid shut—wham!—fastened the nine bolts and threw the box into the lake.

The snake was enraged. He began twisting and writhing inside the box, creating a terrible torrent of motion, causing the waters of the lake to toss and roll and splash at the rocky shores.

To this day, even when the wind couldn't dislodge the slightest pebble on the rocky hillside of the Gap, the waters of Black Lake are seen in continual motion—but only the people of Killarney know why.

MR. SNAKE OUTWITS ST. PATRICK

What if Mr. Snake did manage to perform a "Great Houdini" feat and escaped the box in the bottom of Black Lake after all? What then? St. Patrick would have to think of another trick to capture this devious snake, such as building an irresistible trap, enticing the snake to the surface of the lake with a favorite meal or story, capturing it with a fish net or other conniving trick. The group can work together in teams of two and create short skits about how St. Patrick outwitted the vain snake. One team member can play the snake and the other St. Patrick, while using Envelope Puppets.

TO MAKE A SNAKE ENVELOPE PUPPET

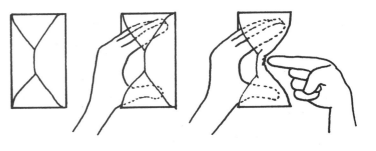

Materials: 6-1/2" × 3-1/2" letter envelope, construction paper, fabric, yarn and trim.

Construction: Tuck flap of envelope inside. Place hand inside envelope as shown. Gently "bite" finger of other hand to form mouth. Straighten out mouth if wrinkled. For snake, add a long strip of fabric or paper to back of envelope in shape of snake. For St. Patrick, add a paper nose, yarn or fringed paper hair and a green body.

Mr. Snake planning his great Hondini escape trick

56

POT OF GOLD

Read the poem that follows as you animate the leprechaun up and down the rainbow.

I'll tell you a tale
A tale so old.
Of a little old leprechaun
Ever so bold!
He searched for a pot.
Do you know what it holds?
All sparkly and shiney.
You guessed it!
GOLD!

He climbed up a rainbow,
'least that's what I'm told
And slid to the end
Where lo and behold
Was a pot.
Is it black?
Is it shaped like a bowl?
What is inside it?
You guessed it!
GOLD!
　　　　　　by Tamara Hunt

LEPRECHAUN'S RAINBOW AND THE POT OF GOLD
by Tamara Hunt

Once there was a leprechaun who lived in Ireland. He had heard that if he looked very hard, he would find a pot of gold at the end of the rainbow. First, however, he would have to find a rainbow and then he would have to slide down to the other side. Now he was a very young leprechaun and had never seen a rainbow before. So he asked some children, "What is a rainbow?" (Children respond). "What colors are in the rainbow?" (Children respond). He listened to what the children said, then went looking for the right colors. He found red, orange, yellow, green, blue, and violet (give children time to color the rainbow with the correct colors).

When all the colors were side by side the leprechaun climbed to the top and slid down to the bottom. Sure enough, there was a pot of gold at the rainbow's end. He shared the gold with all the children who had been so helpful.

A rainbow story and "sparkling" poem about leprechauns' gold make glittering settings for a miniature theater. Each child may wish to make up his or her own story and theater about how the Leprechaun found gold and what he did with it afterwards (give it away, spend it on something special, etc.). Or, you may wish to use the following ready-made story and poem with the accompanying miniature theater.

Begin the story with the rainbow uncolored. Ask the children to color in the rainbow as the story is being told. Then pass out gold (foil) pieces to the children in the end.

TO MAKE A MINIATURE RAINBOW AND FINGER PUPPETS THEATER

Materials: Photocopy of patterns, heavy paper, stick

Construction: Glue and cut out Rainbow Stage photocopy. Cut out Stage opening. Attach rod to back of Rainbow Stage.

Cut out Finger Puppet along bold line and tape ends together as shown.

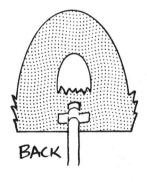
BACK

BACK

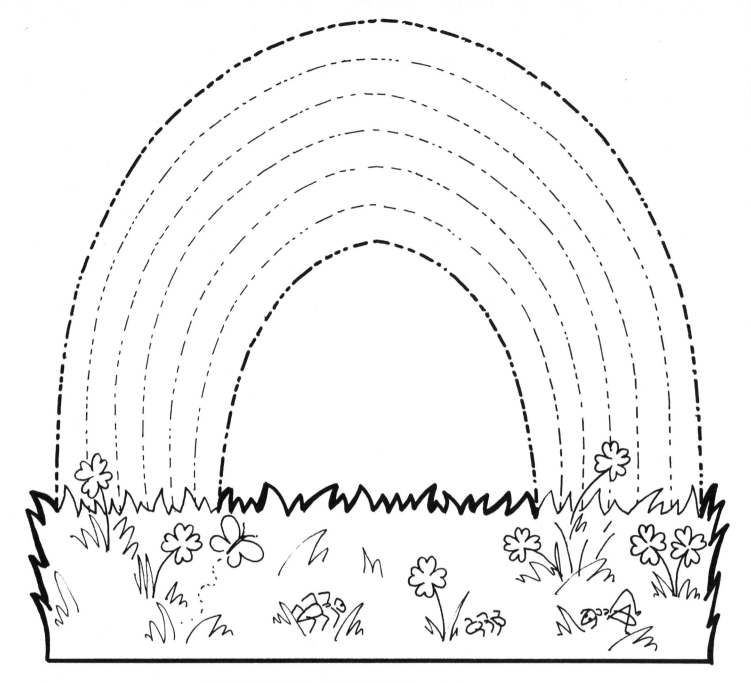

RAINBOW THEATER PATTERN

LEPRECHAUN

POT OF GOLD

58

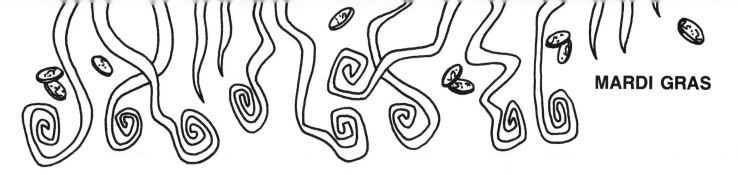

LET THE GOOD TIMES ROLL!

"Hey, mister! Throw me something!" chime the spectators as a rainbow of doubloons—purple, green and gold*—are thrown from spectacular floats. The crowds compete madly for who can gather up the most trinkets, necklaces and doubloons to take home as souvenirs. Suddenly, in this whirl of madness, a grotesque mask atop a body painted half purple, half green, makes an appearance. A lively jazz band beating out some Dixieland music overwhelms the scene, and gradually the spectators' search for treasures diminishes as they are distracted by the continuing parade of dazzling floats with new booty. Revelers are attired in the most absurd, fantastic costumes—dresses made from Spanish moss or uncooked pasta or gilded bodies in colorful bikinis. Harlequins and pirates add to the rainbow of colors in a parade that is a feast to any imagination.

"Laissez les bon temps rouler!" (Let the good times roll!) And so they do in New Orleans as in other parts of the world. Mardi Gras is a time for carnival and unsurpassed joviality, rowdiness and frenzied party-making. Mardi Gras, party of all parties, is a French term meaning, "Shrove Tuesday" or "Fat Tuesday" and is clearly the final feast before Lent and self-imposed fast as initially practiced by the Catholics, but celebrated by all. Capping the fun, the official theme, "If I Ever Cease to Love" is heard everywhere. On the twelfth night of celebration a cake, the King Cake, is cut and the finder of a bean hidden therein becomes the king or queen to rule the celebrations. These grand balls of royalty continue to set the pattern for the elaborate pageantry that follow. King Rex rules over all and each year a new king is selected from the most popular young men to lead the spectacular parade and masked balls that highlight the event. Queens are also selected.

A Mardi Gras parade is composed of actually many parades, with representatives from the various Krewes joining each one—Rex, Zulu, Comus, etc. In addition numerous marching brass bands join in, each band led by a flamboyant leader carrying an umbrella.

No matter how Mardi Gras is celebrated, when the feast has ended, it is time to fast. The stroke of midnight is a pronouncement that begins a strict severance of all worldly indulgences for all devouts observing the Lenten season.

*The official Mardi Gras colors.

DAZZLING MARDI GRAS

Join in the carnival spirit by having various groups work on preparing a Mardi Gras setting:

Decorate the Room. Prepare the room for a Mardi Gras. Any party decorations will add to the festivity—balloons, crepe paper, streamers and other items. Particularly focus on the Mardi Gras colors yellow, purple, and green. Set up a chair to serve as a makeshift throne with crown and scepter ready for the King or Queen. Children may research some original doubloons to create a large round version to hang on the walls.

Build Floats. A colorful float can be built on a wagon or back of a pickup truck (if held outdoors). Decorate the float with crepe paper, paper flowers, cardboard cutouts of nobles and royalty. The king or queen can ride in a wagon or truck while jazz band and/or masked attendants march alongside throwing doubloons and trinkets. If a float is not possible, then the royal court can march without one.

Improvise a Jazz Band. If real instruments such as banjos, drums and clarinets are not available, use the imagination and gather up a collection of found instruments. Let the good times roll!

    Inverted large tin pans and pots can be tapped with the hands, for tinny sounds.

    Taut rubber bands plucked on open boxes or a Y twig.

    Scrub brushes and kitchen utensils rubbed over cheese graters or wash boards.

    Large round or square boxes used for percussion sounds.

    Coat hangers or other metal items used for chimes.

    Cardboard tubes blown for wind instrument.

    Cans and plastic jars filled with pebbles and beans for rattles and shakers.

Make doubloons and necklaces. It is traditional that marching royal attendants throw generous supplies of gold doubloons and jewelry (plastic necklaces) to parade spectators, as gifts. Have students create doubloons from gold and silver foil. Necklaces can be made from any assorted materials. Use cording or yarn as a base and add bits of foil, beads, or macaroni painted vivid colors.

Bake a King's Cake. This colorful cake is readily available in bakeries around New Orleans at Mardi Gras time, decorated in a rainbow of pastel-tone sugar. The lucky person who finds a pecan or bean inside his or her slice of cake is proclaimed king or queen for the day.

While this is prepared as a yeast cake in a large doughnut or ring shape, any basic white cake will suffice for the classroom occasion. Consider using a ring style cake mold in baking. Create a thin white icing for the cake (a ready-made commercial icing can be used) and dribble it over the entire cake. Decorate the cake by sprinkling green, purple and yellow sugar crystals over the top of the icing in stripes. Garnish with marashino cherries and citron candy. (Don't forget to add a pecan half or trinket to the batter before baking.)

Design Mardi Gras Masks and Costumes. Large cereal boxes (with backs cut away), paper plates or poster board make easy mask construction. Have on hand a glittering selection of decorating materials such as party ribbons and boxes, holiday tinsel and wrapping paper, and aluminum foils. Fabric and newspapers and large supermarket bags can be fashioned into imaginative costuming.

KING'S CAKE

HA, HA...I FOOLED YOU!

A duck in the pond,
A fish in the pool.
Whoever reads this chapter,
Is a big April Fool!*

A year without a Fool's Day would be a dull year indeed. This special day, reserved for mischief and tomfoolery, is a holiday for tricksters of all ages around the world. Gluing a penny to the sidewalk, filling a sugar bowl with salt, placing a "kick me" sign on someone's back are some of the oft-repeated deceptions invented by joking children.

It will be fun to ask children to discuss the April Fool's tricks they have played on others, or others have played upon them. Go further with the children and help them discover some new tricks for this years' tricks that are funnier than ever before, but that do not hurt anyone. By the way, did you know your shoelace is untied—ha, ha, I fooled you!

*A popular Fool's Day rhyme by children in New Zealand.

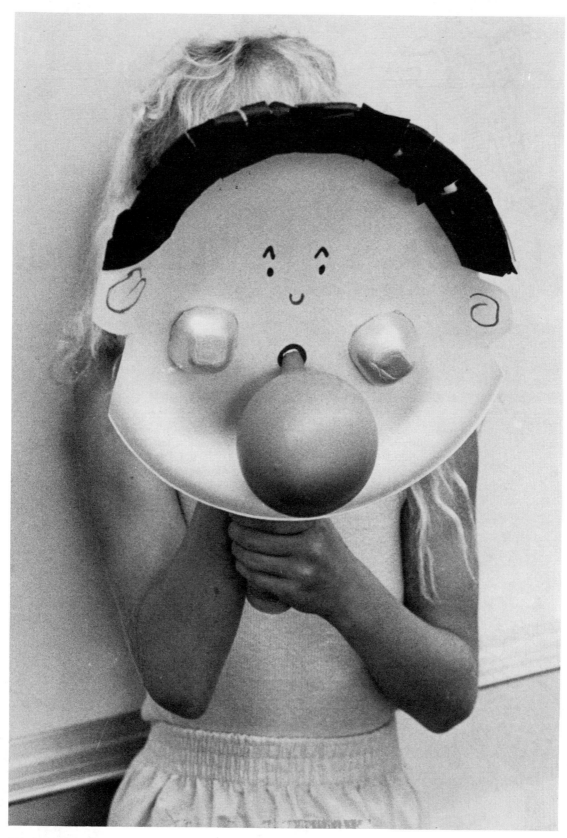

Blowing up a trick puppet.

FOOL'S RHYMES

"April Fool's a-coming and you're the biggest fool running" (United States)

"Up the ladder, and down a tree, You're a bigger fool than me!" (United States)

"April fool, eat a herring, Wash it down with muddy water" (Sweden)

It is okay to be a fool at least one day of the year. Have children create Trick Fool Puppets by assembling a character from a variety of junk. When completed, have them create original Fool's rhymes or repeat those practiced around the world for their puppets to recite. Rhymes can be written on the backs of the puppets (like cue card) for easy reading to the class.

TO MAKE A TRICK FOOL'S PUPPET

Materials: Items from *Wish List* (paper plates, cups, straws, clothespins, cardboard tubes, egg cartons, balloons, etc.), construction paper, yarn, fabric and trims, rods.

Construction: Experiment with different ways junk can be combined to form a unique puppet. Concentrate on animation: a pop up wig or funny hat, reversible turn around puppet, movable limbs (by means of paper fasteners). Use paper, fabric and trims to define features, costuming and other detailing.

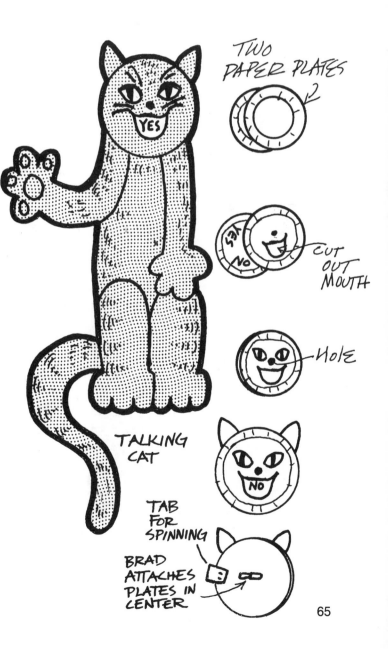

TWO PAPER PLATES

CUT OUT MOUTH

HOLE

TALKING CAT

TAB FOR SPINNING

BRAD ATTACHES PLATES IN CENTER

YARN

PAPER PLATE

TUBE

DOWEL

POP-UP MAN

A FOOL'S GIFT

Let everyone in the group create a "Ha, ha...I fooled you!" gift to present to another member of the class or a friend. This can be constructed from two paper plates, that picture a "nice" gift on the outside, but when it is opened reveals a surprise or joke inside. For example, the outside of the plates might picture a glittering diamond necklace. Open up the plates and out pops a sinewy, glistening, coiled snake! Have children think of other surprises to include, such as:

Nice Gift	Joke Gift
Big, Juicy Hamburger	Liver and Spinach Sandwich
Gold Coins	Rattlesnake
Beautiful Flower	Thistle with Thorns
Big Smile	Terrifying, Growling Monster Mouth
Pussycat	Ferocious Tiger

TO MAKE A FOOL'S GIFT

Materials: Two paper plates, two medium sized rubber bands, construction paper, scraps of fabric.

Construction: Staple a rubber band across the back of each plate approximately two inches down, as shown. Line up rubber band ends of plates and bind together at one point to serve as a hinge. Create a "gift" image on outside plates by drawing or gluing on gift image. Make a joke image from paper and scrap materials on the inside of the plates. To operate, put fingers under top rubber band and thumb under bottom. Open and close hand to reveal surprise inside.

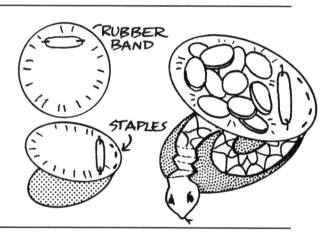

THE WISE FOLKS OF GOTHAM

This old legend is about King John when he was ruler of England, way back, many centuries ago. Some say it is a story about how April Fools' Day began. Before reading the story let the group share the funniest tricks that they have themselves played on others for April Fool's Day, or those about which they have heard. Discuss the meaning of the words "fool" and "foolish", and the distinction between being a fool or just acting the fool. Tell them you know of a King who lived among some very foolish people.

Read the story to the children. Afterwards have each child make a Tube String Puppet of a person who does something foolish. Props may be added (real or paper) to define the basic idea. Have each child demonstrate the puppet's foolish action to the group.

For example, a foolish character could:

Walk upside down
Wear a big fish for a hat
Wear roller skates on the hands
Make a pot of stone soup

The Wise Folks of Gotham

Once upon a time, a long time ago in England, there lived a king named King John. How he loved to stroll and was often seen pompously walking over his countryside with his cane, making a survey of his magnificent kingdom. Now, there was a custom in those days that any ground area that the king walked upon became a public road. The people of Gotham thought this custom most absurd and did not want their lovely meadows turned into ugly roads. So they protested and kept the king out of the meadows.

Of course King John was very angry. "Nonsense", he growled this is pure nonsense." So he sent his chief officer to find out why the people in his kingdom were so rude to him. He thought perphaps that he might even go so far as to punish them.

When the people of Gotham heard that the chief officer was coming to spy on them they quickly called an emergency meeting. Putting their heads together they came up with a superb idea. They would pretend that they were all fools, this way the king would not punish them.

So when the chief officer came this is what he saw.
Some people trying to drown a fish in a pond.
Some people trying to put lard on a cow.
(They said this would help the cow make butter)
Some people rolling cheese down a hill.
(They said it would find its way to the Nottingham Market)
Some people hanging potatoes on a tree.
(They said it would make the tree grow tomatoes)

When the king's chief officer saw all this, he was flabbergasted. He told the king that they were all nothing but a bunch of fools.

The king decided not to bother punishing them.
And that, say some, is how April Fools' Day began!

The End

TO MAKE A TUBE STRING PUPPET

Materials: Cardboard towel tubes, construction paper, string.

Construction: Cut out a paper head and attach to top of tube. Cut out and pleat strips of paper for bouncy arms and legs. Add paper or cardboard hands and feet. Make paper props, or use found objects, and attach to puppet as required. Attach lengths of string to hands or feet (two to three strings maximum). Attach opposite ends to tube controls.

HA, HA

PESACH

Passover, Pesach in Hebrew, the holiday of freedom, tells the story of the Jews' slavery in Egypt and their flight to freedom. It is a time of celebration and remembering—celebrating freedom and remembering a time when Jews were not free. At Passover, even while rejoicing in their own freedom, Jews take time to remember those who are not yet free. They tell the story to their children of a time when their ancestors were slaves in Egypt and give particular concern and direct actions toward the rights of people in places who are still trying to be free—in their bodies, free in their spirits, free in the land of their birth and free in the land of their soul.

The story of Moses leading his people out of slavery became a source of inspiration and hope to the slaves in pre-Civil War South. They composed many songs of freedom with biblical themes, one of which ("Go Down Moses") even uses the same words that Moses spoke to Pharoah, "Let my people go".

The holiday takes its name from the tenth plague, when the Angel of Death "passed over" the houses of the Jews and went only to the Egyptian houses. The Passover Ceremony—the seder—retells the story of the Jew's life in Egypt and their escape to freedom. The symbols of the Seder—which means "order"—come from the exodus from Egypt. Jews had to leave in a hurry, so there was no time for the bread to rise, hence a thin, unleavened cracker-like substance called *matzoh* is eaten.

Each of the symbols of the Passover seder relates to the flight of the Jews from Egypt:

Hard-Boiled Egg—The hardness of the egg stands for the strength of the Jews.
Roasted Lamb Bone—Reminder of lambs that were sacrificed so that God would pass over the Jewish houses.
Salt Water—Stands for the tears shed by Jewish slaves in Egypt; also the salty Red Sea, and the tears of all people in bondage.
Greens—Parsley and celery are dipped into the salt water as a reminder of the parting of the Red Sea; also symbolizes springtime and hope.
Bitter Herbs (maror) horseradish—recalls the suffering of the slaves.
Charoset—Made from chopped apples, nuts, cinnamon and wine, as a reminder of the clay/mortar mixture the slaves used in making bricks for the Pharoah.

The Story of Passover

The story of Passover and the Jews' time in Egypt is framed by two dreams. The first involves Joseph who was sold into slavery by his brothers because he was the father Jacob's favorite son. While in Egypt, he was asked to interpret the dream of Egypt's ruler a dream in which seven skinny cows devoured seven fat ones. When Joseph heard the dream, he told the ruler that the dream meant there would be seven years of abundance followed by seven years of famine and he urged the king to stockpile food during the plentiful years to last through during the lean years. And so it was that Egypt was the only country—thanks to Joseph— to thrive during the seven years of famine. People came from far away to buy grain from Egypt and it was in this way that Joseph met his brothers again and forgave them. He was re-united with his father and for many years afterward, life was good for the Jews in Egypt because the ruler was so pleased with Joseph's counsel and advice.

Generations passed and the new Pharoah knew nothing of Joseph's help. He enslaved the Jews and made their lives very bitter and hard. One day, he had a dream in which he saw an old man holding a scale. On one side was a little lamb; on the other side were all the great men of Egypt, and the scale was tipped so that the little lamb outweighed all greatness of Egypt. When the Pharoah's advisers told him that the lamb represented the Jews, Pharoah ordered all the first-born Jewish sons killed. He thought that by killing the children, he would prevent the prophecy from coming true.

The life of the Jews as slaves in Egypt was very hard and bitter. Through the ingenuity of his mother, a baby named Moses was saved from the Pharoah's decree and was raised by the Pharoah's own daughter. He grew to be respected and strong, and one day, when he could no longer tolerate the way the Jews were being treated, he struck down an Egyptian taskmaster then fled to the desert and there he was instructed by God, in the form of a burning bush—to go to Pharoah to free the Jews from Egypt. However, when he went to Pharoah saying, "Let my people go," Pharoah only laughed at him and refused.

Moses told Pharoah that unless he let the Jews free, God would send terrible plagues to the Egyptians, and because Pharoah did not believe him, the plagues came—one more horrible than another, until Pharoah finally agreed to let the Jews free from slavery. Their flight to freedom was hasty. There was no time for bread to rise and so, a flat cracker-like unleavened bread, called matzoh, was eaten then and again now during the holiday of Passover.

Passover Activities Follows:

Do an interview of a famous Biblical figure, like Moses or Pharoah. Children, either as themselves or using puppets (Paper-Plate, Envelope or other) to dramatize the action, can "become" the character, with the adult helping to guide the interview. Ask questions like:

What was life like in your time?
What was the biggest problem that you faced?
How did you solve it?
What did you think of your solution?
Would you do it again, based on what you know now?

Personalize the symbols of the Passover's seder. For example, with maror—bitter herbs—which represents the bitter life of the Jews under slavery, ask the students to think of what represents the maror, the bitter part, of their own lives. Furthermore, ask them to think of what represents the bitter parts of life in the world. (Ex.: miscommunication, arguments with parents or friends, not feeling understood, not being popular—personal issues; hunger, poverty, war—global issues).

Go one step further and ask the students to think of possible remedies for the problems of the bitterness of life. Allow any answer to be given, both the plausible and the implausible, and discuss with sensitivity and respect, any issue that the students might raise.

Create a Seder Plate. The middle piece ot matzoh is hidden—called the Afikomen—and until it is found, the Passover seder cannot be concluded. Children often receive presents in exchange for the Afikomen. Play: "Hide the Afikomen." You may substitute a cracker if matzoh is hard to obtain.

An extra cup of wine is poured for the prophet Elijah, in hopes that he will come on this night, and the door is left open as a sign of welcome. Also, strangers are welcomed into the family festivities on this night.

Present the four questions. As asked on Passover night by the youngest child about why this night of Passover is different than any other night. The Passover seder answers these questions.

The answer is given in different ways for the four kinds of children so that each one might understand to the best of his ability: the *wise* who is given a full explanation, the *simple* one who needs a simple answer, the *bad* one who doesn't want an answer at all and the one *who asks no* questions.

Have the students (or puppets) think about which kind of child they most resemble, and group themselves in each corner of the room with others of that type. In a group, let the students discuss times they were wise, times they were bad, times they couldn't understand something and times in which they were uninvolved while something important was going on around them.

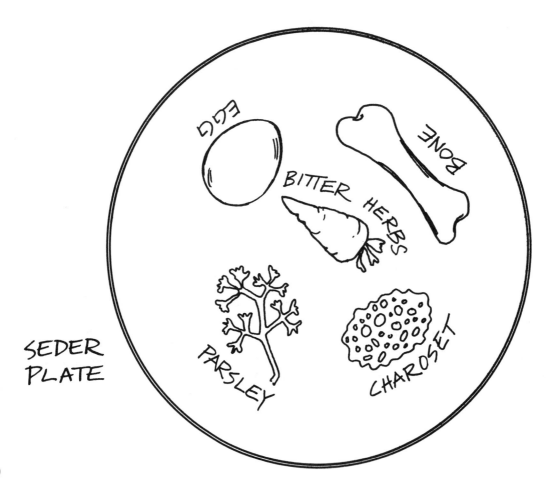

SEDER PLATE

CHAD GADYA
One Kid (Little Goat)

One little goat, one little goat,
  My father bought for two zuzim.
One little goat, one little goat.
Then came a cat and ate the goat
  My father bought for two zuzim.
One little goat, one little goat.
Then came a dog and bit the cat,
  That ate the goat
My father bought for two zuzim.
One little goat, one little goat.
Then came a stick and beat the dog,
  That bit the cat that ate the goat
My father bought for two zuzim.
One little goat, one little goat.

This appealing song is sung during Passover and tells about a father who bought a goat for two coins. It is a cumulative song with characters following one another in sequence. Sing the song with the children, using the puppets provided below to illustrate the actions. These novel puppets are graduated sizes and can swallow one another. Children may wish to add larger animal characters to fit the same format.

1. One lit-tle goat,_____ one lit-tle goat, my__

Chorus begins ... *Chorus ends*

fa-ther bought for_ two _ zu-zim. One lit-tle goat,_____ one lit-tle goat.

2. Then_ came the cat and ate_ the_ goat, my___

(Chorus)

fa-ther bought for_ two_ zu-zim. One lit-tle goat,_____ one lit-tle goat.

TO MAKE A SWALLOWING ANIMAL PUPPET

Materials: Photocopy of patterns, construction paper.

Construction: To make animal, cut out and color photocopy of pattern; cut out mouth hole area. Trace and cut out animal outline onto a sheet of construction paper. Glue outside edges of paper (back of animal) and photocopy (front of animal).

To make goat, cut out and color photocopy of pattern. Bend tab to fit finger.

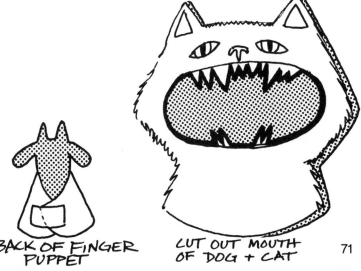

BACK OF FINGER PUPPET

CUT OUT MOUTH OF DOG + CAT

71

DOG

CAT

GOAT

MAKE
2" LONGER

AN EASTER EGG-STRAVAGANZA

Striped, speckled, spotted—undoubtedly one of the most appealing aspects of Easter to children around the world is the kaleidoscope of egg masterpieces reputedly painted by that mad artist, the Easter Bunny. How thoughtful that he should leave such priceless creations behind, hidden in nooks and crannies for children to find on Easter morning. In some parts of the country, particularly the South, another custom is practiced—that of "nicking" eggs. Two children, each with an Easter egg (hard boiled!) in hand, knock the eggs together. The one whose egg cracks the least under the tap appropriates the egg of the other. Besides eggs and other more significant aspects of Easter, this holiday also provides a backdrop for seasonal activities that coincide with the bursting of spring.

Mr. B's garden (Paper Bag Puppets)

MR. B'S GARDEN

Everybody needs a home and the Easter Bunny is no exception. And what could make a nicer home for him than a magnificent garden, tenderly hoed, with blooms of every color and description? It's the perfect place to nestle in after a hard day's work delivering Easter eggs.

To motivate the children, bring in some flower books to share with the group and discuss the most popular flowers, the most unusual, any aspect that piques the children's interest. Roses, daffodils, jack-in-pulpit, lady slippers, tulips are all fascinating subjects with their different shapes and coloration. Create a garden with the group's cooperation, asking each child to make and "plant" a Paper Bag Flower Puppet in the designated garden patch. Flowers can be propped over weighted boxes or pastic bottles.

Use flower puppets for sing-alongs ("Here Comes Peter Cottontail"), or as discussion starters. Ask each flower to tell a secret about the Easter Bunny who hides in the garden. For example, a child may tell something the Easter Bunny likes to eat or do, where he hides his eggs, or some such detail. Of course, the garden is not complete without the master artist, the Easter Bunny himself. Make a Paper Bag Easter Bunny (using the pattern that follows) or Duck or Chick Puppet. These puppets can be used with the poems or songs in this section, or arranged in the garden with the Flower Puppets when not in use.

TO MAKE A PAPER BAG MR. "B" PUPPET

Materials: Small sized paper bag, cotton or large party pom pom, yarn.

Construction: Cut out and color photocopy of patterns. Glue head portion to upper part of bag and body parts to lower part as shown. Attach cotton tail to back of bag and yarn whiskers to face.

TO MAKE A PAPER BAG FLOWER, CHICK OR DUCK PUPPET

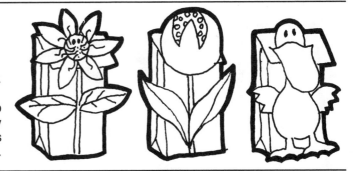

Materials: Small sized paper bag, construction paper.

Construction: Add flower petals or face features to upper flap of bag and additional flower petals or body features to lower part of bag, as shown. Place fingers inside flap, and move up and down to operate mouth.

TO MAKE A GARDEN PATCH

Materials: Cardboard boxes, plastic bottles, green or flower print fabric, construction paper.

Construction: Spread out fabric or paper over tabletop or floor area to represent the garden home. Open out and prop each puppet over a weighted cardboard box or plastic bottle. Paper or real eggs can be hidden among or under the flowers.

MR. B. PATTERNS

HERE COMES EASTER BUNNY

Here comes Easter Bunny
Hop, hop, hop!

"Please Mr. Easter Bunny
Stop, stop, stop!
I don't have any eggs today!"

So he put one in and bounced away!

Here comes Easter Bunny
Hop, hop, hop!

"Please Mr. Easter Bunny
Stop, stop, stop!
I only have one egg today!"

So he put in a second and leaped away!

Here comes Easter Bunny
Hop, hop, hop!

"Please Mr. Easter Bunny
Stop, stop, stop!
I only have two eggs today!"

So he put in a third and leaped away!

There goes Easter Bunny
Hop, hop, hop!

"Thanks Mr. Easter Bunny
You're tip top!
See you again next Easter Day!"

Flippity flop! He hopped away!

by Tamara Hunt

This poem provides plenty of action for Easter egg delivery fun. Let each child make a paper Easter egg and bunny ears beforehand. The basket can be held by the leader as the poem is read and different Easter Bunnies hop by to insert a paper egg. Repeat the poem so all the Easter Bunnies have had a turn.

TO MAKE BUNNY EARS

Materials: One white paper plate, string or ribbon.

Construction: Cut a paper plate as shown. Fold ears forward. Staple the ends of the plate together to form a crown to fit child's head and attach string or ribbon to be tied under the child's chin. The ears can be colored.

Idea from *Storytimes for Two-Year Olds* by Judy Nichols

TO MAKE AN EASTER BASKET

Materials: Photocopy of pattern, heavy paper, paper bag.

Construction: Glue pattern to heavy paper, cut out and color. Staple a paper bag to back of pattern to catch the inserted eggs. Cut out eggs and glue to heavy paper.

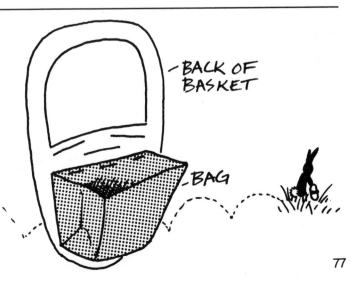

BACK OF BASKET

BAG

77

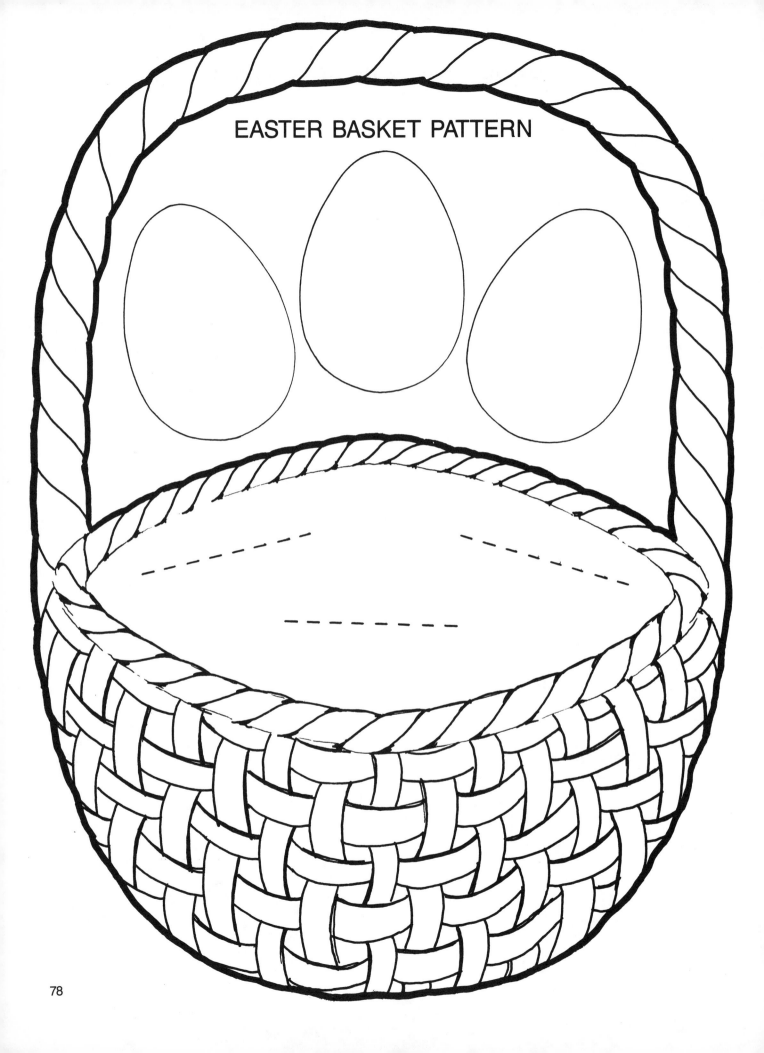

EASTER BASKET PATTERN

78

EASTER BABIES

One little bunny twitches her nose.
Two little bunnies wiggle their toes.
Three little bunnies go hop, hop, hop!
Here comes Mother Bunny, she says, "Stop!"

One little duckie waddles away.
Two little duckies swim and play.
Three little duckies go, "Quack, quack, quack!"
Here comes Mother Duckie, "Please walk on back!"

One little chickie packs for grain.
Two little chickies catch the rain.
Three little chickies go, "Peep, peep, peep!"
Here comes Mother Chickie, "Go to sleep."

by Tamara Hunt

CUT ALONG
DOTTED LINES
ON HATS

HATS

Friendly Easter animals make a cheerful cast for participatory experiences. Divide the class into three animal groups (bunny, duck, chick). Have each child make a Finger Puppet with the patterns that follows of one of the animal groups. As the poem is read, animals in each group can respond by hopping, waddling or pecking at the grain. The leader can play the three mother roles using the same finger puppet patterns with the addition of Easter bonnets.

Cut out and color photocopy of patterns on this page. Cut out finger holes.

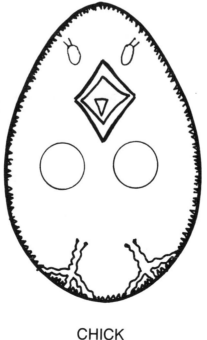

CHICK

DUCK

BUNNY

I FOUND A LITTLE EGG

I found a little egg.
I took a little peek.
Out came a chick
With a "Cheep, cheep, cheep!"

I found a little egg.
I gave a little tap.
Out came a duck
With a "Quack, quack, quack!"

by Tamara Hunt

One of children's most enjoyable activity at Easter is decorating the eggs, a traditional custom practiced in many parts of the globe. Paper plates make an ideal surface for creating a colorful Pop-Up Easter Egg appropriate for a baby chick or duck to be hatched. Ask children to make either a chick or duck for their egg and recite the poem as they pop their creature up.

TO MAKE A POP-UP EASTER EGG

Materials: One full and one half (cut in zig zag fashion) paper plates, construction paper, blunt wood skewer, dowel, straight twig or other rod six inches or longer.

Construction: To make egg, line up edges of half plate with the whole plate. Staple edges, leaving bottom free. Decorate plates with a colorful pattern with coloring media. Make a chick or duck image from construction paper and attach to end of rod. Insert rod through space in bottom of plates and hide puppet inside plates ready to pop up on cue.

THE DAY THE JELLY BEAN MACHINE MADE CANDY CANES

The local grocer's jelly bean machine may be just the thing to inspire thematic story searches for Easter Day. Perhaps everytime someone puts a coin into the machine it goes haywire and spurts out candy canes. (And its not even Christmas!) The grocer in dismay, has to find a solution! Does he call the Easter Bunny, Santa Claus or a mechanic to fix it?

Form the group into teams of three to four members each to develop short puppet skits based on one of the titles above, or another added to the list. Use a puppet idea found in this book for construction.

HELP! SOMEBODY KIDNAPPED THE EASTER BUNNY

That mad artist, the Easter Bunny, appears once again as the lead star in the following story. It is written in the form of a play script for easy participation by the children. The left column contains the narration script to be read by the leader, while the right column describes the actions that accompany the narration. Be sure to strive for contrasting voices where possible when reading the script.

For puppets, use patterns shown earlier in this section and make a Paper Bag Bunny and Flower, and Finger Puppet Duck and Three Little Bunnies. Also prepare a Chick-in-Egg from pattern that follows.

Gather together the following props; cloth square, real or cardboard decorated eggs (one for each child); some plain *blue* eggs; an artist's paint box or palette and paintbrush. Hide all of the props, *Easter Bunny* and *Chick-in-Egg* puppets in your apron pockets or a bag tote.

Cast the following roles: Leader operates the *Easter Bunny* and *Chick-in-Egg* puppets.

Children use puppets to play the parts of *Dooper Duck* (give blue eggs to Duck to hold), the *Three Little Bunnies* and *Flower,* . Two other children play the kidnapper and officer, without puppets. Arrange the cast in the playing space in order of appearance. The Duck can pretend to be in a pond (a small rug), and Flower and little Bunnies in a garden. Let the remaining children pretend to be other flowers (with or without paper bag puppets) in the garden. Cue the children on the story's actions.

A lapboard will make it easier for the Leader to handle the various items. Bring out a few decorated eggs, paintbrush and the paint box before the story begins and lay them on lapboard.

Introduce the Story by having the children share their Easter egg coloring experiences and how they like to decorate their eggs. Ask them, "What do you think Easter would be like if someone happened to kidnap the Easter Bunny?" Introduce your *Easter Bunny* puppet and begin the story.

CHICK IN EGG PATTERN

THE STORY BEGINS

NARRATION

It was the night before Easter and the Easter Bunny was having the grandest time. He was dabbling with his paintbrush, painting spots and dots, and lines and swiggles all over his wonderful eggs. In fact, he was so busy that he simply didn't notice that something or someone was slinking about nearby. When all-of-a-sudden, that something or someone jumped in front of him, threw a cloth over his head and zipped him away. Oh dear, isn't that a most dreadful event. Somebody *actually* had the nerve to kidnap the Easter

ACTION

Bunny dabbles with brush.

Kidnapper sneaks up, throws cloth over Bunny and dashes off.

NARRATION	ACTION

NARRATION

Bunny. It was in the newspapers. It was on the radio. It was even on television! And all the little children found out about this terrible, terrible event. They would not have any lovely eggs this year with spots and dots, and lines and swiggles all over them. They were all sad indeed.

But who wants to sit and mope about it. Let's go find somebody else who will decorate those eggs for us. "Look! There's Dooper Duck in the duck pond now. Dooper! Oh, Dooper Duck! Dooper! Come on over here!" Sure enough Dooper comes waddling along the surface of the pond and says, "Quack, Quack! Wanna fish? Wanna fish?"

Dooper waddles across designated pond area and quacks.

"Oh, no. not today, Dooper," I respond. "We have more important things to think of now." "Listen Dooper, how are you at painting Easter eggs?"

He answers, "Quack, Quack, Quack! Super! Just super dooper!"

"Oh that's great," I reply with a sign of relief. "Now we shall have those eggs in time for Easter after all."

So Dooper puts the paintbrush in his beak, for he claims that for duck artists, this is the best method he knows for painting eggs. Then feverishly he sets to work and paints the eggs. He dips his brush in and out of the pond with every other dab. How convenient to be a duck artist!

Puts brush in his beak and paints eggs, dipping brush into pond occasionally.

At last he finishes and shows the eggs to me. But do you know what he did? He made every single one of those eggs *blue!* ugh! All blue eggs! I just can't believe my eyes for they are all dull, dull, dull! And do you know what he says? He says, "Quack, Quack, Quack! Can't be fussy. Can't be fussy. The pond is blue and the sky is blue. I *love* blue! Quack, quack, quack!" And huffily he waddles off.

Shows eggs to Leader, who looks at them in dismay.

Just then three little bunnies come by, playing a hopping game. So I stop and tell them all about the dreadful kidnapping case and ask if they will finish the eggs for me. Surely, being bunnies themselves, however little, they must know just how to paint eggs. They are so cooperative and altogether say, "Yes, yes, yes!"

Little Bunnies hop all about.

So, I give them the paintbrush and do you know what happens? They all start to fight over it! Ugh! They simply can't agree who will be first to use the brush. So, I snatch the brush away from them and leave. For surely I'll find someone else who can finish these eggs.

Together they say "Yes, yes, yes☆"
They all fight over the brush.

Just then I come to a flower garden with a lovely flower standing in the middle. Ahh—it smells so sweet. Naturally, flowers know all about colors. They are so colorful themselves. So I tell the flower about the dreadful kidnapping and ask if she will mind completing the eggs. "Why of course, my dear," she chimes sweetly, "We flowers are master artists. Certainly you can tell from looking at me that I have a wonderful sense of color."

Smells flower and smiles.

NARRATION	ACTION
"Yes, you are truly gorgeous, I admit."	
So, I give her the paintbrush and to my dismay discover she starts to paint the other flowers! "No, no Flower!" I interrupt. "I need *Easter Eggs* painted, not flowers!"	*Flower uses brush in mouth and paints other flowers.*
"Well, she says huffily, "I don't happen to feel like painting Easter eggs today. I'd much rather paint other gorgeous flowers, like myself. Besides, I hate eggs! Yuk!"	
So, I take the paintbrush away from her and begin to sulk. Well, I guess all those children will just have to be disappointed this year because it looks like there won't be any Easter eggs. One little tear rolls down my cheek. But that's all. After all, what's done is done. And if you can't do anything about it, why sulk about it?	*Takes brush and sits despondently.* *Looks sad and wipes away tears.*
Then, suddenly, there is a knock on the door. Do you know who is there? A Police Officer holding our dreadful, awful kidnapper by the collar. And in the kidnapper's dreadful hands is the Easter Bunny!	*Police Officer knocks on door and holds out robber with Easter Bunny.*
And do you know what the kidnapper does? He very gently hands over the Easter Bunny to me with fine apologies. (You can be sure he didn't come up with such fine manners all by himself!)	*Hands over Easter Bunny to Leader.*
"Thank you," I say, and they hurriedly leave. Now, we will have Easter eggs after all. "Hurry!" "There's still time to finish the eggs." I tell the Easter Bunny.	*Officer and kidnapper leave.*
So the Easter Bunny merrily sets to work painting his spots and dots, and lines and swiggles all over the wonderful eggs.	*Bunny busily paints eggs.*
At last every one of the eggs are done! And do you know what the Easter Bunny does? He gives one of his precious eggs to each and every one of the children, who in turn gently pet him and say, "Thank you!"	
He gives one egg to (child's name) _____	*Gives one egg to each child. Each child, in turn, pets Bunny and says, "Thank you ☆ "*
At last his work is all done. Oops! But what's this? One last Easter egg left. Isn't it strange, isn't it odd? Hummmmm—and it doesn't even look at all like the other ones.	*Leader looks questioningly at egg.*
'Peep—peep—peep!" Do you hear that? Oh, my—what's this? "Peep—peep—peep!" (Noisily)	*Leader holds up egg to ear while making peeping sounds.*
Its a baby chick! Now that is what I call the very best Easter Surprise of all!	*Open egg and pop out the chick surprise.*
By Nancy Renfro	**The End**

MERRY MAY

May Day is a festive holiday, celebrating spring in many places around the world. Traditionally, going to the surrounding countryside and picking flowers, bough branches and bringing them home is the symbolic act of "bringing home the May," This sense of bringing new life, bringing spring, and the process of rebirth/regeneration itself into the village is a custom of European derivation. Thus flowers have become a universal symbol for the sharing of love and friendship.

Flowers can be arranged in many interesting forms and shapes, with the most common for May Day celebrations being wreaths, garlands, and baskets. In Hawaii, May Day is celebrated as "Lei Day" when garlands of flowers are placed around people's neck.

Maypole dances are performed at May Day celebrations, the first of May. This symbolic dance features a tall central May pole with colorful ribbon streamers held by children or young garlanded maidens. The dancers dance in two opposing circles, weaving in and out in such a way as to create a colorful inter-twining of the ribbons into a braid-like pattern. Many similar ribbon dances are performed in other countries such as Germany, India, Mexico and the Soviet Union. These ribbon dances are intriguing options to explore with children together with the related activities that follow.

HIBISCUS

PLUMERIA

TUBEROSE

ORCHID

GARDENIA

PASSION FLOWER

LEI DAY GIFTS

Children may also make regional Leis. For example, Texas might have a lei made of bluebonnets; Georgia, magnolias; and New York, daffodils. Let your region be represented, or go further. Incorporate a geography lesson into the botany possibilities of lei creation, as state flowers from around the United States are interwoven in a long garland or individual leis. Children can be assigned a specific state flower to research, sharing their findings both creatively and botanically with the rest of the class.

In Hawaii, May Day is also called "Lei Day" when garlands of sweet-scented, beautiful flowers are given to be worn around the neck. Although leis are presented as gifts year round, they are especially featured on May Day. To celebrate Lei Day, consider inviting "Lei" the Flower Pig to the classroom to assist in making leis with the children. Lei loves, more than anything to smell and pick sweet flowers as shown in the story that follows.

TO MAKE A HAWAIIAN FLOWER LEI

Materials: Photocopy of patterns, large paper plate.

Construction: Cut out a large hole in a paper plate to leave a 1"-1½" wide ring. Let children choose their preferred flowers from patterns to cut out and color. Glue flowers on ring. Cut out an opening at one point in ring and slip lei over the child's neck.

Floral magazines and mail order catalogues also may be cut up for flower imageries; or, consider making tissue or crepe paper 3-dimensional flowers as alternate ideas.

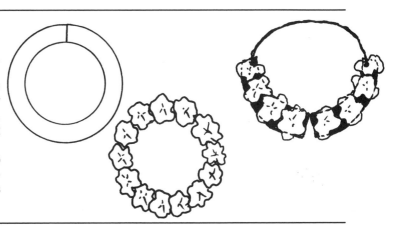

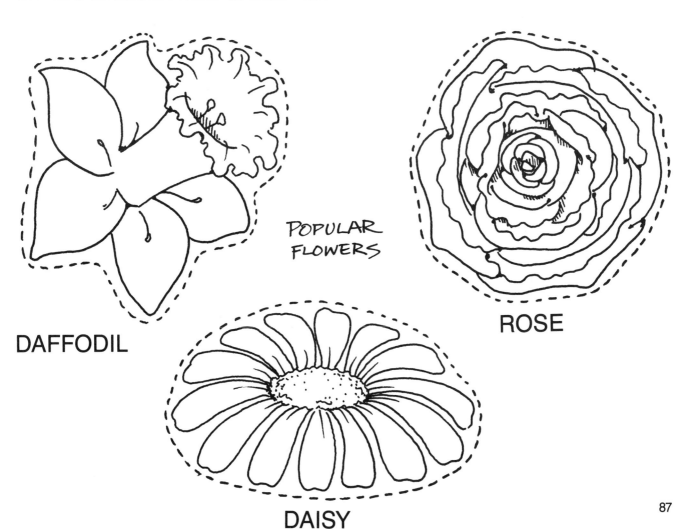

DAFFODIL

POPULAR FLOWERS

ROSE

DAISY

FIVE LITTLE FLOWERS

Five little flowers on the first of May
Were tucked in a basket to be given away.
The first one said, "Where will we go?"
The second one said, "I don't know."
The third one said, "Who will it be?"
The fourth one said, "Let's wait and see."
The fifth one said, "Oh my it's getting late."
So they closed up their petals to wait, wait, wait.

by Tamara Hunt

Cup Flowers are a good, fun-filled way to involve children in botanical study. Ask the children, "What do you like best about flowers"? "What is your favorite flower?" Talk about May Day and the popular tradition of giving flowers as tokens of love and appreciation. Have each child make a Cup Flower and perform in groups of five the poem's actions.

An alternate idea for the teacher is to create a Garden Patch Theater with paper or pictures (from mail order catalogues or magazines) of flowers on drinking straws.

TO MAKE A CUP FLOWER PUPPET

Materials: Two styrofoam or paper cups, construction or tissue paper, blunt skewer or drinking straw.

Construction: Make a flower face with coloring medium or construction paper on one cup.

Create petals with tissue or construction paper on second cup.

Puncture a hole in bottom of both cups. Insert and glue end of skewer or straw in hole of face cup; insert opposite end through hole in petal cup. Pop face cup up and down to give illusion that petals are closing over face.

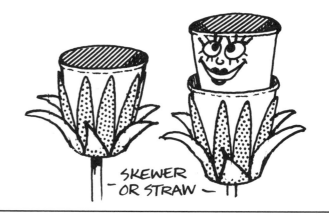

TO MAKE A GARDEN PATCH THEATER AND PUPPETS

Materials: Cut down cereal box, construction paper or flower pictures, drinking straws.

Construction: Cut out and color a garden patch from paper; glue to face of cut down cereal box. Punch five holes in bottom of box.

Attach each flower to end of a drinking straw; insert opposite and through punched hole in box. Pop up each flower as the poem is read.

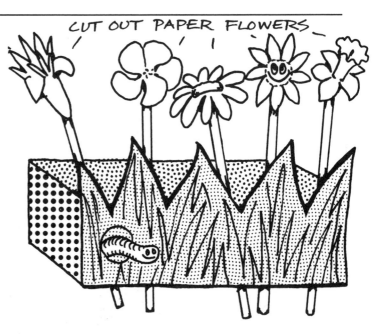

LEI, THE FLOWER LOVING PIG

Lei, the flower loving pig and accompanying story makes an endearing introduction for teaching children about friendship as well as an appreciation for flowers while learning about the Hawaiian custom of giving flower leis as gifts. Have each child make a flower lei, using either the flower pattern included in this section or a customized page of other regional flowers to use with the story. If you wish, customize the story by substituting the name and location where Lei lives, and the children's names, where she visits to make new friends. The leader should play Lei the Pig with a Supermarket Bag Puppet. Assign some children to play the Muddy Pigs (the additions of paper piggy ears, snout or paper curly tail suggest character). The remaining children can be the new Friends with flower leis ready to place around Lei's neck.

Set the scene of the farm by designating rug or other areas to be the muddy pens and the flower gardens (with some real plant prop).

TO MAKE A LEI BAG PIG

Materials: Large supermarket bag, pink construction paper or poster board, scrap fabric and trims.

Construction: Create a pink pig face and ears on upper section of bag's flap and body on lower section. Add pink paper or poster board arms and legs, and a curly paper tail on back of bag. Improvise a frilly fabric skirt, big colorful bow or other costume detail. Cut a hole directly behind flap mouth to insert hand through and comfortably operate flap.

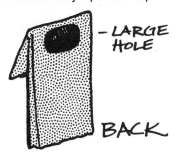

LEI, THE FLOWER LOVING PIG

NARRATION	ACTION
Lei was a very fat and funny Pig who lived on a farm on the island of Maui in Hawaii. She did not like the common pasttime of wallowing in mud baths like most pigs (she thought that a senseless hobby). She was bit uppyish in that she much preferred to wallow in flowers. Lovely, sweet smelling flowers. Bright red ones, yellow ones, pink ones, and purple ones. Oh, how they delighted her.	*Lei explores flowers in garden.*
She spent all her spare time in the neighborhood flower gardens, snorting and sniffing each particular flower while trying to detect what makes one flower so much sweeter or more special than another. It was truly a mudless and wonderful world and made her feel so giddy and happy.	

Lei thinks her flower necklaces smell sweet

NARRATION	ACTION
The other pigs on the farm enjoyed rolling in the mud. They really thought Lei was outrageous and as a whole paid little attention to her. They just left her alone with her silly flowers. When she wanted to play games with them, they laughed and said, "Go away Lei! You are disturbing our mud bath. We want to play Ring Around the Mud." So they all held hands and danced in a circle as they sang:	*Pigs roll in the mud.*
"Here we go around the yucky mud bath;	*Pigs dance around mud pen.*
Yucky mud bath,	*To tune of "Here we go Around the Mulberry Bush"*
Yucky mud bath.	
Here we go around the yucky mud bath,	
This bright and muddy day."	
So Lei didn't have any friends. This sometimes bothered her because she didn't see anything wrong with a pig loving flowers. So the flowers became her *only* friends. She also decided that since people grew the flowers that maybe she could find people friends who understand her sensitivity. Besides she was lonely.	
So one day she waddled away from the farm and took a journey into the neighborhood. She came to a friendly looking house and knocked on the door.	*Lei knocks on door.*
(*Child's name*) answered and said, "Hello."	
"Hello, I'm Lei! Do you like flowers?"	
(*Child's name*) answered, "I grow lots of (*flower description*). Here is a flower necklace for you!" (*child's name*) puts the necklace around Lei's neck.	*Child puts necklace around Lei.*
Lei was very happy that she made a new friend. She said, "Thank you." They shook hands and off Lei went to the next house and knocked on the door.	*Lei knocks on door.*
(Repeat last three paragraphs until all children have a turn).	
Now Lei was very, very happy indeed for she had made many new friends in one day. She went back to the farm and the other pigs saw all her colorful flower necklaces hanging around her neck. They were so envious that they gathered aruond her to admire them.	*Pigs admire necklaces and each says a compliment.*
"Oh, they smell so sweet!" said one pig.	
"I love the colors on that one," squealed another.	
Well, Lei, being a generous pig, decided to let bygones be bygones and shared her flower necklaces with all her muddy pig friends. She put a necklace around each pig's neck. The pigs were so charmed that they jumped up and down and snorted, "Let's play a game! Let's play a game!"	*Pigs jump with excitement.*
They all joined hands and formed a circle around Lei as they sang and danced.	
"Here we go around our friend Lei pig,	
Friend Lei pig,	
Friend Lei pig,	
Here we go round our friend Lei pig,	
This bright and mudless day."	
Lei had made enough friends for one day!	

by Nancy Renfro

The End

STARS AND STRIPES

It was said that General Washington once described the flag by saying, "Take the stars from heaven, the red from the Mother Country, separating by white stripes, thus showing that we have separated from her; and the white stripes shall go down to posterity representing liberty." Every part and every color of this noble flag has a world of meaning. The colors remain symbolic—red for courage, white for liberty, and blue for loyalty.

Everyone knows that Betsy Ross had the honor of making the first flag. She copied the original design exactly as it was presented to her, except for one suggestion, she made five points on each star rather than six. It is said that George Washington argued for a six-pointed star. Since there would be so many to cut, Betsy took out her scissors and took liberties to cut a perfect five-point star—and that was that!

In the evolution of the flag's design, the thirteen red and white stripes symbolized the thirteen Colonies that stood side by side and fought for freedom. The thirteen stars in the original flag were placed in a circle on a sky blue field to signify the never-endingness of the Union and to symbolize the equality of the states. As the union has grown in size, so too have the stars in the flag increased in number.

The flag's strong symbolism can be communicated to children through the flag projects that follow.

FLAG PARADE

50 Stars and 13 Stripes
Is what I like to see
'Cause when I wave my little flag
It waves right back at me.

Blow the horns and beat the drums
Let's have a big parade
And I will proudly wave my flag
'Cause it's the one I made.

by Tamara Hunt

Children love parades! Assign children to form the drum and bugle corps with improvised instruments, such as, pot lid and spoon cymbals, cardboard box drums, or cardboard tube horns (pinch one end together for a mouthpiece) for horns. Or, if a more realistic effect is desired, toy or real instruments may be substituted.

Have each child create a Paper Bag Flag Puppet for the parade, using bold and decorative patriotic motifs of their compositions. Completed puppets can be used to sing songs about America such as, "America the Beautiful," "Oh, Say Can You See" and "Yankee Doodle." Or, they may use the poem above as they march.

TO MAKE A PAPER-BAG FLAG PUPPET

Materials: Paper bag, red, white, and blue construction paper or paint, aluminum foil.

Construction: Cut off the bottom of the bag so to achieve a horizontal flag proportion. Add bold stripes and areas of color with red, white and blue paper or paint. Aluminum foil may be used for stars (use rubber cement to glue down). Flags may take on personalities with added features such as mouths and eyes.

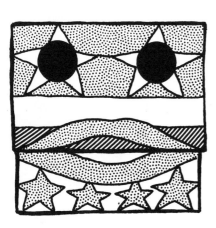

POP, BANG. . .BOOM!

Pop, Pop, Pop, Pop!
Firecrackers never stop!

Pretty colors soaring high
Firecrackers light the sky.

Bursting Bright, in the night
Firecrackers! What a sight!

Wizz, Bizz, Tizz, Sizzle!
Firecracker slowly fizzle.

by Tamara Hunt

What could be more dazzling than a spectacular, sizzling fireworks display in the sky? This splendid event is something all children look forward to. The "Glorious Fourth" is among our most patriotic of holidays as the Liberty bell rings accompanied by a thirteen guns salute (at Independence Hall in Philadelphia) and church bells still peal at various locations in the country to proclaim the adopting of the Declaration of Independence on July 4, 1776.

SIZZLING FIRECRACKERS

Every firecracker seems to have its own personality when celebrating the glorious Fourth. Safe, but noisy (as noisy as children are) Firecracker Tube Puppets can be fashioned from cardboard tubes that feature pop-up sparklers. Have children develop their own individualized fireworks sound track to accompany the puppets in conjunction with the poem.

Afterwards, have children sit in a circle formation with puppets to participate in a dazzling fireworks display. Pretend to light each child's puppet, while the child demonstrates its sound followed up with one statement about what the child is proud of or likes best about being an American (going to a baseball game, being free to express a viewpoint, a picnic, hearing rock music, seeing a parade, visiting another city, riding the train, etc.)

TO MAKE A FIRECRACKER TUBE PUPPET

Materials: Cardboard tube, red tissue paper, foil or tinsel, dowel, blunt skewer or other stick, construction paper, aluminum foil.

Construction: Create a funny face on the tube. Make a nose and features from construction paper. Decorate tube with aluminum foil, paper or paint. Red, white and blue stripes and foil stars may be appropriate motifs to add, but other colors can be explored.

Attach fringed red tissue paper or foil to end of stick for sparkle effect. Insert stick through tube and pop up and down.

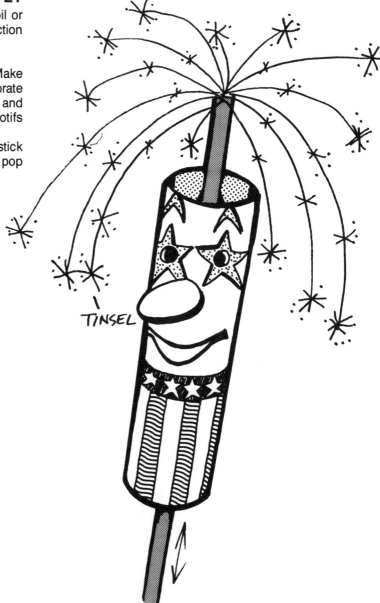

TINSEL

FAMILY FUN

In a world of changing parental roles and responsibilities, Mother's and Father's Day can become a time to celebrate what being a family means to the children. Emphasizing the many different kinds of family units will help make each child feel comfortable that his or her home composition is just as important as that of another child. Stepparents, Grandparents, Aunts, Uncles, Cousins, and special "adopted" relatives are all important but do not have special days in their honor. Thus, we suggest Family Day! In any event you may wish to share with the children Mother's and Father's Day traditions and origins as well as invent new traditions honoring special family members.

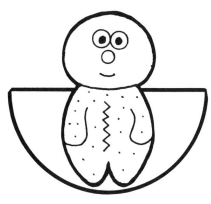

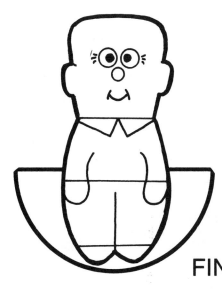

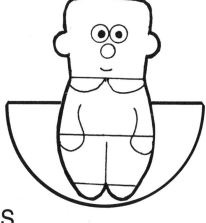

FAMILY
FINGER PUPPET PATTERNS

MITT PATTERN

MY MOM, MY DAD AND ME

My Mom, My Dad Reversible Mitt Puppets provide an opportunity to share parent-children activities with all members of the family, including parents, step-parents, grandparents or other relatives. Simple paper mitts provide a space for a child's image on the thumb, and parent or other relative image on both sides of the finger areas.

Each child can have a turn introducing the relative to the group and telling about memorable experiences shared together.

TO MAKE A MY MOM, MY DAD PUPPET

Materials: Photocopy of pattern, cardboard, supermarket bag, fabric, cotton, yarn and trims.

Construction: Cut out a master cardboard mitt shape following the pattern. Use this shape to trace a copy of mitt on flattened supermarket bag.

Cut out two thicknesses of bag, following shape outline resulting in two identical pieces. Line up the pieces and staple or glue edges together, leaving bottom free. Draw a child image on thumb area, and parent or relative on opposite side of mitt. Yarn, cotton, fabric and other odds and ends can be used to decorate costume areas. Another parent or relative can be created on opposite side of above.

BECAUSE YOU'RE SPECIAL

A customized greeting card made by children and presented to a special person, family member or otherwise, can be a meaningful experience all around. Use the following patterns for a Special Finger Puppet Card for each child to copy. There is a space on the card to write a poem or personalized message and drawings.

TO MAKE A SPECIAL FINGER PUPPET CARD

Materials: Photocopy of patterns, yarn, cotton, sequins (optional).

Construction: To make card, cut out and color the photocopied card with pictures of hobbies, interests and other imageries that reflect the special person. A poem or note can be written in the block area.

To make puppet cut out and color photocopy appropriate pattern from Family Fun introduction page. Curve sides around and tape at back.

BACK OF FINGER PUPPET PATTERN

You're Special!

cut out

CARD PATTERN

WHO LIVES IN OUR HOUSES?

Imagine a miniature town in the classroom with houses created by class members to reveal what is most special about home and family. To create such a town of composite "favorite spaces," ask each child to convert a shoebox or food box into a model house. One room, several rooms, or the exterior alone can be represented. They can do their actual favorite room or a room of their dreams.

Arrange the boxes on a tabletop or floor surface and link them together with paper strips, sidewalks and roads. Add families by using photographs brought from home as models for making walking finger puppets of the people who live in the house. When not on display, children can improvise scenes of what they enjoy doing at home with their families. Children with two homes can be encouraged to create scenes of both locations. Those who finish early may want to create "extra" scenic suggestions like trees, the school or a favorite store to give an even more realistic neighborhood feeling.

TO MAKE A WALKING FINGER PUPPET

Materials: Photocopy of pattern, heavy paper, yarn or cotton, small rubber band.

Construction: Cut out and color pattern. Reinforce by gluing to heavy paper. Glue on yarn, fringed paper or cotton for hair. Staple a small rubber band across back of puppet to slip fingers through and walk puppet.

PUPPET PATTERN

GIANT LABOR DAY FESTIVAL

A grand marshal with impressive hat and huge baton takes the lead and is followed by a lively brass band—tuneful French horn, blaring trumpets and tubas. Not far behind, march formations of jewelry workers, bricklayers and other craft workers all celebrating new liberation in labor laws as they hold their first festival in New York City in 1882. It was indeed a moment to commemorate as working conditions then were often very harsh and trying. People worked long hours (twelve to fourteen hours a day) and were paid minimal wages for their endless labors. Wages were often so low that in order for families to survive, little children had to pitch in and worked almost as intensely as the adults.

When things became so tough, craft unions formed, many of the workers in craft unions in New York City were immigrants from other countries who wanted to realize their dream in America of success, prosperity—and some leisure time to spare.

ALL KINDS OF PEOPLE

Who brings your newspaper right to the door?
Who grows the food that you buy in the store?

Who helps you learn lots of new things at school?
Who guards the children who swim at the pool?

Who flys the planes that you see in the sky?
Who sells you bread, donuts, cupcakes and pies?

Who makes you well when you feel really sick?
Who builds you houses from wood, steel or brick?

Who brings you letters and gifts in the mail?
Who keeps the speedy train "straight on the rail?"

All kinds of people who work for their pay
To them we say "Thank you" on this labor day.

by Tamara Hunt

The people who work in a community make it a special place to live. Discuss the people who work in the children's communities. Who are some of the key people and what their primary functions are in the community?

Recite the poem. Afterward, ask children to create Community Helper Puppets. This can be done by using the basic S/He pattern in section one and the basic costume pattern included here. Each child can choose a worker to depict. A modern interpretation would be to create a motif or symbol on the costume following popular T-Shirt fads to represent a profession. For example: a cake (baker); tool (carpenter); apple (teacher).

CHOOSE A JOB

Choosing future careers, or asking children what they want to be when they grow up is always a curious question to pose. Exploring the spectrum of job opportunities and roles people play in the community through puppetry is a good way to broach the subject of Labor. Have children choose jobs and create Paper-Plate Worker Puppets to represent chosen professions. Cardboard or improvised props can also be made to enhance the character's role, such as a police car (cardboard cutout on a stick) for a police officer;

hammer for a carpenter; computer (constructed from a box) for an engineer; cake for a baker; or paint brush and palette for an artist.

Organize a Giant Labor Festival parade with a makeshift band up front and a Grand Marshal with baton and top hat to lead the parade. Afterwards, each child can make a speech about his or her job (what is done at work; what products, services or goals are achieved).

TO MAKE A PAPER-PLATE WORKER PUPPET

Materials: Two paper plates, two medium sized rubber bands, construction paper, mural paper, fabric, yarn and trims.

Construction: Staple a rubber band across the back of each paper plate, about two inches down from the top. Line up rubber band ends of plates and staple plates together, as shown.

Create a face on plate. Teeth, tongue and mouth features can be detailed inside bottom plate. Yarn or fringed paper make good hair.

Have children trace their body outlines on sheets of mural paper to cut out and decorate. Attach body to bottom plate. Or, an alternate idea is to make smaller body versions from construction paper.

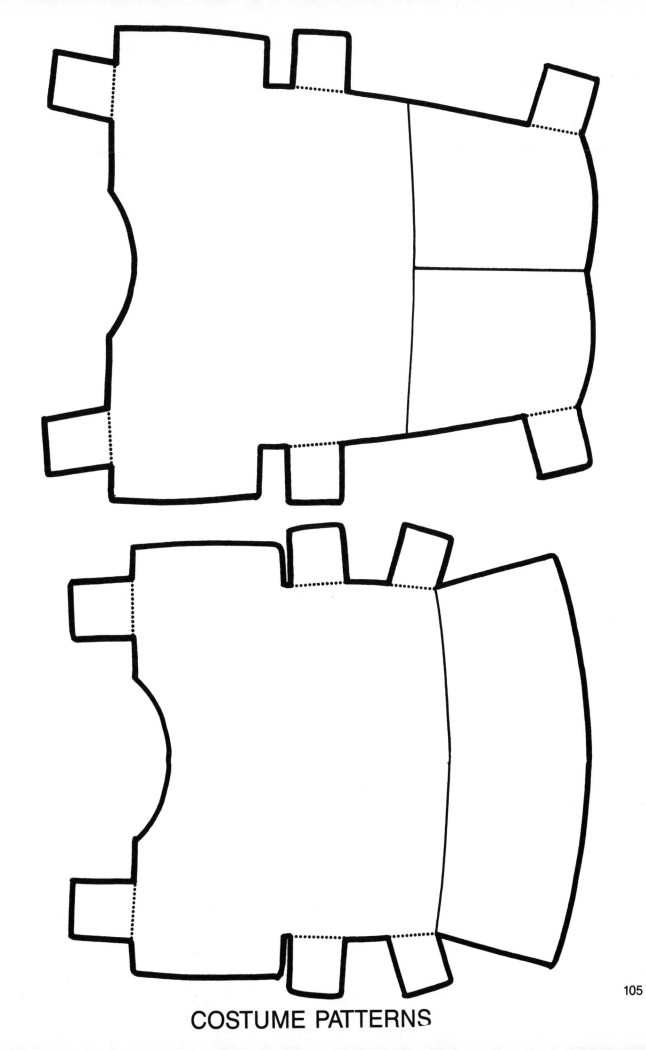

105

COSTUME PATTERNS

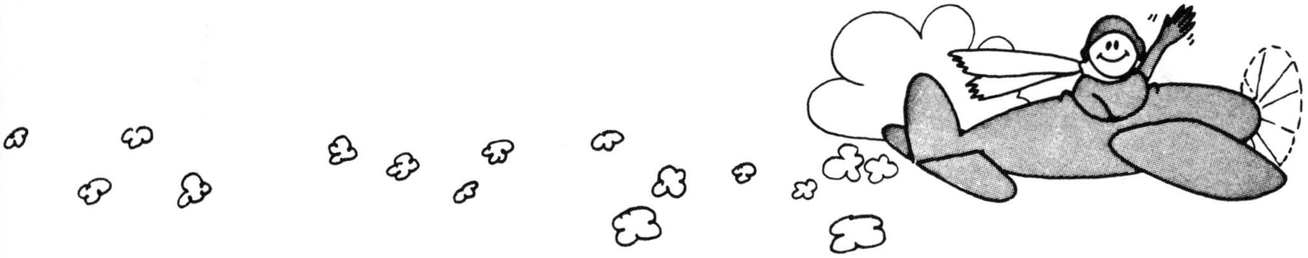

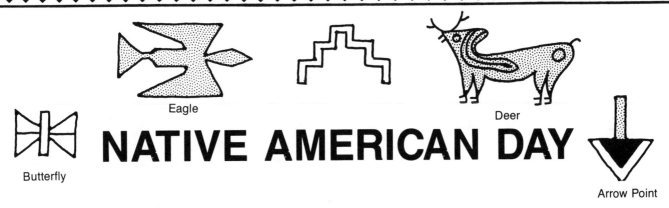

Eagle

Deer

Butterfly

NATIVE AMERICAN DAY

Arrow Point

At one time, Pah-ince, the beaver, was a great and proud fellow. Pah-ince possessed one of the most beautiful tails in the animal kingdom. It was covered with thick, soft, black fur as bushy as a bramblebush. One day he tried to steal fire from the Fire Indians. In the process, he was pounced upon by the Indians, and to save his own life, narrowly escaped by jumping over the fire. To his dismay, his tail caught fire and suddenly burst into flames. By the time he reached home, there was not a single hair left. And that is why beavers today have a flat, smooth and shiny tails.

A Pahute Tale (Utah)

There are many other such similar tales as *The Beaver's Tail. How The Turtle Got Its Cracks, Why The Porcupine Cannot Throw Its Quills,* and *How The Seasons Came To Be Set* are all part of the immensely rich lore of Native America. To have the privilege of sitting around a campfire under an illuminated night sky of shivering desert stars and listening to the narro-gwe-nap (official storyteller) tell legends is an honor indeed.

Storytelling as well as music and dance and feasting are all joyous aspects of the Powwow still celebrated, by tradition, in many parts of the country today. This Native American ceremony, sometimes called a Tribal Fair is an event that blends old and new traditions, with its main purpose to bring family members together and link tradition Dancers participate sometimes wearing fanciful beaded costumes for more colorful events, the pulsating of drum beats constant background.

Powwows are still held on special occasions, usually at reservations or at rodeos and fairs.

Native American Day is an official holiday in various parts of the country and offers an opportunity for children everywhere to become more aware of this country's rich heritage. To celebrate this day, take a regional tack. Have children work in teams of three or four members each to research interesting data on local Native American culture and lore. Perhaps even invite a member of the Native American community (or other knowledgable person) to speak with the class. Hold a Powwow highlighting authentic costuming, dance, food and crafts (weaving, bead work, building a Tipi, hunting tools, etc.).

Another approach, for bringing children closer to Native American culture is to have teams present Native American lore. If local stories can be found, they could serve as ideal material. Another source is to use one of the selections as retold by modern authors (Such as McDermotts *Arrow in the Sun.*)

A popular theme is coyote, a reoccurring character in many Native American stories. He is known as a most devious fellow, always on the sly and doing his best to outwit those who reside in the human world.

Have the group create stick masks from paper plates or boxes for pantomiming the roles in this story as it is narrated by the leader. Three or four members can form a Tipi with their bodies serving as the central focal point of the story. A fabric bundle or pillow case with a beach ball "sun" inside and tied to a stick can be arranged inside the Tipi for the Coyote to take away with him. Designate a path around the room that the Coyote can follow in his travels.

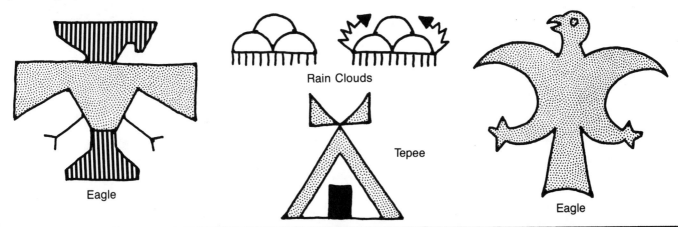

Eagle

Rain Clouds

Tepee

Eagle

The Man of the Tipi — (Paper Plate Stick Mask)

Coyote Tries to Steal the Sun

One time when Coyote was traveling around the country he came to a tipi. He said to the man of the tipi, "Little brother, I heard you were camped here, and I've come to sleep all night. I'll choose the side I like. I want to pick my own bed." The man said that that was all right.

Coyote looked around and saw a bundle tied over the bed on the west side, so he picked out that wall. At night they all went to sleep except Coyote. When he was certain that all of the others were asleep, he took whatever it was that was tied over him and went out. He kept going and going; he traveled all night, all the next day. By the evening of that day he was wornout and sleepy, so he lay down and went to sleep.

When he woke up he found himself back in the tipi from which he had stolen the bundle, which he had under his arm. The man said, "Coyote, you're crazy, tie that back up where it belongs."

Coyote said, "I put it under my arm to give me luck." He then went out and told the man that he was going away but would be back that night.

He came back that night and slept in the same place. During the night he looked around and saw that they were asleep. He again untied the bundle and told himself he was going farther away than the time before. He went out and started to run. He traveled for two days and two nights this time. Then he was so tired he fell asleep as soon as he lay down. At daybreak he woke up and found himself back under the same tipi poles with the bundle under his arm. The man saw him and said, "Coyote, you tie that back up, you can't get away with it."

"I just want to be lucky, little brother, so I sleep with it under my arm," Coyote replied. But he was mad and said to himself that next time he would go much farther before he stopped.

He went off during the day but came back at night and slept in the same place. When they were all asleep he got the bundle down again and went off. He kept going day and night, day and night, day and night, before he lay down to rest. He fell asleep at once. The man found him sleeping with the bundle under his arm. When Coyote woke up the man said, "Coyote you shouldn't do that. You can't take off with this bundle."

Coyote said, "I don't want to take it. I don't feel good and I only want to sleep with it." He went off that day, but came back that night to try again.

The fourth time he lay down he didn't go to sleep, but untied the bundle as soon as everyone was asleep and started off with it. He traveled on and on and on. For four days and nights he kept going, then lay down to sleep.

When he woke up he saw the same tipi poles over him. The man said to him, "Coyote, you can't take off with this bundle. This is my tipi. The sky is my tipi and you can't get out from under it. This medicine is here all the time."

Coyote then found out that he had been trying to run away with the sun, so he gave up. He knew he couldn't get out from under the sky.

He told the man that he was moving on to the next camp.

The End

Taken from "The Sky is My Tipi" by Mody C. Boatright with permission from the Texas Folklore Society.

TO MAKE A STICK MASK

Materials: Paper plate, cereal or other box, construction paper, ½" diameter dowel, fabric yarn, cotton and trims.

Construction: Use a paper plate or cut out the entire back and bottom end of a box for the mask base. Locate and cut out the eye holes. Paint or use colorful papers, trims and other odds and ends to decorate face and add character. Attach dowel to back of mask and hold up mask in front of face while pantomiming actions.

PAPER PLATE

CEREAL BOX

HIGH HOLY DAYS
ROSH HASHANAH & YOM KIPPUR

The High Holy Days, called the Days of Awe, are the holiest days of the Jewish year and are the beginning of the Jewish calendar. According to legend, the Jewish New Year began when God created the earth. The High Holy Days are made up of Rosh Hashanah (in Hebrew meaning "Head of the Year") and Yom Kippur ("Day of Atonement"), which are times when Jews think over their lives during the past year, their relationship with other people and their feelings about God. They try to correct problems between themselves and other people, and they spend time thinking and praying about how they might live as better people during the coming year.

The major symbols for the holiday is: the ram's horn, which reminds us of Abraham's devotion to God. Instead of sacrificing his only son, a ram was sacrificed instead. The ram's horn, called a *shofar*, has a stirring sound when blown and punctuates the High Holy Day services with its powerful blast.

In biblical times, the shofar proclaimed important moments, such as a call to battle, a newly crowned king, or the beginning of Sabbath. The story of Jonah, who blew the ram's horn, causing walls to tumble, is read at this time.

Some important symbols around High Holy Days follow:

Book of Life
Jews speak of the events for the coming year as being inscribed in the Book of Life. When they greet each other at this time of the year, they say, "May you be inscribed for a good year in the Book of Life."

Apples and Honey
Apple slices are dipped in honey to symbolize extra sweetness for the coming year.

Although there are many lessons of this important holiday period, they can all be summed up in the words of a wise rabbi: "A man should live in such a way that he can truthfully say, 'I have not yet wasted a single day of my life.'" To every Jew, at Rosh Hashanah and Yom Kippur, this challenge is renewed.[1]

Some High Holy Days activities follow:

Ask yourself questions
Think about the year just passed.
What did you do that you wish you could undo?
What did you do that you're proud of?
What happened that you wish hadn't happened?
Is there something you could have done to make things better than they were?
If you could wish something for yourself this coming year, what would it be?—for your family?—for your friends?
If you could wish three things to be better for the world, what would they be?
Can you do anything to make them happen? How?

Act out the story of Jonah, the ram's horn and Jericho with or without puppets.

Dramatize the Yussel's Prayer,[2] the story of a young orphan who is not considered important enough to come to worship at the Yom Kippur by Reb Meir, his employer. Reb Meir tells him to go to the field to take care of the cows because he does not know how to pray. The young boy obeys, but wants to pray so much at this sacred time of year, that he plays music from his heart on a simple reed. Meanwhile, in the synagogue, the rabbi will not conclude the Yom Kippur service until he is sure that a sincere and pious prayer has opened God's heart. People in the synagogue become impatient and wonder, "Why does the rabbi not finish and let us go home to eat." They are hungry since they have been fasting all day. The rabbi waits and waits and finally he hears what he has been waiting for—the sincere prayers that come straight from the heart; it is the prayer of the young shepherd in the field, a voice on whose wings all the prayers of the people are carried to God's heart.

Make puppets of the story's characters and dramatize.

[1]Morris Epstein. All About Jewish Holidays and Customs. New York: Ktay Publishing, 1959, p. 23.

[2]Cohen, Barbara. Yussel's Prayer, a Yom Kippur Story, New York: Lothrop, 1981.

LeSHANAH TOVAH GREETINGS

During the Jewish New Year, families send greeting cards to friends and relatives, often adorned with Stars of David and shofars and other High Holy Holiday images. Have each child create a personalized LeShanah Tovah ("good year" greeting) Card with finger puppet to give to someone special. The pattern below provides the card and finger puppet constructions for children to which they can add designs and special messages, using symbols of Rosh Hashanah. These cards also carry the traditional message *Leshanah Tovah Tiketatevu* or "May you be inscribed in the Book of Life for a good year."

TO MAKE A LESHANAH TOVAH FINGER PUPPET CARD

Materials: Photocopy of patterns.

Construction: To make card, cut out and color a design or message on the card. Cut out finger puppet hole and fold card along crease lines. To make finger puppet, cut out and color pattern. Perhaps glue a photograph of the person's face you wish to give the card or draw in an image. Bend tabs of puppet and glue to fit finger.

PATTERN

LE SHANAH TOVAH TIKETATEVU

CARD PATTERN

AHOY THERE—LAND!

Adventure, tropical islands, thundering storms and a momentous landing! What a fine drama with which to introduce children to Christopher Columbus' renown 1492 voyage across the high seas.

Columbus was born in Italy where he grew up to be an excellent seaman, having spent most of his adult life on the water. He loved to navigate sailing vessels at a time when sailing was considered terribly dangerous and quite foolhardy. In his life, it was believed that the earth was flat as a pancake and, therefore, it would be easy to sail right off its rim! Columbus was so wise in the ways of the waters that famous navigators came to him to consult and often hired him to help make their navigational charts.

But Columbus wanted more; he dreamed the dreams of Marco Polo and wanted to find a new route to India and the Far East. His friends laughed at him when he said he could reach the East by sailing West. Finally, he convinced Queen Isabella of Spain that he could find both a new route to India and rich coffers of gold with which to enlarge her kingdom. Isabella offered to sell her personal jewels in order to pay for his trip.

After much preparation, he sailed off with the famous trio of sailing vessels—the Nina, Santa Maria and the Pinta. At daybreak October 12, 1492 could be heard the resounding words, "Land! Land!" On land, waiting to greet Columbus and his crew were natives who watched the ships with utter amazement and curiosity. Columbus named these natives "Indians" because he thought he had discovered the coast of India which was of course America.*

*America's name comes from Amerigo Vespucci, another Italian explorer, who is reputed to have landed there first.

CHRISTOPHER COLUMBUS

*Christopher Columbus begged his Queen, "Please let
   me go
To take a crew exploring where great western breezes
   blow."
The wise Queen Isabella gave her blessing, bid
   farewell.
And what might be the ending, only history would tell.*

*Christopher Columbus went a'sailing off to the sea.
With the Nina, the Pinta and the Santa Maria three.
All his men got tired as they sailed for days and nights
Wondering if ever there would be new land in sight.*

*Christopher Columbus said, "We mustn't give up now."
His men looked so discouraged as they stood upon the
   bow.
And then one morn, October 12th, 1942
They saw a most amazing sight against a sea of blue.*

*Christopher Columbus heard a voice cry out with joy.
"Tierra, tierra, tierra, look—There's land ahoy!"
And others said, "The grass is green. The rocks and
   earth are brown."
But they had no idea, not a clue of what they'd found.*

*Christopher Columbus said, "Come men let's go
   ashore.
I claim this land for my dear Queen to be San
   Salvadore."
And as the great explorer stood and watched to his
   surprise.
He met the gaze of Arawaks with dark and curious
   eyes.*

*Christopher Columbus then proclaimed for all to hear.
You shall be the Indians of the Western Hemisphere.
And then he told his men, "Set sail. It's time for us to
   leave.
We must return to tell the Queen our goal has been
   achieved.*

*Christopher Columbus, an explorer bold and brave.
America was one of the discoveries he made.
History proclaims his fame and though the past is gone.
His voice still echoes in the wind, "Sail on, sail on, sail
   on."*

by Tamara Hunt

This poem provides background to help children explore details of Christopher Columbus' life and famed journey. Discuss "courage" and compare past adventures requiring courage with modern day explorations requiring courage—space travels, undersea explorations, alpine climbing and other adventures of danger.

Recite the poem using Columbus and three Paper Plate Ship visuals as key focus. Children can play parts of the queen and Native Americans. Arrange them at opposite ends of the playing space (ocean) as the leader or children guide the ships across the space and undulating waves.

Children can all make ships to bring home or to use for sing-along in the classroom to songs as "America the Beautiful" and "Sailing Over the Ocean Blue".

TO MAKE A PAPER PLATE SHIP AND COLUMBUS PUPPET

Materials: Photocopy of pattern, paper plate, two drinking straws.

Construction: To make ship, fold paper plate in half. Cut out white sails from construction paper; attach to a drinking straw and insert in a hole punched along fold of plate. Decorate ship and write its name on sides.

To make puppet, cut out and color photocopy of pattern. Attach to end of a drinking straw; insert opposite end through a second hole punched along plate's fold line.

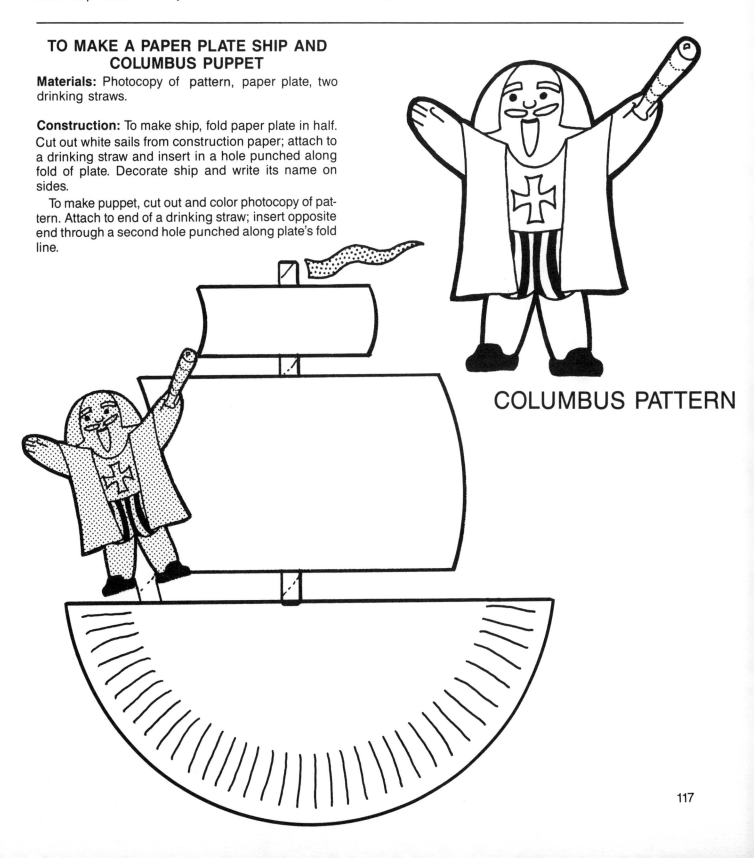

COLUMBUS PATTERN

117

HORRORIFIC HALLOWEEN

On Halloween Eve by the midnight moon
The skeletons dance to an eerie tune,
The bones they cackle and the bones they creak
There's a clickity clacking and a squiggly squeak!

On Halloween Eve by the midnight moon.
Don't open your door, at least not too soon.
For the skeleton's trick, but they never treat
And they might just getcha if you dare to peak!

Skeleton Dance by Tamara Hunt

The midnight moon on Halloween night seems to symbolize all the spooky horrors imaginable—cackling witches on broomsticks; creaky skeletons wth their clicking and clacking bones; mangy black-cats, screeching and scratching; and round orange pumpkins, eerily glowing and moaning. The imagery is endless, but it is all part of the fun that makes Halloween night a time to haunt us earthly creatures.

At one time in Western Europe, witches were believed to ride on broomsticks while menacing ghosts played tricks upon their unknowing victims. It is said that farmers chased away these evil spirits by building bonfires and wearing grotesque disguises to frighten away the evil night air. These disguises became the basis of our present system of wearing costumes at Halloween. The original word Halloween derives from "Holy" or "hallowed" evening because it comes on the day before "All Saints Day", which was celebrated on November 1st.

For the present, however, we are not concerned with these traditional links and Halloween has, instead, been celebrated as the most whimsical and nonsensical of all the holidays. It is a time for fun and hocus-pocus and trickery as wild as the imagination can soar. As the rumpus begins, we continue to pit our puny powers against the night air of this menacing eve.

A CHILLING CLOTHESLINE CAST

Creepy crawlers, bloodthirsty bats and vaporous vampires make a great cast when hung on a clothesline strung across the room, creating a ghastly effect. In conjunction with the decorative element of the clothesline, the characters can be used for dramatizing in the song, "Old Woozer Witch Had a Haunted House," revamped to the tune of "Old MacDonald Had a Farm."

Ask one child to create a ghastly witch image and another, a haunted house from large sheets of construction paper. Then have the rest of the group arrange a cast of suitable tenants to inhabit a haunted house—beasts, ghosts, vampires and bats.

String a clothesline across two points in the room or have three children serve as clothes poles to hold up the line. Give each child a spring clothespin. Begin the song and have the children with the Woozer Witch and haunted house images clip these items to the clothesline with the clothespins. Proceed with the dubbing in new characters, one by one, while adding ghastly sounds for each new character. A verse sample follows.

OLD WOOZER WITCH HAD A HAUNTED HOUSE
(to tune of Old MacDonald Had a Farm)

Old Woozer Witch had a haunted house,
Eee I, ee I, O.
And in that house was a hairy beast.
With a growl, growl here, and a growl, growl there,
Here a growl, there a growl,
Everywhere a growl, growl.
Eee I, ee I, O.

TO MAKE A GHASTLY HALLOWEEN CHUM

Materials: Construction paper, fabric, yarn and trim.

Construction: Cut out character from construction paper. Decorate and add features and details such as wiggly antennas and ears, costumes, horrible warts, gruesome scars and mangy hair, using paper and scrap materials. Certain materials can be used to create special effects: plastic food wrap is good to have on hand for ghostly characters; aluminum foil for a threatening robot.

BOO! I SEE A GHOST

Boo! I see a ghost
Scary as he can be!
Ha! Ha! I fooled you
Look, it's only me!

by Tamara Hunt

A Pop-Up Ghost in a Cup Theater is a nice novelty item for surprising friends. Each child can add a touch of individuality to this idea by drawing a "me" version on the blank side of the ghost section of the turn-around pattern below, or pasting in a photograph of themselves. As the poem begins, the ghost can be hidden in the cup, ready to pop up on ghostly cue, pop down, then reappear in the form of a "me" image.

Utilize this project for opening discussion with children about their fears. Talk to the children about being "scared." Ask, "What are some of the things that make you feel scared? How do you scare others? What is the scariest part of Halloween" End the discussion with elements that reassure: "What is the best part of Halloween? What makes you feel safe after you are scared?"

TO MAKE A GHOST CUP THEATER

Materials: Photocopy of pattern, styrofoam or paper cup, drinking straw.

Construction: Cut out pattern and fold along crease line. Draw a "me" image on the blank section or glue in a photograph head image. Glue or tape one end of drinking straw between a folded ghost. Puncture a hole in bottom of cup and insert other end of straw through hole. Operate straw from underneath the cup.

ATTACH BACKDROP TO CUP

↕ STRAW

SELF/GHOST PATTERN

SILLY SKELETON DANCE

From the head bone to the toe bone, skeletons make an engaging theme for some loose jointed Halloween fun. For this activity, upper grade level children may wish to make a Paper String Puppet based on a skeleton's actual anatomical framework, while younger children might enjoy a silly version of a skeleton utilizing the patterns that follow.

The skeleton constructions can be manipulated to the rhythm of the poem, "Skeleton Dance" included in the Halloween introduction while playing up the sound effects in the poem. Or possibly, the skeletons can dance to the popular "Dem Bones" song (The head bones connected to the neck bones, etc.) Before beginning the puppetmaking session, warm up the group by playing some fast, lively music and have children pretend that they are loose jointed skeletons, dancing and moving in time to the music.

TO MAKE A SILLY SKELETON STRING PUPPET

Materials: Photocopy of bone patterns, paper bag, black construction paper (optional), string, paper fastener brads, cardboard tube.

Construction: Glue sheets of black construction paper onto surface of paper bag (optional). Cut out bones from photocopy and glue to bag surface and glue over bag's surface. Also refer to the Mexican Holiday "Day of the Dead" activity

Extra bones can be linked together with lengths of string or paper fastener brads to make nimble joints.

Attach a length of string to top of bag and tie other end around a cardboard tube handle.

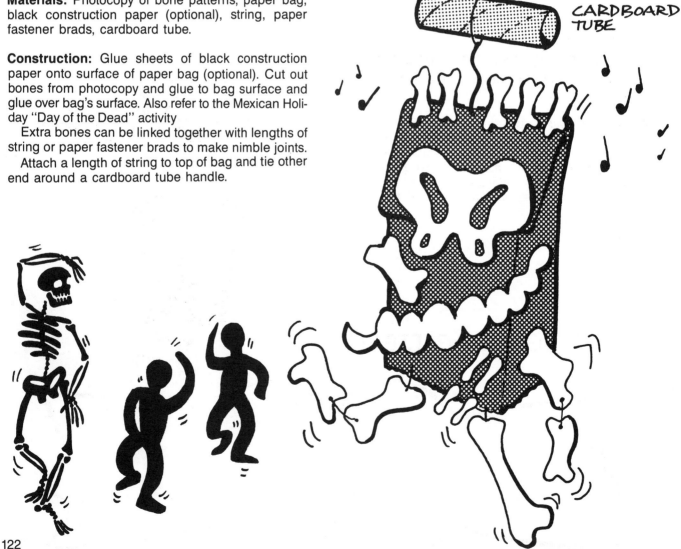

CARDBOARD TUBE

SPOOKY HABITATS

SNIDER SPIDER

Barry Bat's cave, Wanda Witch's haunted house, Snider Spider's pumpkin hide-a-way are a few of the habitats that make permanent residences for such habitants. Have each child create a Spooky Envelope Puppet and matching Bag Habitat. After completion, ask each child to make up a poem or short story about their character and its home. Such questions as the following might spark ideas:

What does your character like to do all day?
Does it enjoy scaring people? How?
What does it like to eat?
Who are its best friends?
What is it most afraid of?

BARRY BAT

TO MAKE A SPOOKY ENVELOPE PUPPET

Materials: 3½″ × 6½″ letter envelope, construction paper.

Construction: Tuck flap of envelope inside envelope. Place hand into envelope as shown. Gently "bite" finger of other hand to form mouth. (Straighten out mouth if wrinkled). Add features to envelope and a paper body to bottom of envelope. Note: Avoid envelopes with overly large V cut into back. Also use sturdy grade envelope rather than the lightweight variety.

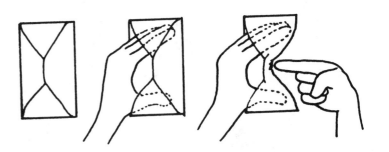

TO MAKE A BAG HABITAT

Materials: Supermarket bag, construction paper.

Construction: Decide how the character will enter the bag. A bat may fly into a cave hole (hole cut in front of the bag), or a ghost shrink down a chimney or tombstone (from the top of the bag).

Decorate the bag with paper details or use coloring medium to create definition such as windows for a haunted house, stones for a cave, or yarn for a spider's web. Real grasses and other natural items can also be glued to the surface of the bag.

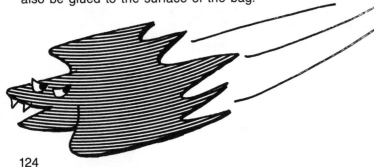

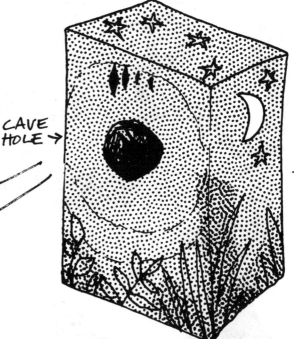

CAVE HOLE →

WITCHES BREW

Biggety, baggety, boggety Boo!
This is the way I stir my stew.
Biggety, baggety, boggety, Boo!
Won't you put something in my brew?

Biggety, baggety, boggety Bip!
Wouldn't you like to take a sip?
Biggety, baggety, boggety Bite!
It will turn you into a fright
On this special Halloween night!

by Tamara Hunt

Children enjoy working magic and seem to take a particular fancy to witches, those wonder-workers that cast spells. Just think of the bogus that can be achieved with a whole woggle of witches casting spells into a shared pot of potent brew! Turn around Bodi-Witch Puppets are the perfect medium as children dramatize this sorcery on the poem above.

Use an oversized pot or bucket as the witch's cauldron, with an oversized spoon, paddle or shovel for stirring the brew. Have one Witch take the lead and stir the brew while the other Witches chant and add their ingredients, one by one. After each Witch takes a sip, the puppet can be turned around to show what it has become.

The verse should be repeated enough times so as to offer all the Witches time to add to the concoction, another horrible "ingredient". (items drawn on paper, or found objects such as a shoelace, rubber spider, bubble gum, etc.)

TO MAKE A BODI-WITCH PUPPET

Materials: Paper plate, 6" wide × 36-40" long strip of dark fabric or crepe paper, construction paper, ribbon or cording.

Construction: Create a witch's face on one side of the paper plate and something into which she will be transformed on the other side. (Monster, pumpkin, frog, or insect, etc.)

Add features with construction paper or coloring medium. Attach a paper witch's hat to top of plate. Staple a strip of dark fabric or crepe paper to bottom of plate and let hang down. Staple a ribbon or cording to the center of top plate.

125

SCAREY STORIES

Based upon the Rorschach test of finding forms in the odd shapes of inkblots, this unusual technique using abstract shapes helps promote children's imaginative powers. They examine abstract shapes to find images that will spark new story ideas that may then be incorporated into puppet shows and/or creative dramatizations.

TO CREATE A SCAREY STORY

Materials: 12″ × 18″ or larger sheet of construction paper, scrap construction paper, fabric, yarn and trims, paper fastener brads.

Construction: Divide the group into teams of three members each. Discuss the kinds of lines that might be used to draw shapes—curved, angular, zig-zagged, wiggly, and so on.

Give each team a sheet of colored construction paper, asking them to draw a fast line on the paper, resulting in two shapes dividing the sheet.

Repeat the process once more until there are three shapes. Study them carefully to see what forms the shapes suggest—animal, person, creature, inanimate object, landscape or anything else that comes to mind that might be translated into a Halloween theme.

Have each team think of a story idea while converting the shapes into characters, scenery, or props. For example, the three shapes might suggest a haunted castle, a two headed ghost, and a whale. The challenge here is to create a unified story around such unlikely story components. In this grouping trio, members will have a challenge pitting their imaginations to insert the whale in the story. At some point, now or later, the story can be developed into either an improvisational outline or a written script.

Story example: A historic castle owned by the townsfolks is faithfully guarded by a whale who daily swims the castle's moat. No one is allowed to enter the castle ever. But, one day a two-headed ghost appears and decides the house will make the perfect home for her n' him. The ghost and the whale encounter many difficulties as they confront one another, before deciding who has rights to the castle. Eventually, they find a way that pleases both to coexist in the castle.

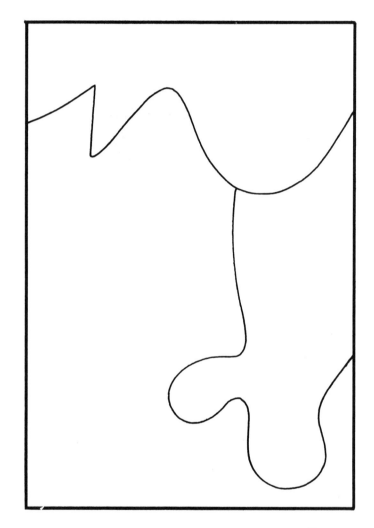

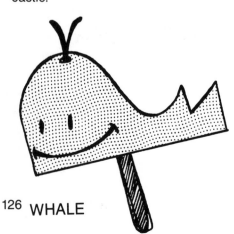

126 WHALE

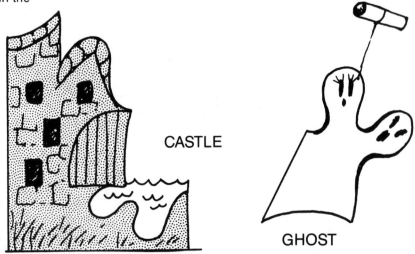

CASTLE

GHOST

FIVE LITTLE PUMPKINS

Five little pumpkins, sitting in a patch
Big and orange and round and fat.
Along came (Child's name) with a wick and a whack.
And one became a Jack-o-lantern just like that! `
Four little pumpkins sitting in a patch, etc.

by Tamara Hunt

With a wick and a whack, children can imagine what it would be like to be a jack-o-lantern. Ask, "What kind of a face would you have? Where would you like to sit? What would you like to do? Who would you scare?"

As an initial activity and without puppets children can pretend to be pumpkins with no expression on their faces, then make their faces "glow" as a jack-o-lantern. Or, other types of facial expressions can be explored: scared, cheerful, sad, frightening, bullying, etc.

Afterwards, the leader can recite the poem with five pumpkins in a Box Theater Pumpkin, turning each pumpkin around to reveal the Jack-o-lantern face.

TO MAKE A BOX PUMPKIN THEATER

Materials: Cut down cereal box, construction paper, 5 drinking straws.

Construction: Create a fence or garden patch facade from paper and glue to front surface of cereal box. Cut out five pumpkins from paper and attach to ends of straws; poke other ends through holes punctured in bottom of box.

WACKY WITCH WILMA

This original Halloween story about an upbeat witch who loves skateboards as a mode of transportation, instead of traditional broom, lends itself well to the overhead projectors for small or large group presentations. Use the patterns for overhead puppets provided at the end of the story to tell the story.

WACKY WITCH WILMA

NARRATION

Once upon a time there was an old haunted and decrepit house (whoo...whoo...), where a wacky witch named Wilma lived. Why was she wacky ? For a very good reason. She didn't follow tradition and fly through the sky on a broom like ordinary witches do, but instead preferred travelling afar on a zooming skateboard. Wow! Was she a champion, too. She could do the loop-de-loop-oh-la-la up the wall, over the ceiling and down again better than anyone in the neighborhood.

But, like all witches she had her good days—and her bad days (Of course, she loved her bad days better than the good ones.) On the good days, none of her magic seemed to work. But on the bad days, oh what fun she had being bad. Today she was having one of her bad days. It was Halloween and she felt particularly devilish as she shot along on her skateboard. "Whee... Look! Look at me!" she cackled "Ha...ha. I can go faster than any other witch around."

Well one day as she was showing off particulary fancy loop-de-loop-oh-la-la when suddenly she slid off balance and fell. Whoops. Perlunk! Right on her prized witching warty nose. "Oh, toad warts!" she moaned as she slowly got up. Her nose became so out of shape and swelled up all ugly like. She looked at herself in the mirror and whined.

"Oh, how terrible, I must be the ugliest witch in the world. That's what I get for trying to be so wacky. What am I ever going to do?" she moaned. "I can't possibly go out on this terrible night without a proper nose." Just then her pet crow, Zachery swooped down and perched on her nose.

He cawed "What's this? A tree branch to sit on. Sit on. Sit on. What's this?...caw, caw. Love it!"

"Oh, shut up!" screeched Wilma. "Can't you see you are sitting on my very sore nose? Shoo—get off!"

And the bird flew away cawing mockingly.

"I know." squawked Wilma, "I will go and look for a nose doctor who will know how to mend a wacky nose." So off Wilma skidded on her high powered skateboard.

Zoom...over the field.
Zoom...over the graveyard.
Zoom...she shot at super speed doing another loop-

ACTION

Begin with house and moon set.

Wilma zooms along on skateboard around perimeter of class area.

Repeats actions and falls on face. Fold out and extend nose as she gets up.

Zachery perches on nose.

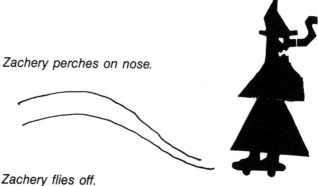

Zachery flies off.
Remove house and moon.
Wilma zooms off.

Bring on graveyard scene.

Wilma does another loop and gets stuck between trees.

NARRATION	ACTION

de-loop-oh-la-la between two narrowly spaced trees. Oops! When suddenly Wilma got stuck between the trees.

"Oh, my nose still hurts," she moaned as she slowly got up and realized her body had stretched long and crooked like from the force of speed as she shot and was wedged between the trees. She gazed at her reflection in a pool of water.

Wilma gets up. Expand body.

"Oh, toad warts," she screeched. "Now look at me. I'm a disgrace and could never get a job haunting houses looking like this. I'm too tall for a witch. I must find a doctor who knows how to shrink witches." So off she went into the black, eerie night once more to find a nose doctor and a shrinking doctor.

"I'll go even faster on my skateboard," she boasted as she skidded through the cemetery. And just then a hairy toad leaped out from behind a tombstone and startled her. She fell kerlump! Right over a tombstone. "Oh, toad warts!" she groaned louder than ever. "My nose hurts worse than ever. My body feels taller than ever." She put out her hand to feel her nose only to discover that both her arms were bent entirely out of shape. Oh, this is a terrible, terrible thing to happen to a witch.

Toad leaps out and she falls again.

Fold out and expand arms.

And at that moment a ghost came oozing out of a grave pit, took one look at Wilma and flew off in absolute terror. "Whoo..." it cried. "I see something wacky."

Ghost appears.

As Wilma stood there, absolutely stunned and in a state of shock, a horrible vulture came swooping down and perched on her arm. "Oh, what a marvelous, yucky, wacky tree this is. It screeched. "I will make it my home and build a nest, and stay here forever and ever."

Vulture perches on her arm.

And so Wilma decided at that point on to become a wacky tree instead of a wacky witch. She gave up her skateboard (and all her other worldly witch possessions) and grew lots of strong roots and new branches, to make a place for vultures to nest.

And every year, baby vultures would hatch in the nest she protected much to her joy. What a wonderful wacky world it is!

Put baby vultures on arm.

by Nancy Renfro

The End

TO MAKE OVERHEAD PUPPETS

Materials: Photocopy of patterns, heavy paper, drinking straws, acetate, plastic sandwich bag.

Construction: Cut out photocopies of patterns. Glue to heavy paper, to reinforce. Cut and split apart end of drinking straw and attach split end to back of image (with masking tape or staple) for handle.

Wilma Witch has expandable nose, body and arm parts. Fold over these parts, as shown on crease lines; secure in place by means of small pieces of double-stick tape. To make ghost, attach eyes to a sandwich bag. Attach straw handle to eyes.

Make acetate photocopy of graveyard scene to color with marker pens. (Vis a Vis brand or water based)

You will need:
Puppet Characters
Wilma Witch
Zachery bird
Toad
Ghost
Vulture
Baby Vulture

Props and Scenery
Haunted house and moon
Graveyard scene
Branches for Wilma
Vulture's nest

129

MOON

VULTURE

HOUSE

FOLD
LINE

Baby Vulture

CROW

FOLD
LINE

FROG

DRINKING STRAW

GHOST EYES

SANDWICH
BAG
GHOST

WILMA WITCH

130

Refer to "It was the Night before Christmas" activity in the Christmas section for overhead shadow construction. Make printed acetate copy of scene on right page.

An acetate strip can be used for handling quick on and off characters. Attach strip to character and glide along glass.

Print on Acetate

A THANKFUL THANKSGIVING

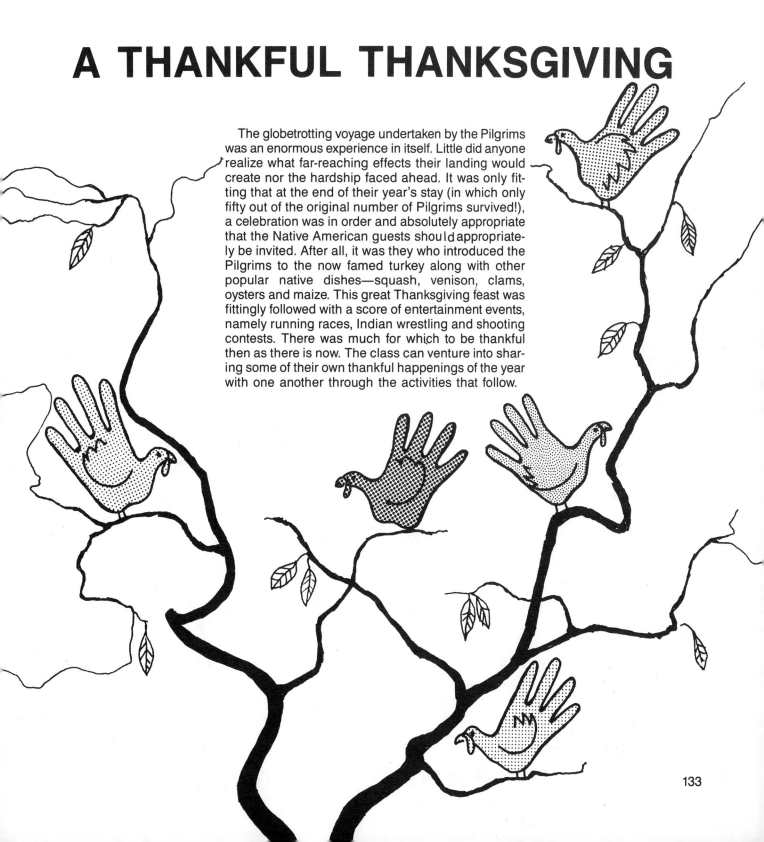

The globetrotting voyage undertaken by the Pilgrims was an enormous experience in itself. Little did anyone realize what far-reaching effects their landing would create nor the hardship faced ahead. It was only fitting that at the end of their year's stay (in which only fifty out of the original number of Pilgrims survived!), a celebration was in order and absolutely appropriate that the Native American guests should appropriately be invited. After all, it was they who introduced the Pilgrims to the now famed turkey along with other popular native dishes—squash, venison, clams, oysters and maize. This great Thanksgiving feast was fittingly followed with a score of entertainment events, namely running races, Indian wrestling and shooting contests. There was much for which to be thankful then as there is now. The class can venture into sharing some of their own thankful happenings of the year with one another through the activities that follow.

TABLETOP VILLAGE THEATERS

Wandering through a Pilgrim Town or Native American Tribal Village make a fascinating tour as children act out simple historical scenarios with Walking Finger Puppets in Tabletop Theater settings. Divide the class into two groups to build the village sets. One group can focus on the Pilgrim Town while the other create the Native American Village. Search out some picture books of Pilgrim lodgings and tribal dwellings to show the group. Discuss some of the distinctive features that the villages might include such as tepee decorations, skin-drying, food preparation, etc. that might be incorporated in the set to give authenticity. Also share with the children activities that the Pilgrims and Native Americans performed daily. Discuss those that were alike and those that differed. Patterns are provided below of basic characters for use with Finger Puppet play that children can use to enact village happenings.

TO MAKE A TABLETOP VILLAGE

Materials: Mural or brown wrapping paper. Assorted throwaways such as boxes (milk cartons, pudding, small milk cartons, jewelry boxes, etc.), cardboard tubes, construction paper, sand, dried weeds, stones, shells and other nature items.

Construction: Lay mural or wrapping paper over tabletop and securely tape all around table so it lays flat. The bare table can also be utilized if no mural paper is available.

Create dwellings from small boxes. A pint sized milk carton covered with brown paper is ideal for making a log cabin. A paper triangle shape can be glued to the side of a box for a tepee. Trees can be assembled from cardboard tubes as shown.

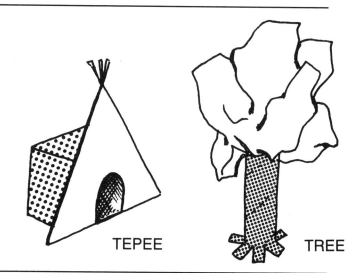

TEPEE   TREE

TO MAKE A WALKING FINGER PUPPET

Materials: Photocopy of pattern, stiff paper, small rubber band, yarn, real feathers (optional).

Construction: Cut out and color photocpy of pattern. Reinforce by gluing to stiff paper. Staple a small rubber band across back of puppet. Add bits of yarn for hair, or a real or paper fringed feather for Native American character.

FINGER PUPPET PATTERNS

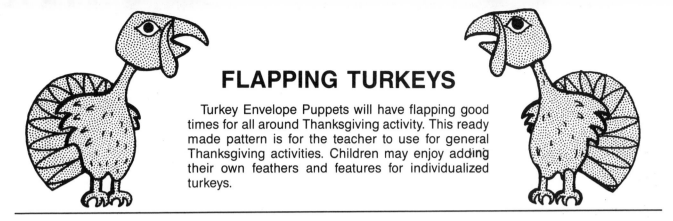

FLAPPING TURKEYS

Turkey Envelope Puppets will have flapping good times for all around Thanksgiving activity. This ready made pattern is for the teacher to use for general Thanksgiving activities. Children may enjoy adding their own feathers and features for individualized turkeys.

TO MAKE A TURKEY ENVELOPE PUPPET

Materials: Photocopy of patterns, 6½″ × 3½″ envelope, construction paper.

Construction: Tuck flap of envelope inside. Place hand inside envelope as shown and gently "bite" finger of the other hand to form mouth (straighten out mouth if wrinkled).

   Color beak and fold along crease line. Glue to upper section of envelope.

   Color body and attach to bottom back section of envelope.

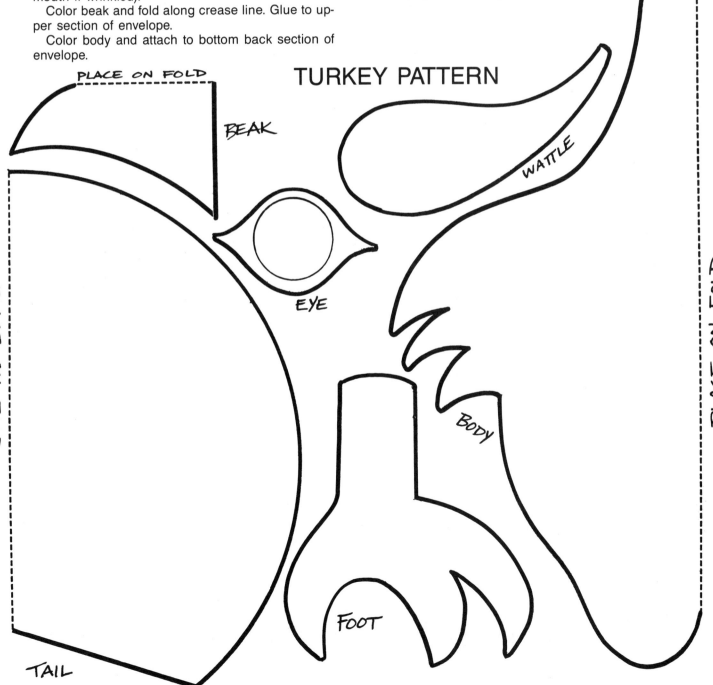

TURKEY PATTERN

PLACE ON FOLD

BEAK

WATTLE

EYE

BODY

PLACE ON FOLD

PLACE ON FOLD

FOOT

TAIL

THANKS-A-LOT!

This "hands-on" project is true to its word and serves a double role for Thanksgiving exchange. Traced cutouts of the children's own hands are just the thing for hearty handshakes as children give "thanks-a-lot" greetings to one another for special deeds done throughout the year. Flip the hands over and convert the backsides into flapping turkeys to use with the poem.

FIVE FAT TURKEYS

Five fat turkeys sitting in a tree
Five fat turkeys feeling fancy tree.
The first one sighed, "November's in the air" (child recite)
The second one lied, "I don't care (child recite)
The third one replied, "We'd best beware" (child recite)
The fourth one spied, "Pilgrims over there!" (child recite)
The fifth one cried, "Tomorrow's turkey day!" (child recite)
So they flapped their feathers and flew away.

by Tamara Hunt

TO MAKE A HAND/TURKEY PUPPET

Materials: Construction paper, strip of cardboard or ice cream stick.

Construction: Trace outline of hand on a sheet of construction paper. Glue cardboard strip or ice cream stick to bottom area of hand to serve as a handle. Decorate one side of hand shape with bits of construction paper feathers and other features to create a turkey, let other side remain plain for a hand.

BACK

THE PILGRIM'S HICCUPS

There are many known cures for a Pilgrim to get rid of the hiccups? She could be dunked in a pond, eat a dozen ears of corn on the cob, or be chased by a wild and woolly turkey? But how does this tale of woe end? Does she finally find a cure or, is she doomed to hiccups forever? Have the children become storytellers and create some solutions of their own to present to the group.

Divide the class into groups of two or three members each and have each group choose one of the story starters below. A puppet construction found in this book can be used in presenting these mini-dramas.

The Pilgrim's Hiccups
The Turkey Who Was Too Skinny
The Indian Who Loved to Eat
Wow! Look What I See on Land
The Pilgrim and Indian Who Met for the First Time

SHIPS AND TEPEES

An enactment of a flotilla of pilgrim's ships sailing the high blue seas can make their historic landing to Plymouth Rock, Massachusetts, and be greeted by Native Americans dwelling in colorful tepees. Divide the class in half and have one half create Paper Bag Ships with Pilgrim String Puppets and the other half Paper Bag Tepees with Native American String Puppets. Tepees can be arranged at one end of the space while ships sail across the room (waters) to arrive at the tepee village in time for each pilgrim to greet a Native American on a one-to-one basis. A rock strategically located will help to symbolize the occasion.

TO MAKE A PAPER BAG SHIP OR TEPEE

Materials: Supermarket bag, construction paper.

Construction: Create an image of a ship or tepee on outer surface of bag. Have some books on hand showing pictures of sailing ships and also some decorative tepees with Native American motifs to inspire detailing of the bag. When completed open out the bag and place habitant inside ready for action. A doorway may also be cut out of a tepee design for the character to enter.

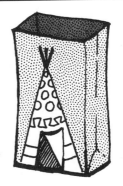
TEPEE

SHIP

TO MAKE A PILGRIM OR NATIVE AMERICAN STRING PUPPET

Materials: Two small paper plates, 2″ wide cloth strip, four 1½ inch wide strips of construction paper, assorted colored construction paper, string, cardboard tube.

Construction: Use one paper plate for the character's body and the other for the head. Staple the strip of cloth strip between the two plates to serve as the neck. Pleat narrow strips of construction paper for bouncy arms and legs and attach to body plate. Add paper hands and feet. Create features and costuming details from construction paper or coloring medium to define character. Attach a length of string to head as shown. Tie other end of string to cardboard tube handle for operating. Puppets can be hidden inside bag and bounce out.

CARDBOARD TUBE

PAPER PLATES

PLEATED PAPER

A THANKFUL GIANT'S FEAST

A mouthwatering array of colorful foods fit to feed a giant is a sure way of brightening up the classroom holiday time. Mountain-sized mounds of mashed potatoes, peas the circumference of golf balls, mammoth turkey, and a lake full of cranberry sauce would all challenge the colossus appetite of a thankful giant, especially a Pilgrim Giant who is very hungry after toiling in the new land.

Ask each child to dream up a harvest food or research popular foods* in the days of the Pilgrim's landing to serve the giant's Thanksgiving feast. Food selection can be made from large sheets of construction paper. Be sure that there is a varied menu to appease the giant's mammoth appetite and to insure that he receives all his proper vitamins and nutrients. Display the culinary delights on a clothesline strung across the room with spring clothespins. Invite the Pilgrim Puppet Giant to the fantastic feast to share with the group.

Fantastic Feast Activity

A creative drama activity can revolve around the Giant Puppet and various food images. Ask each child to pin his or her food image onto the body somewhere to serve as a Bodi-Picture. Have all the food stand in a circle formation with a child operating the Giant Pilgrim Puppet in the center space. The giant then recites:

"Fee, Fi, Fo, Fum,
I'm very hungry
Yum, Yum, Yum!
Give me some_____(food choice).
Yum, Yum, Yum.

Then have the child with the corresponding food image move to the center of the space and give appropriate movement and/or sound in the space for the food represented. For example; mashed potatoes—limp movements with slushy sounds; peas—rolling or circular movements; turkey—stiff flapping movements (this is a cooked turkey!)

After the child has completed the movement, have her remove the food image off her body and place it into the Giant's tummy pouch.

TO MAKE A PILGRIM GIANT PUPPET

Materials: Two large supermarket bags, newspaper, cording, construction paper.

Construction: Cut out notches on the sides of one supermarket bag so that bag sits on the child's shoulders comfortably. Locate eyeholes and remove bag from child. Cut out eyeholes in bag. Add oversized giant features such as ears, nose and mouth.

Create the giant's tummy from the second supermarket bag and tie opened bag around child's waist with cording.

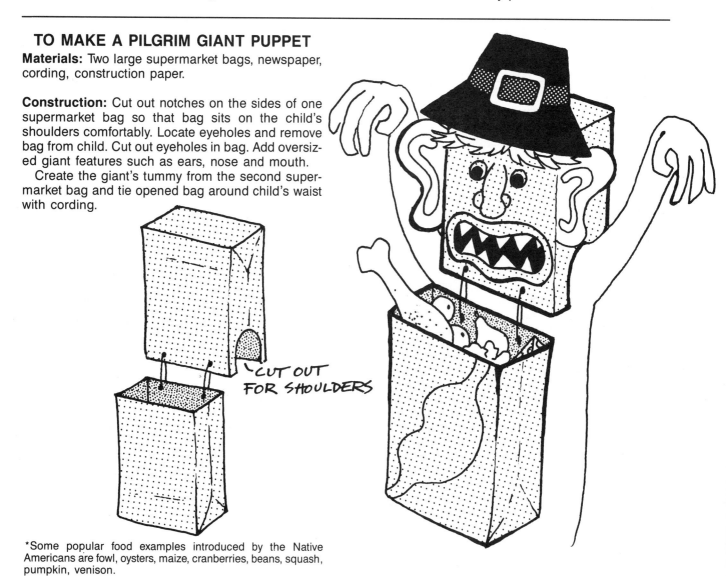

CUT OUT FOR SHOULDERS

*Some popular food examples introduced by the Native Americans are fowl, oysters, maize, cranberries, beans, squash, pumpkin, venison.

THE FESTIVAL OF LIGHTS

Hanukkah—a time of glowing candles, the tantalizing aroma of potato pancakes, and the laughter of families playing the dreidle game and exchanging holiday gifts. How did Hanukkah, the holiday whose name means "dedication," come to be celebrated with burning candle lights? And how did Hanukkah which commemorates the first victory for religious freedom in the world come to be celebrated with joy, dreidle games and festivities by young and old alike?

The story begins around 165 B.C. in the hills of Judea (modern day Israel) under the rule of a harsh ruler, King Antiochus (pronounced An'tee-ah-kus) the Fourth of Syria. He ordered the Jews to worship pagan gods instead of their own God and made it a crime for them to observe their religion—or even to study their Bible.

The Story of Judah Maccabee—The Hammer

One day, in a small town called Modi'in, the king's soldiers ordered an old Jewish man to bow down to a pagan statue and sacrifice a pig. This old man was Mattathias, a brave man with five sons, who said, "No, I bow down only before God, and never will I bow down to any other." The soldiers did not know what to do, because they had never heard such an answer before. Although he knew he would be punished, Mattathias continued, saying, "I will not hide. The time has come to fight for our beliefs. Whoever is for the Lord, follow me!"

Over the next several years, a series of remarkable battles took place between the Jews, who were principally farmers and shepherds, and Antiochus' mighty army. The leader of the Jewish farmers was Judah, the eldest son of Mattathias, who was known as Judah Maccabee (the hammer) because his strikes against the armies of Antiochus were steady and strong. As his father Mattathias said to him, "You are called Maccabee, the hammer. Train our people to be hammers, too.[1]

After the struggle was over, Judah and his men succeeded in driving the armies of Antiochus out of Jerusalem and regaining control of the Holy temple. As they began to clean the Temple, they noticed that the Eternal Flame was dark. This flame, called "Ner Tamid," should always be lit since it signifies God's presence among each one of us, but when the Maccabees looked around, they could only find a bit of oil, enough for only one night. It is said, "A great miracle happened there (or in Israel, they say "happened HERE") because instead of burning for only one night, the bit of oil burned for eight days and eight nights, enough time for the Jews to get more oil so that they could keep the flame of light burning.

The End

Since that time, Jews have lit an eight-pronged candle holder called a "Menorah," in memory of the eight nights on which the oil burned. They light one candle on each night, with the aid of the helper candle, called a shamash, until finally, on the last night, all eight candles are lit. In addition, a special delicious potato pancake is eaten at Hanukkah which is fried in oil, to remember the oil that burned for eight days. Gifts are exchanged, in some families on all eight nights, in other families, just the first night or two.

A special spinning top, called a dreidle, is a favorite Hanukkah game, with players paying into the pot or taking out of the pot, according to the spin of the dreidle. Peanuts or pennies often comprise the pot.

Songs are sung, games are played and a special glow hovers over the house with the light of the shimmering candle during Hanukkah, the Festival of Lights.

Some Hanukkah activities follow:

Make a four-dimensional dreidle and teach children how to play. Use a box or small milk carton for the dreidle, poking a stick through the bottom as a spinner and through the top as a handle. Draw one Hebrew symbol on each side, as shown.

Rules: Each player puts a nut in the center. Spin dreidle. If it lands on:

"Gimmel" stands for great	—	The player gets all the nuts in the pot.
"Nun" for miracle	—	The player gets nothing.
"Hey" for happened	—	The player gets half the nuts.
"Shin" for there	—	The player adds a nut to the center.
A great miracle happened there.	—	Each spin comprises a round of the game. You play as long as you like, counting the totals when you stop. Whoever has most points, nuts, coins, etc., wins.

JUDAH MACCABEE—THE HAMMER

One of the most tenacious stories in Jewish history is the story of Judah Maccabee and how he led his people to victory over the soldiers of Antiochus. Have the children divide into teams or work together as a class to present a puppet performance using Stuffed Paper Bag Puppets (or consider an overhead shadow presentation) to portray the characters. Discuss some of the scenes they may wish to highlight and how they can be dramatized effectively:

— *Antiochus said all Jews must stop practicing their religion, worshipping pagan idols instead.*

— *An old man named Mattathias refused to bow to idols. He urged others to follow their beliefs.*
— *His son, Judah, became known as Judah Maccabee (the Hammer) and led the Jewish shepherds and farmers to fight against the army of King Antiochus.*
— *After several years of struggle, the Jews defeated the Army and regained control of the Holy Temple in Jerusalem.*
— *Cleaning the Temple, they found only enough oil for one night. The miracle is that the oil lasted for eight nights.*

TO MAKE A STUFFED BAG HEAD

Materials: Small or medium sized paper bag, newspaper, short cardboard tube, construction paper, fabric, yarn and trim.

Construction: Stuff a paper bag with crumpled newspaper until nearly full. Insert and glue a cardboard tube up neck of bag. Tightly gather the opening of bag and wrap it with masking tape to secure. Add paper features, egg carton eyes, yarn hair and other details.

Add a fabric body, using pattern provided, cut out two pieces. Sew side seams with right sides together, turn. Hem bottom. Glue neck opening to tube neck.

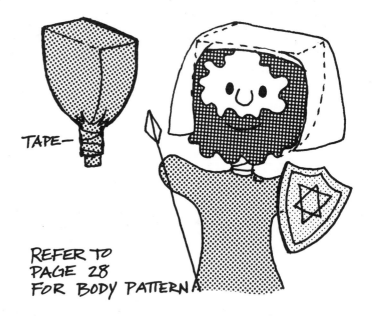

TAPE—

REFER TO PAGE 28 FOR BODY PATTERN

EIGHT LITTLE CANDLES

Eight little candles one by one
Waiting to join the holiday fun.

The first little candle standing in the row
Said, "Light me now, so I can glow".

The second little candle joining the plea
Said, "Light me too, so I can see".

The third little candle wanting a turn
Said, "Light me now so I can burn".

The fourth little candle standing in line
Said, "Light me too so I can shine".

The fifth little candle hoping for the same
Said, "I will dance if you light my flame".

The sixth little candle wished and wished
Said, "Give me a light so I won't be missed".

The seventh little candle was happy tonight
Said, "It's my turn now to get a light".

The eighth little candle waiting so long
Said, "I may be last, but my light is strong".

Now all eight candles are burning bright
Filling the world with the "wonder of light."

by Jean Warren
(TOTLINE newsletter—see bibliography)

Jewish children and family members gather around the menorah in great anticipation each evening for the eight nights of Hanukkah when the candles are lit, and blessing of thanks are offered. In Israel, menorahs are aglow everywhere and during this Festival of Lights, Jerusalem is fittingly called the "City of Lights".

The tradition of lighting a menorah occurs at sundown on the first night of Hanukkah when the first candle is lit and the holiday festivities begin. An extra candle, the Shamash, or "servant," is also lit each night and used to assist the lighting of the other candles. On the second night, two candles are lit in addition to the shamash. On each night thereafter, one more candle is added until all eight candles plus the shamash are aglow. Candles are lit from the left towards the right side.

Let children use Tube Candles Puppets to form a Jewish Menorah and to use with the poem. Make one candle larger than the rest, use a towel cardboard tube and longer stick and let one child use it for a (Shamash) and light the other candles.

Invite eight puppeteers to be the Menorah. As the "Candle Helper" puppet "lights" each of the eight candle-puppets, ask the remaining children to think of a gift they would like to give someone on Hanukkah evening. Although the ceremony actually takes eight days to perform, the children will enjoy lighting all the candle-puppets at once. Children "animate" the flame up and down inside the tube as each candle is lit.

TO MAKE A TUBE CANDLE

Materials: Cardboard tube, construction paper, stick or drinking straw, string red foil.

Construction: Cover tube with paper. Attach a red foil (or paper) flame to end of stick or straw; insert through tube. Pop flame up and down.

SWALLOWING THE LATKES

Potato latkes are popular traditional Hanukkah foods. Some people believed that the Maccabees ate latkes because they were easy to make and helped to fortify them during hard times. Still others believed that latkes were fried in oil and this symbolized to them the burning of the oil. These little pancakes, made from potatoes and onions, can be found in every Jewish home, in a holiday flourish, frying dozens of latkes for eager recipients.

Children might wish to make a puppet character that swallows paper latkes. A song or poem may be improvised to use with the puppet based on, for example, a *Five Little Latke* or *I Know An Old Lady Who Swallowed A Fly* theme (instead of animals consider big, little, lumpy, delicious, etc. latkes).

TO MAKE A SWALLOWING BOX PUPPET

Materials: Cereal or detergent box, construction paper, fabric, yarn and trims.

Construction: Slit box along three edges, as shown, and bend upper portion back. Cut out a head and body from papaer; glue head to upper box and body to lower. Add fabric costuming, yarn hair and paper features. Cut out finger holes in back, as shown, to operate puppet. Cut out paper latkes or model some from play clay.

A HAPPY HANUKKAH APRON

A simple little, entirely paper, apron made from an opened out large supermarket bag and festooned with **Hanukkah** motifs such as a menorah, Jewish star, and dreidle pockets could provide spaces for children to tuck Hannukah puppets for stories and sing a long, or little presents for each other.

TO MAKE A HANUKKAH APRON

Materials: Supermarket bag, colorful ribbon or cording.

Construction: Cut off entire back of bag. Cut and open out bag. Lay flat on a surface. Cut out and color imageries such as a menorah, star, latke and dreidle; glue bottom and side edges of each image to bag in random places to serve as pockets. Staple a length of ribbon to four locations of apron as shown for tiering onto body.

CUT BAG AS SHOWN

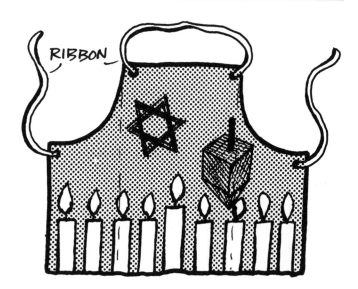

RIBBON

A SHOW OF STARS CHRISTMAS

Christmas is a jewel of a holiday with imageries that abound and delight children's imagination, and that of their parents as well. Santa Claus, round bellied and smiling, Rudolph, the reindeer with a spectacular nose and Frosty, the snowman with a melting heart are a familiar cast that never ceases to appeal to audiences with their yearly appearances. The children will enjoy seeing these traditional characters, and meeting other characters play totally new roles as they participate in the activities that follow.

A STAR TOPPED CHRISTMAS TREE

What would Christmas be without a Christmas tree, a dazzling, sparkling, twinkling tree? The specially designed modular tree described below provides a splendid team project, as well as a festive touch to any wall. It features ornament pockets in which to tuck Christmas cards and small gifts.

TO MAKE A CHRISTMAS TREE

Materials: 12″ × 12″ × 12″ triangular shapes from green construction paper, corresponding number of small, 6″ paper plates, cardboard, aluminum and colored foils, glitter and trims.

Construction: Give each child one precut triangular paper and a paper plate. Locate the paper plate in center of triangle, and glue or staple edges of bottom half of plate to paper, leaving the upper half free in which to insert items.

Decorate the plate as one would an ornament, using foils, glitter, trim, or other coloring items.

Tuck cards and gifts inside the plate ornaments. When ornamented triangles are complete, glue them together into a single tree shape as shown.

Create a bold star from cardboard and cover with aluminum foil or glitter. A smiling face on the star makes a friendly rendition!

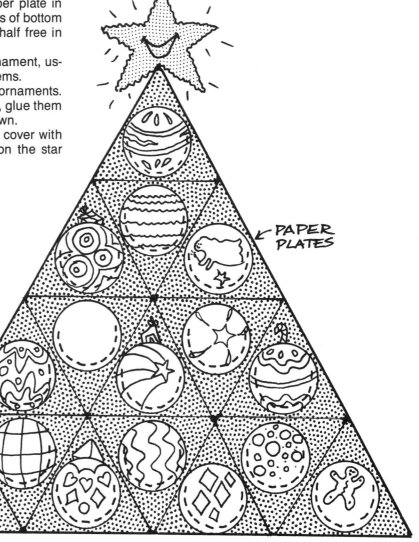

PAPER PLATES

REINDEER

FOUR LITTLE REINDEER

Four little reindeer waiting by the sleigh
The first one said, "Tomorrow's Christmas day."
The second one said, "It's time to get-a-way."
The third one said, "My nose will light the way."
The fourth one said, "So what's the delay?"
Out came Santa with a big "Ho! Ho!"
He jumped in his sleigh and he said, "Let's go!"

by Tamara Hunt

SANTA

A scenic bib panel depicting a wintery wonderland and Santa's workshop makes an ideal background for four frisky reindeer eager to take off and make their yearly rounds. You might want to discuss Santa's reindeer friends with the children. "What do you suppose Santa's reindeer do at the North Pole?" "If you were a reindeer, what would you do to help Santa?" "What do you suppose reindeer see while flying through the sky?"

Recite the poem while wearing the scenic bib panel. Hold the hand in an upright position with a Reindeer Finger Puppet on each finger and Santa on the thumb. Keep Santa only in a folded down position. As the poem is read, fold down each Reindeer on cue, then finally, up pops Santa!

As an alternate presentation, children can play the Reindeer parts using Reindeer Tube Puppets riding them hobby horse style and a Santa mask. As a follow up activity, the group can enact short skits based on reindeer situations.

Santa's Sled is Broken
The Reindeer Who Forgot How to Fly
The Missing Reindeer (a hide and seek approach)
The Time the Bags of Toys Didn't Fit Into the Sleigh

TO MAKE FINGER PUPPET REINDEER AND SANTA

Materials: Photocopy of patterns, cotton, double-stick tape, glove.

Construction: Cut out and color patterns. Glue cotton to Santa for a beard. Attach images to a glove (rubber household glove is excellent) with double-stick tape.

—GLOVE

TO MAKE REINDEER TUBE PUPPETS

Materials: Photocopy of patterns, cardboard towel tube.

Construction: Cut out and color opposite face patterns. Attach a face on opposite sides of cardboard tube. Glue snout section of faces together to secure.

—CARDBOARD TOWEL TUBE

TO MAKE A SANTA MASK

Materials: Photocopy of pattern, cotton, string, bell (optional).

Construction: Cut out and color pattern. Glue cotton to hat trim and beard area. Attach a small bell to end of hat. Puncture holes on each side of mask to tie lengths of string through and secure to head.

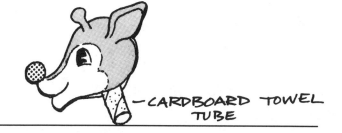

CUT OUT CIRCLES FOR EYES

COTTON

145

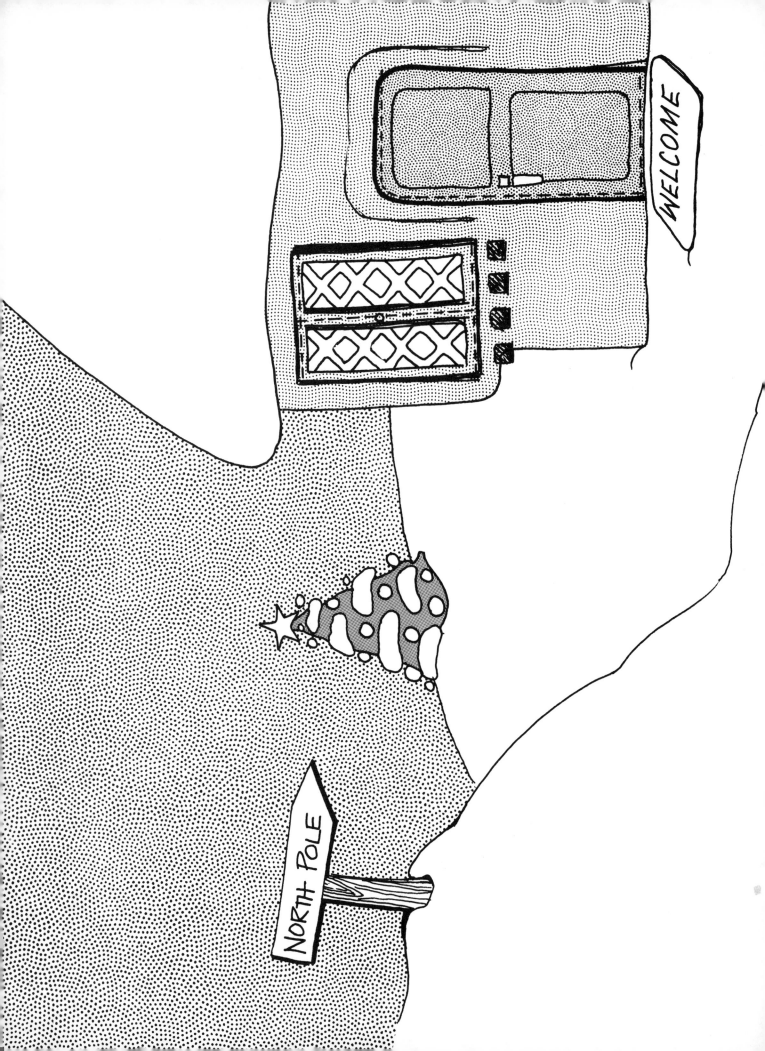

SANTA MASK   147

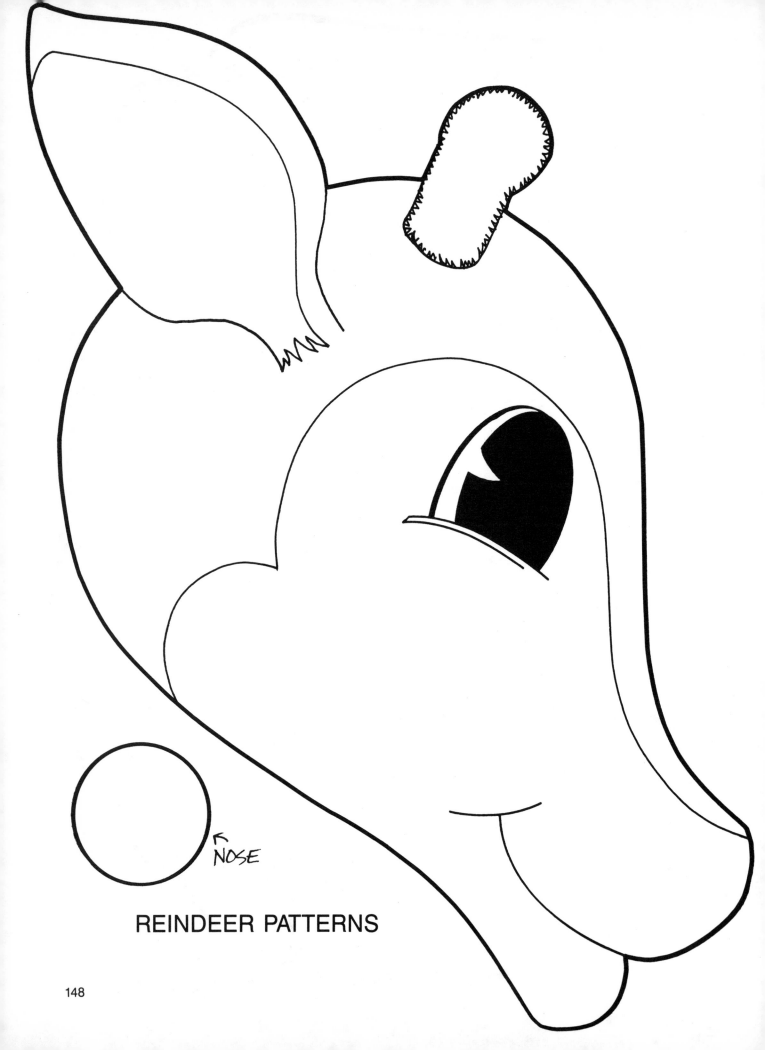

NOSE

REINDEER PATTERNS

148

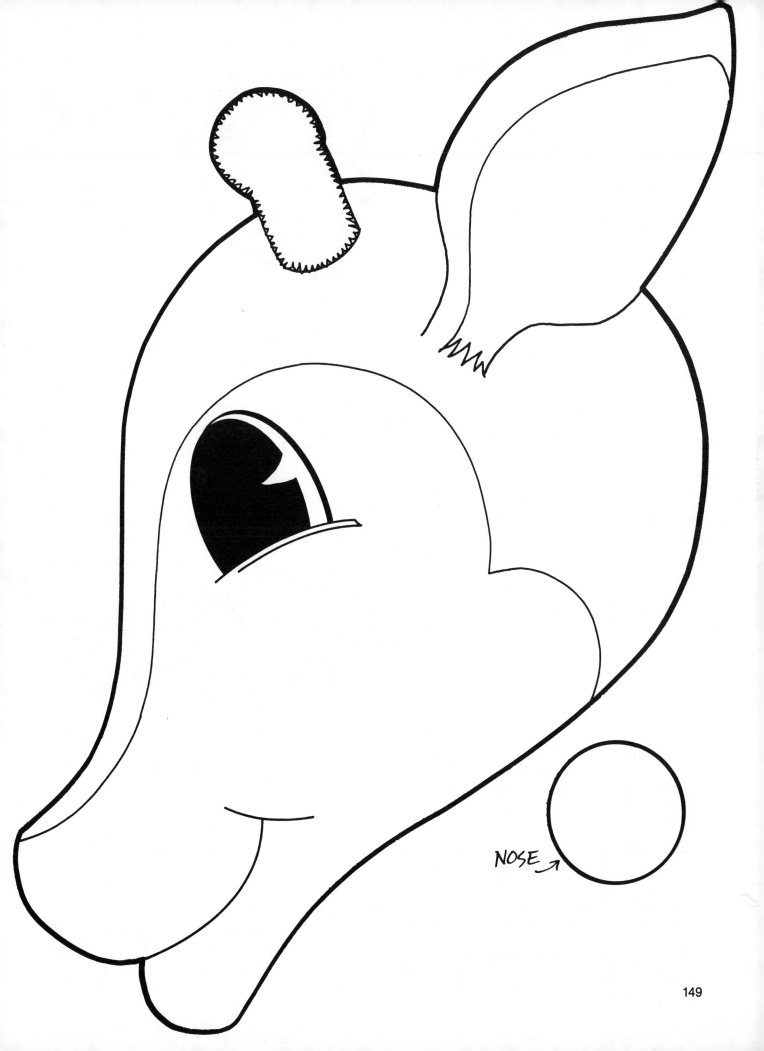

NOSE

149

DANCING SNOWFLAKES

Silver white snowflakes sprinkling from the sky
 Floating to the white, wet earth
  Quietly they lie.

Tippity tap, tippity tap, tippity tap toe.
How many snowflakes are caught in winter's glow?

Silver white snowflakes sparkling everywhere
 Waiting for a friendly child
  To make a dancing pair.

Tippity tap, tippity tap, tippity tap toe.
Everybody find a partner, whisper soft "hello."

Silver white snowflakes with the friends they found.
 Whirling, twirling, circling as a
  Winter merry-go-round.

Tippity tap, tippity tap, tippity tap toe.
Children and snowflakes dancing in the snow.

by Tamara Hunt

A winter wonderland of falling snowflakes is an enchanting backdrop with which to bring the winter spirit to the classroom. Children can pantomime the actions of this poem while floating Snowflake String Puppets down from the sky, befriending them and bringing them to life as they dance together.

TO MAKE A SNOWFLAKE STRING PUPPET

Materials: 12″ diameter white construction paper circle, 1″ wide white strips of paper, length of string, scrap construction paper.

Construction: Create a snowflake from a white paper circle in the traditional manner by folding paper circle in half, then again in thirds, and fold the thirds into halves again.

Cut out hole designs from folded paper as shown. Unfold paper to reveal symetrical snowflake pattern.

Pleat white paper strips and attach to bottom of snowflake for legs. Add paper eyes and other features.

Attach a length of string to top of snowflake and tie finger loop at opposite end for holding. Bounce puppet up and down to make it dance.

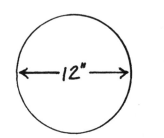

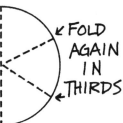

SNOWMAN JOE

I just made a snowman from two little balls of snow
Mom gave me a carrot and I used it for a nose.
Dad suggested buttons and shiny chunks of coal
And Grandpa loaned me his blue hat, why look—It's
Snowman Joe!

Birds perch on his twiggy arms and sing him happy
*   songs.*
Squirrels and mice dance round his feet 'til children
*   come along.*
Mr. Sun comes out to play and waves a big "Heigh Ho!"
But gosh! Oh gee! He stayed too long, Oh my—Where's
Snowman Joe?!

By Tamara Hunt

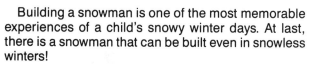

Building a snowman is one of the most memorable experiences of a child's snowy winter days. At last, there is a snowman that can be built even in snowless winters!

Recite the poem while one team member builds a Snowman on the other member, using crayons or marker pens to draw the coal detail, and double-stick tape to attach the nose and hat. In the second verse, the leader can perch the bird on each Snowman's twiggy arm (child's own outstretched arms), dance the squirrel and mouse at their feet and finally hold up the sun to melt the Snowmen to the ground. Repeat the poem so children can reverse Snowmen building roles. Afterward, expand the activity by creating original dialogue and/or skits. For example:

The Snowman comes to life and ventures out in to the world. (What does he discover first?)
The Snowman makes friends with some animals. (What do they think of him and he of them?)
The Snowman is too cold and tries to get warm. (What happens?)

Following the directions below, prepare a basic paper plate Snowman body for each child to wear. As extra props for the poem, create Animal and Sun Stick Characters.

TO MAKE A PAPER PLATE BODI-SNOW PUPPET

Materials: Two paper plates, cording or ribbon, orange and blue construction paper.

Construction: Staple together two paper plates as shown. Attach a length of cording or ribbon to top of one plate; tie around a child's neck. Let plates hang in front of child's body.

Cut out a carrot nose and blue hat from paper. Crayons can be used to draw the buttons and coal features. Put some double-stick tape on backs of carrot and hat to secure to puppet.

151

THE NIGHT BEFORE CHRISTMAS

"His eyes, how they twinkled! His dimples, how merry! His cheeks were like roses, his nose like a cherry!" These happy images of Clement Moore's well-loved poem are easily brought to life through the magic of the overhead projector. The patterns below provide a ready cast with which to present the poem to the class or even to large groups in the auditorium. Photocopies of the poem can be given to children so that they may follow the words as each character appears. Or consider having an acetate copy made to project the text onto a second screen with another projector. Special effects such as twinkling bells during the visions of sugar plums, clattering of inverted bowls for hoof sounds, and ho-ho-ho, full-bellied laughs for Santa will add a realistic touch.

You will need:

Puppet Characters
   Mouse
   Father
   St. Nicholas

Props and Scenery
   Interior house scene
   Sugar plums
   Sleigh
   Bells

MOUSE

ADD YARN TAIL   ADD THREAD WHISKERS

FATHER

BAG

SANTA

PRESENTS

TO MAKE OVERHEAD SHADOW PUPPETS

Materials: Photocopy of patterns, heavy paper, drinking straws, acetate.

Construction: Cut out photocopies of characters and props. Reinforce by gluing to heavy paper. Split and spread apart end of drinking straw; tape split end to back of character image to serve as a handle.

Color in an acetate photocopy of interior house scene to use as background for the entire poem.

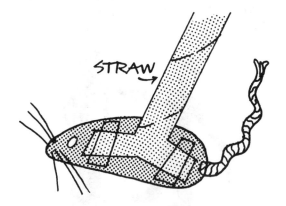

STRAW

THE NIGHT BEFORE CHRISTMAS

NARRATION	ACTION
"Twas the night before Christmas, when all through the house,	
Not a creature was stirring, not even a mouse;	
The stockings were hung by the chimney with care,	Mouse peeks out.
In hopes that St. Nicholas soon would be there;	
The children were nestled all snug in their beds,	
While visions of sugar-plums danced in their heads;	Sugar plums dance.
And Mama in her 'kerchief, and I in my cap,	
Had just settled our brains for a long winter's nap;	
When out on the lawn there arose such a clatter,	
I sprang from the bed to see what was the matter.	Father springs from bed and runs to window.
Away to the window I flew like a flash,	
Tore open the shutters and threw up the sash.	
The moon, on the breast of the new-fallen snow,	
Gave a lustre of mid-day to objects below,	
When, what to my wondering eyes should appear,	Sleigh appears.
But a miniature sleigh, and eight tiny reindeer,	
With a little old driver, so lively and quick,	
I knew in a moment it must be St. Nick.	
More rapid than eagles his courses they came,	
And he whistled and shouted and called them by name;	
"Now, Dasher! now, Dancer! now, Prancer and Vixen!	
On, Comet! on, Cupid! on, Donder and Blitzen!	Sleigh dashes to house top.
To the top of the porch! to the top of the wall!	Bell sounds.
Now dash away! dash away! dash away all!"	
As dry leaves that before the wild hurricane fly,	
When they meet with an obstacle, mount to the sky;	
So up to the house-top the couriers they flew,	
With the sleigh full of Toys, and St. Nicholas too.	
And then, in a twinkling, I heard on the roof	Hoof sounds.
The prancing and pawing of each little hoof—	
As I drew in my head, and was turning around,	
Down the chimney St. Nicholas came with a bound.	St. Nicholas comes down chimney.
He was dressed all in fur, from his head to his foot,	
And his clothes were all tarnished with ashes and soot.	
A bundle of Toys he had flung on his back,	
And he look'd like a peddler just opening his pack.	
His eyes—how they twinkled! his dimples how merry!	
His cheeks were like roses, his nose like a cherry!	
His droll little mouth was drawn up like a bow;	
And the beard on his chin was as white as the snow.	
The stump of a pipe he held tight in his teeth,	
And the smoke it encircled his head like a wreath.	
He had a broad face and a little round belly	
That shook when he laughed like a bowl full of jelly.	Ho-ho sounds.
He was chubby and plump, a right jolly old elf,	
And I laughed when I saw him in spite of myself.	
A wink of his eye and a twist of his head,	
Soon gave me to know I had nothing to dread.	
He spoke not a word, but went straight to his work,	He fills stockings.
And fill'd all the stockings; then turned with a jerk,	
And laying his finger aside of his nose,	
And giving a nod, up the chimney he rose;	
He sprang to his sleigh, to his team gave a whistle,	He goes up chimney.
And away they all flew like the down of a thistle.	
But I heard him exclaim, ere he drove out of sight,	
"Happy Christmas to all, and to all a good night."	

The End

An acetate strip can be used for handling quick on and off characters. Attach strip to character and glide along glass.

SLED

SUGAR PLUMS

Print on Acetate

PIPE

HOUSE

THE RUNAWAY CHRISTMAS COOKIE

Did anyone see the Christmas Cookie? Well, it ran away just as I was about to put it into the oven. In fact, on the way, it swiped a skateboard still wrapped and waiting under the Christmas tree and rolled quickly on its way. I grabbed my bicycle and dashed after it, but just as I was about to catch it...

Christmas themes, combined with new story twists, afford special opportunity to motivate children and expose them to enriching language arts projects. Children may wish to work in teams of three or four members in developing Christmas-related skits using puppet constructions of paper plates, paper envelopes or other ideas as described elsewhere in the book.

On flash cards, write down a series of interesting story starters centered around Christmas themes from which teams choose to originate a story, such as:

> *The Christmas Cookie that Ran Away*
> *The Night Rudolph's Nose Wouldn't Shine*
> *Why the Snowflake Turned to Gold*
> *The Christmas Wish*
> *What Happened When Santa Got Stuck in the Chimney?*
> *The Time Santa's Sleigh Collided with a Space Ship*

A MERRY CHRISTMAS APRON

A seasonal apron for each child will bring extra Christmas cheer when worn while providing pockets to store Christmas puppets and surprises. This apron is made from a large supermarket bag and has a selection of Christmas motifs to serve the pockets—a glittering tree. star. and gingerbread cookie. Puppets can be tucked into pockets for holiday stories and sing a long.

TO MAKE A CHRISTMAS APRON AND PUPPET

Materials: Supermarket bag, colorful ribbon or cording.

Construction: Cut away entire back of bag. Cut and open out bag as shown and lay flat on a surface. From scraps of paper bag cut out and color tree, star, cookie or other image. Glue bottom and side edges of each image on the apron bag, leaving top open. Attach a length of ribbon or cording to four locations to tie on body.

REFER TO PAGE 142 FOR HOW TO CUT

155

CHRISTMAS SONG FEST

The spirit of Christmas is illuminated, perhaps more than anything else with the wide assortment of popular Christmas medlies and songs. Puppets, with a few voice lessons, make perfect choral members, joining in the merrymaking and giving a new twinkle to traditional music. You may wish to try one of the following ideas:

Rudolph the Red Nosed Reindeer—Refer to the *Four Little Reindeer* activity in this section and use the Reindeer Rod Puppet construction for this song. Let each child create a Reindeer Rod Puppet as described. Add a paper red nose to one of the Reindeer to portray Rudolph. One child can be chosen to play Santa.

As the song begins children can make prancing movements. Some bells on a string would add a nice musical effect. The Reindeer can pretend to be playing together, Santa arrives and hooks the Reindeer to his sled, putting Rudolph in the lead and guides the entire sled team around the room. Children can pantomime the actions of the song while using their Rod Puppets.

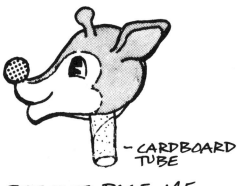

— CARDBOARD TUBE

REFER TO PAGE 145

The Twelve Days of Christmas —Create Paper Bag Puppets for a sing along with this popular song. Assign the twelve featured characters to twelve children. If there are additional children they can play "extras" for some of the following characters:

1	partridge	7	swans a-swimming
2	turtle doves	8	maids a-milking
3	french hens	9	ladies dancing
4	calling birds	10	lords a-leaping
5	golden rings	11	pipers piping
6	geese a-laying	12	drummers drumming

To simplify the puppetmaking task, ask each child to make a *single* representation of the assigned character on the front of the paper bag and write its corresponding number in bold letters on the back of the bag.

Begin the song by lining up the children in front of the room with numbered sides of their puppets facing the audience. As the song is sung, each character is flipped around at the appropriate time to face the audience. Once a character appears it should remain still and in full view until all of the characters have appeared.

TO MAKE A PAPER BAG PUPPET

Materials: Small or medium size paper bag, construction paper, fabric, yarn, trim.

Construction: Create eyes and upper face features of character on flap portion of bag, as shown. Create remainder of character on lower portion of bag. Upper mouth can line flap edge with lower mouth located on lower portion. For ring character consider a ring that also has a moveable mouth.

Place fingers inside flap and move up and down to make a bag sing.

ADD FACE FEATURES

BACK

Up on the Housetop —Children will delight in seeing Santa Claus coming down a Chimney Box Theater laden with gifts to share. The leader may wish to make a Chimney Box Theater for sing-along purposes or, if time permits, each child can make their own Theater and pop-up Santa to cue during the song. This visual is also excellent to use with "Jolly Old St. Nicholas".

TO MAKE A CHIMNEY BOX THEATER AND SANTA PUPPET

Materials: Photocopy of pattern, pudding or pint sized milk carton, cotton, drinking straw.

Construction: To make theater, cut off the top of box. Decorate outside as a chimney. Cut a hole in bottom of box and poke other end of straw with Santa attached through hole. Hide Santa in box and pop him up and down on cue.

To make Santa, cut out and color Santa photocopy. Add a bit of cotton to beard area. Tape Santa image to end of drinking straw.

Jingle Bells—A merry note accompanies the tinkling of bells with this clever Sled and Mouse in disguise, Santa Puppet. Ask the group to sit in a large circle formation on the floor and pretend that they are in a big field covered with snow. The leader should begin the song while undulating the sled prop in rhythm and popping the mouse Santa up and down to the laughter. As the song is sung, pass the sled on to the first child to the right, offering a turn guiding the sled. Continue to pass the sled along in this manner while repeating the song as many times as necessary until everyone has had a turn operating the sled.

TO MAKE A SLED AND MOUSE SANTA PUPPET

Materials: Photocopy of patterns, heavy paper, cotton, string with bells, tongue depressor or ice cream stick, sequins or fancy trim (optional).

Construction: Cut out and color patterns. Reinforce by gluing them to heavy paper.

To make sled, decorate with fancy trim or sequins (optional). Cut a slit in sled on dotted line for inserting Santa.

To make mouse Santa, add a bit of cotton for beard, then attach to end of a tongue depressor or ice cream stick. Insert other end in slit on sled.

"Frosty the Snowman"—Utilize the Paper Plate Snowmen Puppet construct as described in this section for pantomining the song's actions.

MOUSE

SLED PATTERN

SANTA PATTERN

158

THE TINIEST ELF

Even a tiny elf can be helpful during the holidays. This story shows the problems a tiny elf can experience and how she overcame them. Ask the children, "What do you suppose it would be like to be an Elf in Santa's workshop? What would you help her make? If you were a very tiny Elf, what special jobs could you do or not do?

Present the story, *The Tiniest Elf*, while using the following cast and props:

> *Elves* (Mandy, Jinx and Dandy)—Three children wearing caps
> *Tiniest Elf*—Finger Puppet
> *Santa*—Finger Puppet
> *Sleigh*—Shoe box with sleigh facade
> *Bells*—Real bells
> *Toy*—Train, hammer, blocks, car or available toys can be substituted
> *Glue Bucket*—Real bucket with make believe glue
> *Santa's Bag*—Small sack

The leader plays the role of the Tiniest Elf and Santa using finger puppets. A story apron or other storage item can be used to store puppets and props. A tabletop or lapboard will provide a good surface on which to arrange items as the story is told and where most of Tiny's and Santa's actions can occur. The three elves can sit nearby pretending to work on various toys, placing them in Santa's sack and other appropriate actions. They may also participate in dialogue if desired.

Afterwards, each child can make a Tiny Elf Finger Puppet to bring home as a memory of the story.

TINIEST ELF PATTERN

BACK

SANTA PATTERN

THE TINIEST ELF
by Jeannette S. Miller

NARRATION	ACTION

Long ago in the North Pole, on a snowy eve before Christmas, three Elves, Mandy, Jinx and Dandy were making toys in Santa's workshop. Suddenly, a very little Elf appeared on the workbench.

Elves busy making toys. Tiny appears before elves.

"Who are you?" asked Mandy.

"I'm Tiny. I've come to help Santa get ready for Christmas."

"Why you're the tiniest Elf I've ever seen," said Jinx.

"There's lots to do," said Dandy, "and we only have until tonight to finish everything."

"Here, this choo-choo train needs finishing," said Mandy. "You get the hammer and I'll get some nails."

Mandy gives her train.

Tiny went to the train corner of the workshop. She tried lifting the hammer. No matter how hard she pulled, she couldn't carry it.

Tiny tries to hammer.

"It's too heavy," she said.

"It's not too heavy," laughed Mandy. "You're just too tiny."

"I need help painting these blocks," cried Jinx.

Tiny went to the block corner of the workshop. She found a brush but couldn't reach high enough to paint the blocks.

Tiny tries to paint blocks.

"These blocks are too big," said Tiny.

"They're not too big," smiled Jinx. "You're just too tiny."

"Come help me glue the wheels on this car," called Mandy. So Tiny went to the car corner of the workshop. She climbed up on the glue bucket and suddenly...PLOP!...in she fell!

Tiny tries to glue wheels.

Tiny falls into bucket.

"Help, help," she shouted. "This glue bucket is too deep."

She struggles in bucket.

"It's not too deep," said Mandy, as he pulled the little Elf out, "You're just too tiny."

Mandy comes up and pulls Tiny out.

Suddenly Santa appeared. "It's almost time to go," he said.

Santa appears with bag and sleigh.

Mandy, Jinx, and Dandy began filling Santa's bag: a cap for Colin, a clock for Jocelyn, a doll for Jesinda, a unicorn for Tara, a truck for Todd, a train for Ty and a car for Ian!

Elves fill bag.

While Tiny watched, a tiny tear fell onto her little cheek. "I wish there was something I could do to help Santa," she thought sadly to herself.

When the bag was full, the Elves lifted it onto the sleigh. It was so big that it almost filled the entire sleigh.

Elves put bag into sleigh.

"This is the biggest bag we've ever had," said Santa happily. "Why there's hardly room for me!"

Santa climbed into his sleigh. The three Elves looked and cried out, "There's no room left for us."

Santa fits into sleigh.

"Nonsense," said Santa. "Someone has to ride with me to ring the Christmas bells."

But no matter how hard they tried, neither Mandy, Jinx, nor Dandy could find a place to sit on Santa's sleigh.

Elves try to fit into sleigh.

"The sleigh is too small," they said.

"It's not too small," replied Santa, "You're just too big."

Then Santa saw Tiny peeking from the Workshop window. "You're the tiniest Elf I've ever seen," he said in amazement. "And just the right size for my sleigh. Would you like to ride with me tonight?"

Tiny smiled a big smile and happily climbed into the sleigh.

Tiny fits into sleigh and rings the bells.

And to this day, the tiniest elf rides with Santa every Christmas eve, ringing the sleigh bells for all the children everywhere to hear.

The End

BIG BIRTHDAY BASH

Growing one year older—What does it mean?
Becoming Bigger,
Becoming Smarter,
Becoming more the person you want to be,
(and maybe even getting your dreams
come true.)
Three hundred and sixty five days, no two ever alike—some somber, some whoop-it-up, whoop-it-down, some too short and some too long. All are days that mark a yearbook of a child's life, making the completion of the year's cycle a perfect occasion for celebration. Children love a birthday bash anytime, but especially when it is their own birthday. To be king or queen for a day is a special treat to be shared with friends. Honking blowers, silly hats, fancy cakes and can't-wait-to-open gifts are the highlights of the event. Traditionally birthdays are heralded by fun and frivolities. However, it is also a good time to augment the experience by helping children understand such concepts as time or seasons.

MERRY MENAGERIE BIRTHDAY BASH

Invite a merry menagerie of party guests to celebrate the Birthday Bash. "Whip up" an oversized birthday cake picture in the center of a large sheet of mural paper. Along the borders, color or paint streamers, festive balloons, horns, or attach party regalia.

For classroom situations: Ask each child to create a chosen guest from construction paper such as a toothy alligator, robust robot or woolly caterpillar and add a party hat. Attach a letter envelope to the front of each of the guests. An individualized note (written by the leader or another child), such as a birthday fortune or riddle can be written and tucked inside the envelope. Seal envelope with a heart or other sticker to be opened on the child's special day. Tack onto the birthday cake mural.

A menagerie of animals celebrating a Birthday Bash (mural)

CANDLE CREATURES

How many creatures sleeping on the cake?
Why don't we count them?
Then they'll awake.
1,2,3,4,5,6! [Turn candles around].

How many creatures looking about?
Why don't we blow them?
Blow them OUT!
1,2,3,4,5,6! [Remove candles, one by one]

by Tamara Hunt

Sleepy candles sleeping on a shoe box birthday cake can each be awakened by the children as they count. Invite the birthday child to come up and pin the appropriate number of Clothespin Candle Creatures onto the cake, with sleeping sides facing out. Recite the poem and let the children help count the candles slowly together as you turn the candles around.

TO MAKE CLOTHESPIN CANDLE CREATURES

Materials: Photocopies of pattern, spring clothespins.

Construction: Cut out and color photocopies of candle patterns. Glue a sleepy image on one side of clothespin and an awake image on others, as shown.

CLOTHESPIN

TO MAKE A SHOE BOX CAKE

Materials: Shoe Box, construction paper, glitter and trims, scissors.

Construction: Decorate the outside of the shoe box into a fanciful birthday cake.

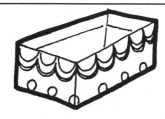

ASLEEP

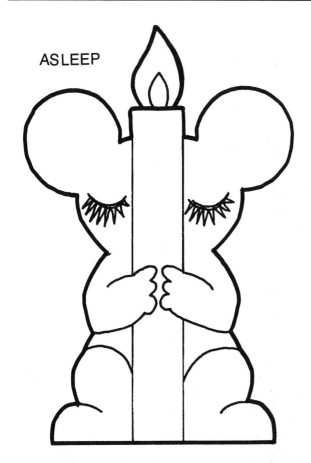

AWAKE

163

SINGING BIRTHDAY CAKES

Any chef would be envious of the array of birthday cakes created by the children. These iced delights also provide appealing companions for birthday sing-a-long and wish giving at the Birthday Bash.

TO MAKE A SINGING BIRTHDAY CAKE

Materials: Small or medium size paper bag, construction paper, double stick tape.

Construction: Cut down a paper bag into a shortened proportion as shown. Decorate the bag and create a masterpiece cake. Draw expressive faces on the cakes as well as elaborate icing designs. Detachable paper candles (use double-stick tape) will provide flexibility for multipurpose usage and counting exercises.

DETACHABLE PAPER CANDLES

ROYALTY AT THE BIRTHDAY BASH

A crown, royal document and king or queen Self-Puppet are additional prepackaged surprises that the birthday child can open on his or her special day and share at the Bash. At the beginning of the school year prepare a manila envelope or paper bag by inserting a photocopy of the crown, royal document and Self-Puppet (see patterns that follow) inside. Each child may wish to decorate the outside of the envelope or bag with a birthday wish, royal treasure or other scene of their choice. On the day of each child's birthday, that child can be asked to color the crown and Self-Puppet and fill out the royal document. This document can then be read to the class by the "reigning" birthday Self-Puppet monarch and the crown worn as the class sings "Happy Birthday".

TO MAKE A KING OR QUEEN PUPPET

Materials: Photocopy of Royalty Self-Puppet, heavy paper, medium rubber band.

Cosntruction: Cut out and color photocopy of Self-Puppet. Glue to heavy paper. Crease fold lines along mouth area as shown and operate mouth with fingers. Staple rubber band across back for slipping fingers under.

RUBBER BAND

BACK OF MOUTH

ROYAL BIRTHDAY DOCUMENT

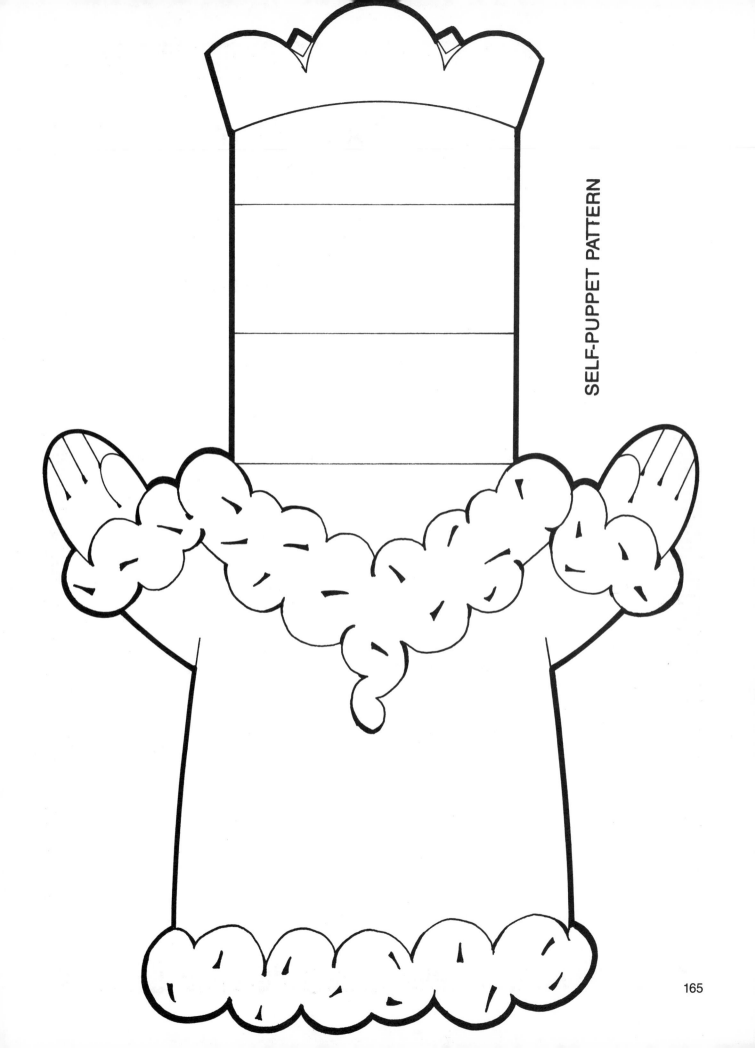

SELF-PUPPET PATTERN

165

Royal Birthday Document

My royal name is _____.

I am _____ years old today.

BECOMING BIGGER

I grew _____ inches this past year.

These are the things that make me look different this year (hair, clothes and other things you can see):

_____

_____

BECOMING SMARTER

These are things I learned and know how to do this year that make me wiser than last year:

1) _____

2) _____

3) _____

4) _____

BECOMING CLOSER TO DREAMS

This is a picture of a dream I hope comes true during this coming year, now that I am one year older:

CROWN PATTERN
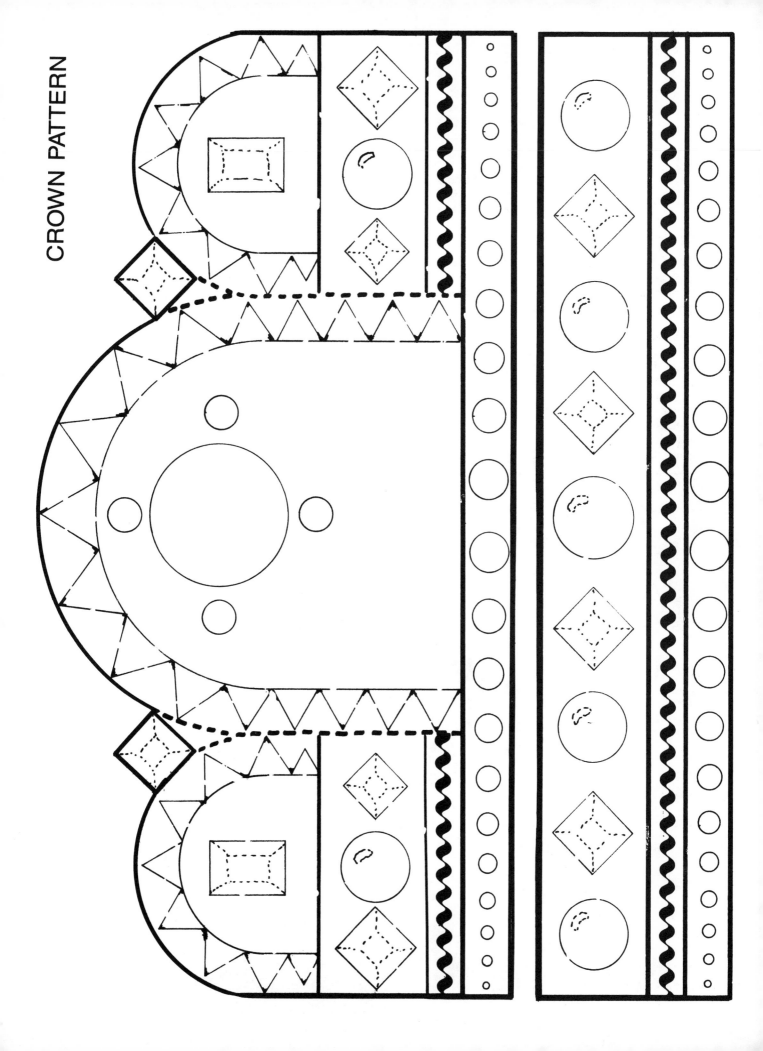

FROG PARTY BLOWERS

Common party blowers take on a novel twist when converted into Party Frog Puppets. Party frogs love to croak in concert to "Happy Birthday" as they stick out their froggie tongues in hopes of catching some tasty bugs.

These friendly reptiles also make perfect hosts for introducing Arnold Lobel's "Frog and Toad" stories to invited guests.

TO MAKE A FROG ENVELOPE PUPPET

Materials: 3-1/2″ × 6-1/2″ letter envelope (search for green envelopes at better card shops, if desired), party blower, green construction paper (optional).

Construction: Tuck flap of envelope inside. Place fingers and thumb inside envelope as shown and gently "bite" finger of other hand, forming two mouth peaks (if envelope appears wrinkled, gently smooth out). Color a face with crayon or felt-tipped marker pens on envelope. Poke a hole in center of mouth area of envelope and insert party blower through hole. Blow party blower from behind envelope. Optional paper bodies can be added to bottom of envelope.

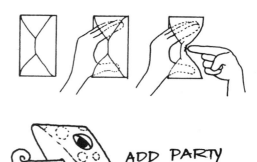

ADD PARTY BLOWER

—ADD BODY

Two frogs join in the fun

BIRTHDAY BAG-PUTER

A Birthday Bag-puter is, of course, the most upbeat item to have in any classroom. The bits and bytes can be supplied by the children themselves as they each are asked to write a gift message out for the birthday child to read. This companionable friend may also have a change over of disks for other holiday programming.

TO MAKE A BIRTHDAY BAG-PUTER

Materials: Two large supermarket bags, 12″ × 15″ piece of cardboard, construction paper, aluminum foil, super plastic junk—(plastic egg cartons, L'egg hosiery container, syrofoam cups, drinking straws, plastic glasses or styrofoam blocks and chips, jar lids, etc., two inch wide strip of paper or roll of adding machine tape.

Construction: Slit all four corners of one bag, approximately 2 inches up. Fold edges out and crease; glue to 12″ × 15″ cardboard base. Open out second bag and slip gently over first bag. Slide bag down approximately 2 inches and glue in place. Add features and control panels to basic Bag-Puter using construction paper and your super plastic junk. Cut out a rectangular slot for the mouth area. Put the paper strip or roll of paper inside mouth and pull out.

Incredible birthday greetings from a Bag-Puter

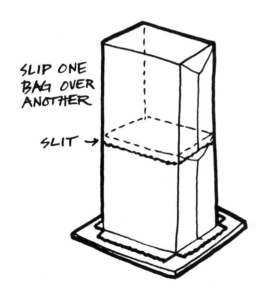

SLIP ONE BAG OVER ANOTHER

SLIT →

INTERNATIONAL HOLIDAYS

HARVEST FESTIVALS

"Help! Someone is stealing our corn!" is the chant heard from children sitting around a fire, nibbling at corn, who have just been robbed by other children of their stock. The robbing of corn continues throughout the day as it turns into a round of good natured free-for-all fun, and the Feast of Nganja finally ends. This is an occasion of celebration as held in Angola during April at harvest time. Harvest festivals are known all throughout Africa as times of hope for a good and productive harvest. It is marked with rhythmic music and dancing, keeping time to the constant tempo of resonant drums heard in the background.

The Congo engages a Leopard Pantomime or Dance as part of their harvest festivities. Traditionally, a small boy is dressed in a leopard mask and leopard skin and pantomimes a scenario of a leopard being pursued by hunters. Tie in with the African harvest celebration by having the children create and wear Paper-Plate Leopard Masks and join in with a Drum Dance.

LEOPARD DANCE

As a warm-up, have the children demonstrate how a big cat moves in the following ways: walk, crawl, leap, dash, creep, pounce and stalk.

Afterwards, introduce the activity by telling the class that drums are very popular instruments in Africa for ceremonial purposes. Play a tempo on the drum (or box substitute) and have the leopards respond by moving in a specific way to a given linear direction. For example:

Four slow beats—crawl slowly in a straight line
Two fast beats—dash in a zig-zag fashion across the space
One slow, two fast beats—pounce!

Experiment with changing tempos and directional patterns. Use more complex combinations according to grade level.

As an extended activity, leopards may be paired with a hunter/warrior to improvise skits whereas the leopard is stalked by the hunter and either captured or escapes.

TO MAKE A PAPER-PLATE LEOPARD MASK

Materials: Paper plate, ribbon or cording, yarn, and construction paper.

Construction: Cut out and locate eye holes on paper plate. Create features on plate with coloring medium or construction paper; add yarn whiskers. Punch a small hole in both sides of plate and tie ribbon or cording through holes. Tie other ends at back of head to secure mask.

Leopards on the prowl

RAT
1936, 1948, 1960, 1972
You are ambitious yet honest. Prone to spend freely. Seldom make lasting friendships. Most compatible with Dragons and Monkeys. Least compatible with Horses.

OX
1937, 1949, 1961, 1973
Bright, patient and inspiring to others. You can be happy by yourself, yet make an outstanding parent. Marry a Snake or Cock. The Sheep will bring trouble.

TIGER
1938, 1950, 1962, 1974
Tiger people are aggressive, courageous, candid and sensitive. Look to the Horse and Dog for happiness. Beware of the Monkey.

RABBIT
1939, 1951, 1963, 1975
Luckiest of all signs, you are also talented and articulate. Affectionate, yet shy, you seek peace throughout your life. Marry a Sheep or Boar. Your opposite is the Cock.

CHINESE NEW YEAR

DRAGON
1940, 1952, 1964, 1976
You are eccentric and your life complex. You have a very passionate nature and abundant health. Marry a Monkey or Rat late in life. Avoid the Dog.

GUNG HAY FAT CHOY

恭　喜　發　財

Dancing lions, Chinese boxers, and a snapping dragon wind down the street in a carnival spirit that encompasses up to seven days of celebration of Gung Hay Fat Choy. Dragon, part beast, part human with its multiple legs, stomps wildly to the beat of noisy gongs and clanking cymbals. These same legs desperately try to avoid the maddening strings of popping firecrackers set off by overeager crowds, wishing to ward off potential evil spirits.

Gung Hay Fat Choy means best wishes and congratulations. Have a prosperous and good year. This Chinese celebration is a time for honoring family members, both present and past, and thanking the gods for their blessings. This New Year event also makes a unique tradition for on this day *everyone* adds a year to their age, no matter when they were born. All of China turns into one colossus birthday party!

Chinese festival dates are determined by an ancient Chinese lunar calendar based on the cycles of the moon. Each New Year is given the name of an animal, allowing twelve animal symbols on the Chinese Zodiac. It is believed that a person born within an animal's year will retain qualities of that particular animal.

The Chinese New Year follows some other interesting customs as well:

•Apples are symbols of good luck for the New Year. Apples and oranges are found in abundance everywhere, and their colors represent the colors of joy.

•Children stay up late on New Year's Eve. It is believed that the longer one stays up, the longer one's parents will live.

•Doors and windows are sometimes sealed with red, good luck paper on New Year's Eve to be unbroken on New Year's morning.

•Incense is burned before a kitchen god which was made at the beginning of the now passing year. Candy or molasses is offered to this paper image in hopes to gum the idol's jaws and prevent his making an unfavorable year (and report bad deeds to heaven). The image is burned and later welcomed back with firecrackers and general rejoicing on New Year's Eve. A new image is made and pasted onto the chimney to start the New Year afresh.

•Gifts are exchanged and just before midnight, the children receive a special gift, called *lai see* (good luck money wrapped in red paper).

•Everyone is expected to be on their best behavior and dressed in new clothes on New Year's Day. It is most important that the New Year is begun on a good note and all ancestors honored properly for the rest of the year hinges on the conduct of this day.

Everywhere people are heard saying GUNG HAY FAT CHOY! No one takes chances.

SNAKE
1941, 1953, 1965, 1977
Wise and intense with a tendency towards physical beauty. Vain and high tempered. The Boar is your enemy. The Cock or Ox are your best signs.

SHEEP
1943, 1955, 1967, 1979
Elegant and creative, you are timid and prefer anonymity. You are most compatible with Boars and Rabits but never the Ox.

COCK
1945, 1957, 1969, 1981
A pioneer in spirit, you are devoted to work and quest after knowledge. You are selfish and eccentric. Rabbits are trouble. Snakes and Oxen are fine.

BOAR
1947, 1959, 1971, 1983
Nobel and chivalrous. Your friends will be lifelong, yet you are prone to marital strife. Avoid other Boars. Marry a Rabbit or a Sheep.

HORSE
1942, 1954, 1966, 1978
Popular and attractive to the opposite sex. You are often ostentatious and impatient. You need people. Marry a Tiger or a Dog early, but never a Rat.

MONKEY
1944, 1956, 1968, 1980
You are very intelligent and are able to influence people. An enthusiastic achiever, you are easily discouraged and confused. Avoid Tigers. Seek a Dragon or a Rat.

DOG
1946, 1958, 1970, 1982
Loyal and honest you work well with others. Generous yet stubborn and often selfish. Look to the Horse or Tiger. Watch out for Dragons.

SNAPPING CHINESE DRAGON

Here he comes with flaming bowl,
Don't be mean to take his toll,
Snip! Snap! Dragon!

Take care you don't take too much,
Be not greedy in your clutch,
Snip! Snap! Dragon!

With his blue and lapping tongue,
Many of you will be stung.
Snip! Snap! Dragon!

For he snaps at all that comes,
Snatching at his feast of plums.
Snip! Snap! Dragon!

Don't ye fear him, be but bold,
Out he goes—his flames are cold.
Snip! Snap! Dragon!

Author Unknown

The Chinese dragon is a most sacred animal and was the Chinese Emperor's insignia representing strength and goodness. Once again the dragon appears to bestow on the Chinese people peace, prosperity and good luck. The Dragon also has remarkable supernatural powers, it is believed, to change itself into innumerous conditions and shapes, become visible or invisible, or shrink to the size of a silkworm or become so large that it can fill the space between heaven and earth. The Chinese dragon (as opposed to it's medieval cousins) is a most friendly creature whose kindliness protects people from potential evil. It is described as having the head of a camel, horns of a deer, ears of a cow, neck of a snake, body of a fish, scales of a carp, claws of an eagle, eyes of the devil and the paws of the tiger. Thus, it is always a popular and colorful guest in punctuating this Chinese celebration.

Have the entire group work together in constructing a dragon from large supermarket bags. Other children can improvise music with gongs, pot lids (or use authentic music recordings) for the dragon to dance in rhythm.

TO MAKE A CHINESE DRAGON

Materials: One large supermarket bag per child, tin can rattle, scrap paper, fabric, aluminum foil, and trims.

Construction: Let each child create one segment of the dragon: Cut out one complete side of bag as shown. Then slit both sides of bag bottom to partially detach flap. Decorate bag with paint splotches, spots, floral designs, or bold geometric designs with coloring medium, scraps of paper and fabric. Link finished bags together by attaching each flap of one bag to the consecutive bag.

Create a head from a full bag for a lead child to manipulate. A tail can be made by pinching a full bag together at bottom end as shown. A can with a lid and pebbles inside makes a noisy rattle for the tail end to shake.

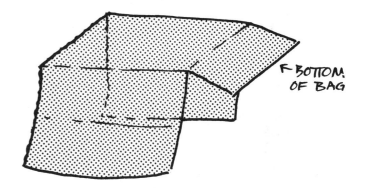

F BOTTOM OF BAG

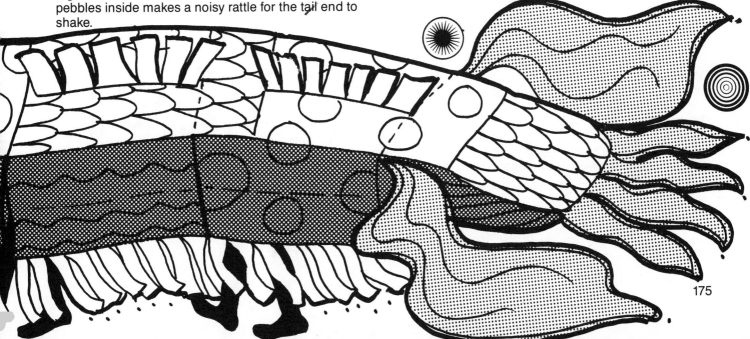

WHATEVER YOU WISH

The Chinese fear of sweeping their luck out the door on New Year's Day prompts them to hide their brooms on this special day. The following traditional story makes appealing subject matter and features a novelty broom puppet with a paper You Yuen woman character hidden inside. Present the story using the three paper puppet characters provided, tube broom shoebox, boat and jewelry props. Au Ming one of the characters, can sit in the boat, cross a make believe lake and throw the jewelry overboard. As the story progresses, present You Yuen to him as a gift. At the end, roll up You Yuen and hide her inside the tube handle of the broom. Children may wish to make their own Yon Yuen and accompanying broom to bring home.

WHATEVER YOU WISH

Long ago there was a merchant named Au Ming. One day he made a business trip by boat and took with him three pieces of valuable jewelry. While the boat was crossing Pan Chick Lake, a storm suddenly broke. He heard a voice from the lake talking about his jewelry. Knowing it was the work of the God of the Lake, he became frightened and threw his jewels into the water to appease the god. Just as suddenly, the storm subsided and he was able to reach the other shore safely.

Upon reaching the shore, Au Ming was met by soldiers who invited him for refreshments. Au Ming was confused and didn't want to go until the soldiers explained that the invitation was to the home of the God of the Lake, who wanted to thank him for his gift of jewelry. The soldiers also hinted to Au Ming that the God of the Lake might wish to give him a gift of his choosing. The soldiers further advised that he should ask for "You Yen."

Sure enough, when Au Ming arrived at the house, the God of the Lake asked him what he wanted. He replied, "You Yuen" and was surprised to discover that You Yoen was the god's maidservant.

Au Ming took You Yuen into his home and married her. She possessed such magic powers that whatever Au Ming wished, she would obtain for him. Over the years, he became very, very wealthy. As Au Ming became prosperous, he became self-important as well. He felt so self important, in fact, that he decided he didn't need You Yuen anymore and began to treat her badly.

One New Year's Day, You Yuen overslept. Now Au Ming really became angry. You Yuen was so frightened she hid herself inside a broom. Au Ming was never able to find her again and from that time on, he began to lose his wealth, until finally he was a poor man.

As the story spread, the people believed that You Yuen was still inside the broom. Therefore, these people would hide their brooms so that You Yuen and prosperity could not leave their homes. It is also appropriate that in Chinese, You Yuen means "whatever you wish."

TO MAKE TUBE BROOM

Materials: Photocopy of basic s/he and costume pattern, cardboard towel (or longer) tube, rafia, straw, fringed newspaper or fringed yellow construction paper.

To Make puppet, cut out and color s/he pattern. (see section one). Color costume pattern and attach to puppet.

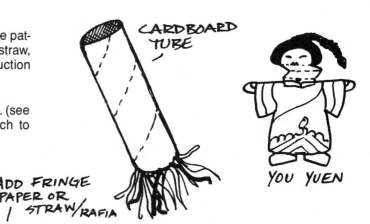

CARDBOARD TUBE

ADD FRINGE PAPER OR STRAW/RAFIA

YOU YUEN

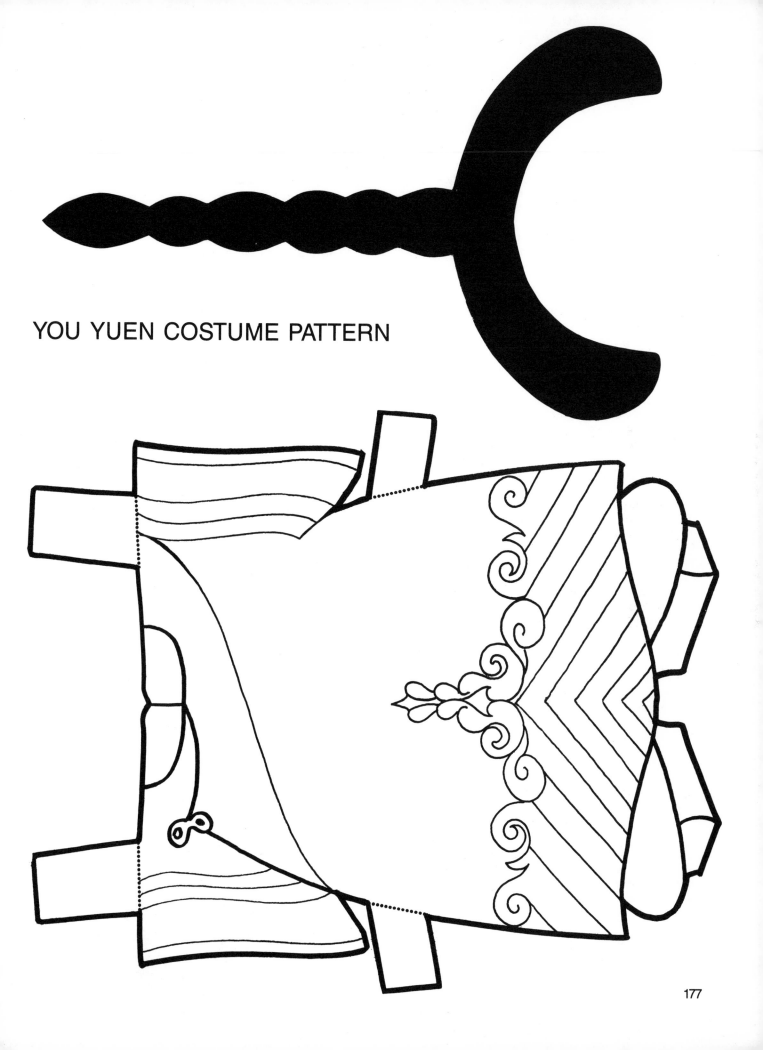

YOU YUEN COSTUME PATTERN

HOLI
Festival of Spring

Small monkeys in frilly skirts chatter and twirl to the rhythm of a drum. Acrobats, ribbons, bangles and sweetmeats filled with exotic spicey flavors set the scene of this important festival. The Holi-Festival of Spring is a harvest festival celebrated in many parts of India during March and April when farmers gather their wheat crops and spring is marked on the calendar.

Holi is also centered around legend. One of the legends is the story about Krishna (who was really Vishnu, the Preserver), who came to earth in a human form. Krishna grew up among cowherds on the banks of the River Jumna in Northern India. As a boy, he contained a mischievous streak and enjoyed playing pranks. He delighted in stealing the sweet butter from the milkmaids' churns and turning over their milk pails. His pranks were many and the cow maids retaliated by squirting colored water over Krishna until he became nothing less than a walking rainbow!

So, during Holi, one sees the chomatic delight of children with multiple streaks of yellow, orange and crimson across their faces and in their hair. The towns abound with carts ladened with different colored powders and liquids for sale to fill revenging squirt guns to spray over friends in good jest. On the other hand, a quiet celebration in an Indian home may involve a bowl of red powder for a friend or family member to dip a finger into and press gently onto another person's forehead as a gesture of good will at Holi.

SHADOW PRANKS PLAYS

Shadow puppets are fascinating puppets used in India for many centuries. They are large and brilliantly colored, intricately pierced for decoration and often made from buffalo hide. They feature moving parts and are operated with rods. The shows performed generally last all night long and involve much action by puppeteers who dance and stamp on sounding boards below the ground and shake bells attached to ankles for special effect. If material is available, share some pictures or real Indian shadow puppets with the children to inspire designs. Have children create simplified, reduced versions of these traditional puppets using the overhead shadow projector as a vehicle of presentation.

Feature an activity to celebrate Holi by having children present, while working in teams of two, shadow shows on the overhead projector. Short skits can be developed using Indian imagery that center around characters playing pranks upon one another as did Krishna. For example:

Put a cow on a rooftop
Offer a friend a bag full of jumping frogs
Jump from a tree and scare a friend
Bring an elephant as a guest for dinner

TO MAKE AN OVERHEAD SHADOW PUPPET

Materials: Light tagboard, manila file folders or other stiff paper, drinking straws, paper fastener brads, paper doilies.

Construction: Cut out image parts from paper or doilies. Cut decorating slits or other features with thread scissors or hole punch. Attach a straw rod control or acetate strip to back of puppet using one of the following methods.

Method A. Using drinking straw, wrap a piece of masking tape around end of straw. Let tape extend at the end of straw 1/2 inch and attach tape extension to back of puppet with another piece of tape.

Method B. Using clear acetate strip, lay tip of strip flat on back of puppet and adhere with double-stick tape. Adding a piece of folded masking tape on end of acetate for hand grip.

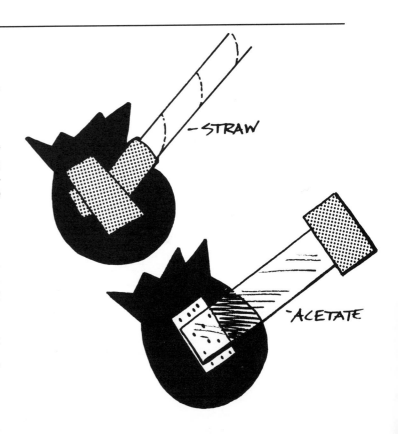

179

DIWALI-HINDU NEW YEAR

This most brilliant of festivals is in honor of goodness in triumph over evil, light over darkness. It occurs at the end of October and beginning of November. As in all New Year festivals, it is a time to look with optimism to the future. It centers around the great Hindu event of a prince named Rama who rescued his wife, Sita, from the ten-headed, ten-armed demon king, Ravana. When they returned from their conquest for their coronation, they were proclaimed by Indians everywhere and thousands of clay lamps (divas) were lit and followed by a magnificent celebation of joy.

It is India's dazzling festival as every home bedecks itself with golden oil lamps. Multitudes of electric lights are hung in public places and fireworks mark the occasion. A revered custom is for every home to be completely cleaned before the festival begins. For on the night of Diwali, Lakshmi (wife of Vishnu, the Preserver) takes care to visit each and every home to inspect its cleanliness. If she is not completely satisfied, she will turn away and prosperity cannot be guaranteed for that family for the coming year.

Children will challenge creating a Ravana, demon king puppet, with its many heads and arms, to manipulate using the pattern that follows. The puppets may be used as a base for class discussion on the virtues of good and perils of evil.

TO MAKE A RAVANA PUPPET

Materials: Photocopy of patterns, two paper fastener brads.

Construction: Cut out and color photocopies. Punch a hole on each arm and both sides of body; link together with paper fastener brads.

HOLES + BRAD

ATTACH STICK

RAVANA PATTERN

BOY'S DAY

The carp is revered in Japan as a fish that symbolizes strength, courage and determination, such admirable qualities that every Japanese wishes to pass on to sons. Boy's Day signified by the carp, transforms the entire country into nothing less than an oversized, above-ground aquarium. Fish fly in the breeze everywhere. Blue spotted, red dotted, yellow striped, all brightly colored and made from paper or cloth. The carp noisily flap and dart, back and forth, snapping in the wind. Huge carp on tall poles and tiny carp alongside tiny babies in cradles.

On this day, each son is honored with a gift from his father of a flying carp. The eldest son receives the largest carp, perhaps as long as fifteen feet, placed in the highest position on the pole that serves this occasion (just under a pinwheel which adorns the pole's top). A notch below it goes each smaller fish, in sequence, according to the number of sons in a family.

All activities on this day are centered around the central theme of giving strength to sons. Traditionally, shelves are arranged with miniature collections of Samurai warriors, swords, and bow and arrows. As many holidays, those old role models are gradually being fitted with new role models. Some other changes have occurred to adjust to modern times. For example, recently the government has reestablished the holiday and now call it Children's Day to honor both boys and girls on the same day.

Ask each child to create a Carp Bag Wind Kite to flutter in an outdoor display or event. Share pictures of some colorful carp to children to inspire design.

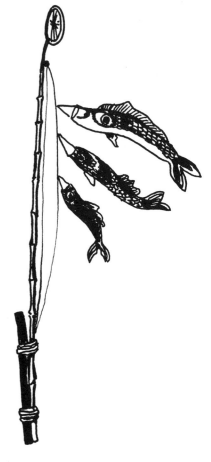

TO MAKE A CARP BAG WIND KITE

Materials: Small or medium lightweight paper bag (consider white bakery goods bag), string, a colored newspaper comics sheet.

Construction: Create a carp design on outside of bag with tempera paint or felt-tip marker pens.

Open out bag and tie a short length of string to both sides of bags at open end. (String should be loose). Put a piece of tape over the string holes to prevent bag from tearing. Tie a long length of string to the center of short length of string.

Cut two or three 1 ½ inch comics sheet strips and tape or glue to bottom of bag for tail streamers. Run with the carp kite in a breeze.

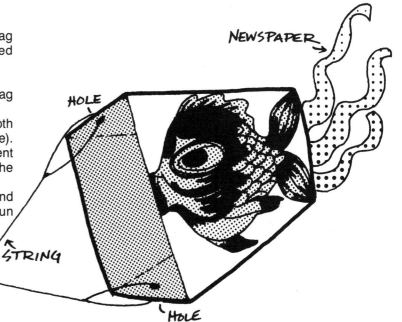

GIRL'S DAY

While Boy's Day centers around the symbol of a carp, Girl's Day pays homage to special dolls called "hinas" which means something small and lovely. The dolls are the center of attention during the Hina Matsuri, or Doll Festival, usually called Girl's Day. It derives from a long ago tradition, a Shinto spring-welcoming ritual. Its purpose was to cleanse away winter's evil spirits. The people believed these evil spirits would vanish from their bodies if they rubbed themselves with small paper dolls, allowing the spirits to leave them and enter into the bodies of the dolls. The dolls were then thrown into rivers to be purified and carried away.

As time went on, dolls were soon contrived from clay and other more recently modern materials. They became such cherished items and seemed senseless to throw away, thus they were stood on shelves to be taken out yearly to display at holiday time. Treasured dolls, often fashioned after elaborate royalty, Japanese emperors and empresses and court (ladies in waiting, ministers of state, court musicians and courtiers) are passed down through generations. There is a large parade of visiting on this day and much fussing and admiration over each family's doll display.

Custom follows that a few weeks before the festival a mother presents her daughter with a gift of fifteen miniature dolls, dressed in stunning brocades and silks.

Dolls are displayed on a special stand with six stepped shelves, covered with bright red cloth to offset the dolls. A certain ritual follows in doll formation: The emperor and empress are placed on the top shelf, in front of a small gold screen. On either side of them is a miniature lantern. On the second shelf, the three ladies-in-waiting are placed to serve the royal couple. Then come the five court musicians, the two ministers of state and the three courtiers with a miniature orange tree and cherry tree on either side of the courtiers.

Tiny pieces of furniture, chest of drawers, dressing table, mirrors, dishes, and a marvelous royal carriage all fulfill the royal couple's needs.

Have children create Tube Doll Puppets using the costume pattern that follows and decorate with intricate floral or other patterns, silky ribbon sashes and trims. Share some picture books of Japanese costuming with children, to inspire designs. Play some Japanese music as children work on dolls.

Afterwards, the tube dolls can be arranged in a special display to be admired.

TO MAKE A TUBE DOLL PUPPET

Materials: Short cardboard tube, photocopy of patterns, white construction paper, black yarn or tissue paper, ribbon, sequins and trims. Scrap part fabric (optional).

Construction: Cover tube with white construction paper. Add a Japanese face to upper area. Form yarn or tissue paper into hair.

YARN OR FABRIC

CARDBOARD TUBE

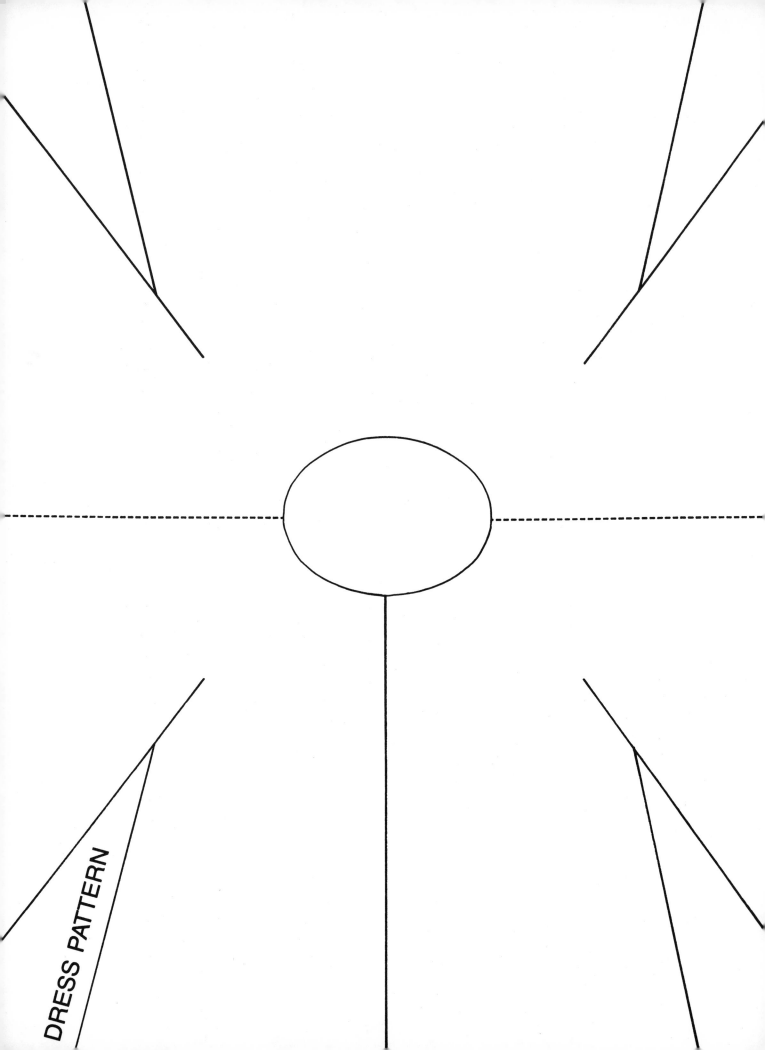

DRESS PATTERN

A MEXICAN FIESTA

"Amigo" is the Spanish word for friend and a Mexican fiesta sets a congenial mood for meeting with friends—old and new. This gay and colorful event is a time marked by the Mexicans to celebrate any one of their many popular holidays such as Cinco de Mayo (Mexico's Independence Day on May 5th), El Dia de Los Muertos (the Day of the Dead or All Souls Day on November 1st), and La Posada (the 9 days of Christmas celebration during the month of December). But no one needs an excuse to hold a fiesta—A fiesta can be held simply for the sake of a fiesta!

A fiesta is a feast not only of zesty foods but also of tantilizing sounds and vibrating colors. A sleepy village is suddenly, magically transformed into a visual and epicurean delight.

Mariachi players with multi-colored ribbons streaming from their guitars stroll by while señoritas twirl in brilliant skirts. Fluffy tissue paper flowers and papier mâché piñatas dangle from paper streamers crisscrossing in the open air. A marionette shouts "¡olé!" as a mustachio merchant sways along singing a song to the clickety-clack of the marionette's wooden feet. When the market unfolds into this exotic fantasy a sense of closeness and community envelopes everyone as grandparents, children, parents and friends all come together to enjoy themselves and participate in the many activities the fiesta has to offer. Mexicans look forward eagerly to this bright spot that punctuates a long year of hard work and checked frugality. For a day at least, they are *all* excited children—whether young or old and they chatter like crickets as they meander among each other's booths.

No one wants this day to end—and, in fact, it really doesn't; there is festive activity all day with only breaks for a siesta!

THE MARKETPLACE

The setting of a fiesta in a marketplace is a project in which the entire group would enjoy participating. To accommodate large groups, plan to use a spacious area such as a cafeteria, gym or outdoor space. However, a fiesta can be fun in any kind of setting, however small. Here are some ideas for pooling together the talents of the group to establish a fiesta mood:

•Hang crepe paper streamers with bright tissue paper banners or paper lanterns in crisscross fashion over the space. The group can make colorful tissue paper flowers to decorate the area. Remember, brilliant colors such as indigo blue, scarlet red, sunshine yellow and other glowing colors are favorites of the Mexicans.

•A piñata should be hung in a special location for all to see. (See latter section this chapter for construction.)

•Paint a colorful background mural of a Mexican village, landscape or other scene to enhance the marketplace.

•Decorate the fiesta area with borrowed clay pots, potted plants, large cacti and wicker baskets filled with festive foodstuff such as mangos, pineapples, papaya, peppers, tomatoes and avocados.

•If the event is held outdoors in the evening, string Christmas lights across the open air and display rows of *luminarias* (paper bag lanterns) along pathways and borders. To make a *luminaria* pour several inches of sand into a medium sized paper bag. Place a short candle in the sand bag and when the candle is lit the bag will glow. Perforated designs or felt-tip colored markers can be added to give the bags a festive touch.

•Improvise booths from desks and tables pushed together or lay down a number of small rugs to serve as booths. As a group, decide what each booth will display and sell. Reserve a space in the center of the booth arrangement for dances, piñata play, and games. One or two members of the group can be in charge of each booth. Here are a few suggestions for items that might be displayed in booths:

Knickknacks and Mexican toys—can be made or gathered by booth members. These might include a clay tree of life, yarn weavings, corn husk figures, masks, marionettes and other Mexican craft objects.

Food Treats—such as chili, pralines, tacos or other dishes made by the group along with fruit and vegetable displays.

Cultural booths—might be set up to give information about Mexican folklore, customs, history and geography. Ask local travel agencies to contribute flyers and posters about Mexico for the occasion.

Use geometric designs and other decorative motifs to make each booth unique. Colorful signs for each craft, food or cultural booth can give it personality such as, "Miguel's Tacos," "Maria's Balloons" and "Pepe's Piñatas".

Hold a contest to judge each booth on quality of its craft or food and the originality of design. Present colorful ribbon awards to the winners.

Although Mexican everyday folk costumes are plain and simple they are functional in many ways. Fiesta dance costumes, however, are their show pieces and iç contrast are highly ornamental. A señorita's dress skirts can weigh as much as thirty pounds and measure eight yards around. As it twirls in a lively dance it spreads out in a large circle that creates a spontaneous blur of pink, yellow, red, orange, blue and purple. The wide-brimmed sombrero of the señor is often the center of attention at a Fiesta during the popular hand clapping "Mexican Hat Dance." Made from felt and decorated with silver embroidery and sequins, it makes an impressive sight.

You may wish to crown a Master or Mistress of Ceremonies with an oversized sombrero in honor of the fiesta.

The group will enjoy making Bodi-Bag Puppets (refer to construction in President's Day section) with their own Mexican costuming designs to help celebrate the fiesta. A supply of brightly colored fabrics, yarn and paper will provide nice touches for improvising colorful details such as found in serapes, dance shirts and other garments described previously. Puppeteers can wear sandals or flat shoes with these puppets.

188   **A Fiesta in full swing — (Bodi-Bag Puppets)**

EL DIA DE LOS MUERTOS

DAY OF DEAD

Up pops the coffin lid—out jumps a skeleton! The children shriek and run. Skeletons, skeletons everywhere. Little hand crafted figurines sitting on shelves (perhaps ironing a pancho or patting out tortillas). Others are human actors hidden behind skull-painted masks and dressed as a bride or bridegroom.

In fact, this oddly placed couple is often seen as part of a mock funeral accompanied by pallbearers carrying a coffin with another jesting skeleton hidden inside. This parody of skeletons is no more frightening to little children in Mexico than some Halloween creatures mght be to children in the United States. The high spirits that prevails during El Día de los Muertos, or the Day of the Dead, (the last day of a three day celebration), is also a solemn occasion. It marks a special day for honoring and remembering family members no longer living. For the Mexican believes that when a person dies, that person goes onto another life, and happier existence. They also believe that their souls come back to visit their families. To assure the event, respect is paid at the cemetery where multitudes of yellow marigold petals are strewn over the graves. The marigold, or flor de los muertos (the flower of the dead), is appropriately named.

On this holiday, when night arrives, tall white candles are lit for each relative who has died and set on the graves. As a combined, communal effort, the Mexican towns ablaze everywhere with the glitter of thousands of flickering candlelights.

Have the class celebrate this special day by creating String Skeleton Puppets. Puppets can be dressed humorously as brides and grooms or other characters. Afterwards, small groups may wish to perform short skits or dances (using some Mexican musical recordings) with the puppets.

A demonstration model or picture of a skeleton will help children better visualize the skeletons framework before construction is begun. Patterns found in the Halloween section may be used for building skeletons or children can create their own framework as described below.

TO MAKE A STRING SKELETON PUPPET

Materials: White construction paper, string, paper fastener brads, cardboard tubes or dowels, fabric, yarn and trims.

Construction: Cut out a selection of various bone shapes and types—long, short, rib cage, pelvic, head, skull, foot, etc. Punch holes at ends of bone shapes and link together with lengths of string or use paper fastener brads.

Tie two to three long pieces of string to hands and head; attach opposite ends to cardboard tubes or dowels, as shown. Add yarn, fabric and trim detailing or costumes.

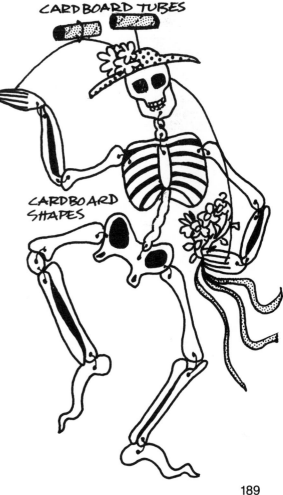

CARDBOARD TUBES

CARDBOARD SHAPES

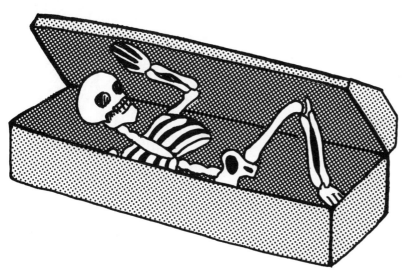

LA POSADA

"Let us in. Let us in!" chime the children disguised as Mary and Joseph seeking lodging in the village.

"There is no room here," is the reciprocating melody sung back to them by the townspeople.

On each of the nine nights before Christmas candle-lit groups of happy children participate in the La Posada and carry a small platform holding clay figurines of Joseph and Mary seated on a burro, (in elaborate events sometimes a real burro and children costumed as Mary and Joseph with accompanying angels lead the procession.) On the last night, Christmas Eve (or La Navida), an infant baby Jesus figurine is added.

After a number of such attempts to find lodging by the La Posada, the children finally find a receptive host (agreed on beforehand) who will accept them and provide accommodations.

"Come in, we will find room," sings the smiling host.

The procession of enlightened children enter and a party begins and refreshments served, mainly of sweets and peanuts. The high point of a La Posada party comes when the piñata is brought out (having been hidden by the host) and strung on the ceiling or outside in the courtyard. Every child knows that it is filled with delightful treats and surprises and hopes he or she will be the lucky one who breaks it apart. Each child has a turn with the stick beginning with the smallest. When broken, treats spill over the ground and all the children dash wildly about to claim their share.

TO MAKE A PINATA

Materials: Large supermarket bag, wrapped candy, peanuts, pennies and small unbreakable trinkets, construction and crepe or tissue paper, aluminum foil and rope.

Construction: Stuff bag with food and trinket items (also some lightly crumpled paper if required to fill space). Tie bag securely at top with a string or tape.

Decide on a character or design for the piñata—a colorful bird, super hero, snowman, mouse, etc. Create features on bag with paper or coloring medium. Crepe or tissue paper can easily be fringed and added for a fluffy or feathery look. Aluminum foil strips will add a sparkling effect or can be used for science fiction characters. Attach a long rope to the piñata at the top of the bag; tie other end to the ceiling on the branch.

Clown Piñata

THREE KINGS' DAY PUERTO RICO
DIA DE LOS REYES

One wise man,
Saw a bright star.
By this sign he knew,
He must travel far.

Two wise men,
Kings, some say,
Looked to the star
To show the way.

Three wise men,
Knew the star was a sign,
That a baby was born,
To mankind.

Three wise men,
Kings we are told,
Carried gifts of frankincense,
Myrrh and gold.

They carried their gifts,
To a far away town,
And gave them to,
The new King they found.

by Lynn Irving

On this day and alongside Christmas festivities, three stately Kings, in the guise of three children, may appear at your door to sing Christmas carols and announce the news of the Magi. The children form chorals in groups of three and are traditionally dressed in the King's symbolic robe colors—red, lavender and yellow. Costumes are topped off with glittering crowns. Rhythm instruments, rattling gourds and clanking sticks, are used to enhance the lively renditions of these carols.

This enchanting custom stems from the story of three Kings—Melchior, Caspar and Balthasar who, two weeks before January 6th, leisurely sojourn towards Puerto Rico on camels (it is uncertain, for some believed they were horses), to visit the homes of all good children. Just prior to their arrival, on the eve of January 6th, custom follows that each child gathers grass or grain and hides it under the bed or in a shoe as food for the Kings' camels. While the children sleep peacefully (and in great anticipation), the Kings visit each home and exchange the gift of grass for a toy or article of clothing. The children wake up happily, knowing the camels will be well fed.

On this note, three Kings' Day has officially arrived and the day is marked with general merriment. After church services there are many festive parties planned for young people throughout the island, with plentiful music and song, and the feeling of good will everywhere.

It may also be of interest that three Kings' Day is also celebrated in Germany, Norway, Spain, Portugal, Italy and other countries with varying traditions.

Children can improvise Kings' costumes and crowns using the crown pattern found in the Birthday Party section. Or, have each child make a King and Camel Puppet with rhythm instrument to use with Christmas carolling or with the poem.

Each child may also be asked to have the King carry a gift or wish written on a note attach to the King's body to give another child, friend or relative.

TO MAKE A KING AND CAMEL PUPPET

Materials: Photocopy of pattern, paper fastener brads, cardboard, blunt skewer or rod, cardboard or tin can, pebbles.

Construction: Cut out and color photocopy of patterns. Create an original crown and robe design on King. Punch holes in camel's body and legs as shown; link together with paper fastener brads.

To prepare rattle, put several pebbles into can. Cut out a cardboard lid and tape onto top of can. Puncture a hole in center of lid, insert a skewer or rod down hole and glue in place; attach other end to camel.

To operate, hold can and rattle as the puppet moves.

TIN CAN

191

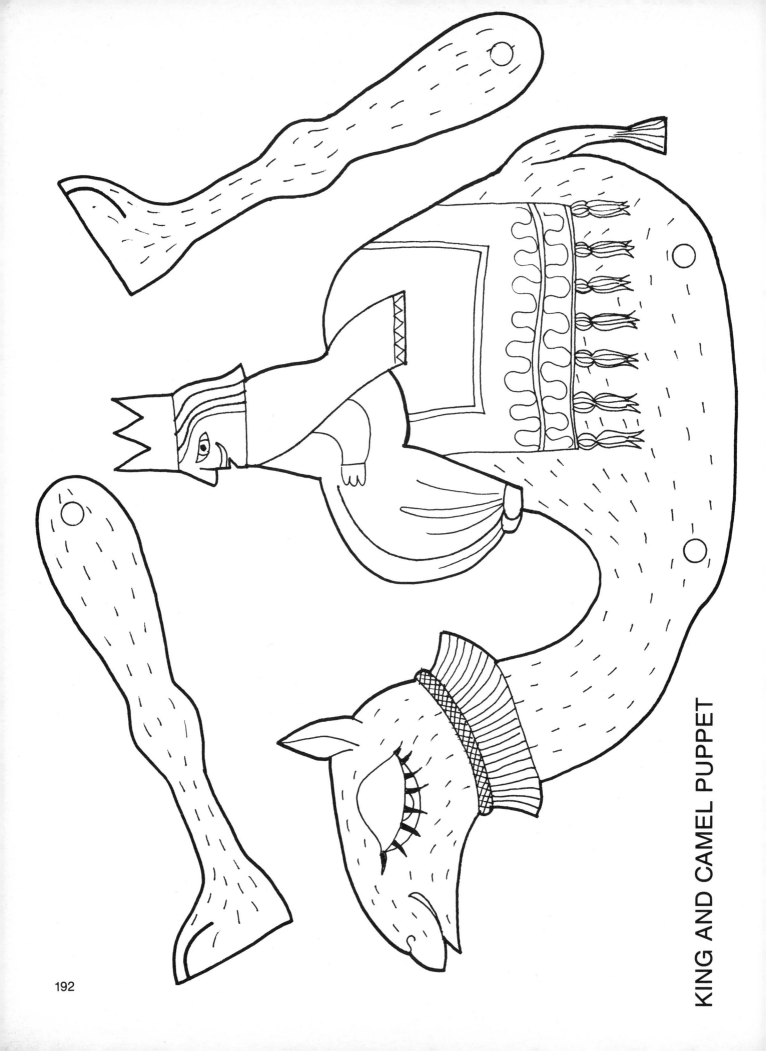

192

KING AND CAMEL PUPPET

MID-AUTUMN FESTIVAL

In many countries, the phases of the moon is carefully observed and often plays a significant role in the marking of holidays. The appearance of the full moon in September (of our calendar) in Viet Nam is so impressive that a special celebration is held to honor it—the Mid-Autumn Festival. At this time the rejoicing of the moon can be found everywhere. The special cake, banh trung-thu, filled with nuts and fruit and as rotund as the moon itself.

Tradition dictates that these moon cakes cannot be eaten until the traditional paper figure of an ancient doctor (no one knows why) placed in the middle of each of the cake trays, is removed, which usually occurs in late evening.

The moon holds such a feeling of beauty and mystery to the vietnamese, that traditionally they enjoy the simple ritual of sitting at night in the outdoor air and staring at the moon while sipping tea and eating moon cakes. Sometimes they even write poems to honor the moon. Mid-Autumn Festival is an especially happy holiday for the children, and is accompanied with lots of gaiety, dancing and music. Best of all are the multiples of glowing, lighted lanterns. These are commonly shaped like the moon, but can take on different shapes and forms such as a fish, plane or animal. A very special lantern favorite is a ring of cardboard that moves inside a lighted lantern to show a sequencing of a fairy tale in silhoutte.

As with Chinese celebrations, the occasion is also marked with colorful dragon dances, clashing cymbals and noisy musicians.

Have each child create a lantern with an inner story script based on a popular legend or fairy tale such as Little Red Riding Hood, Gingerbread Boy or the Three Billy Goats Gruff. Or, an original tale can be created possibly featuring something that occured one night when the moon was full and shining.

TO MAKE A STORY LANTERN

Materials: Paper plate, white tissue or white tracing paper (purchased by roll at drafting supplies stores), aluminum foil, five 1″ cardboard strips, 1″ wide by 30″ long cardboard strip, 4″ wide by 28″ long clear acetate (book report covers purchased in stationery store can be cut and linked in strips) or overhead projector acetate, short candle in small glass or flashlight.

Construction: To make lantern, staple or glue aluminum foil over entire bottom of plate. Staple the five 6″ long strips of cardboard to edge of paper plate as shown; bend strips up in vertical position. Curve and staple 30″ cardboard strip to tops of vertical strips to secure all strips in position. Cover (staple or glue) entire vertical wall area with white tissue or drafting paper.

An alternate version, is to use a large cylindrical shaped ice cream container as the basic lantern walls, if it is well cleaned. Cut out large areas of the container's walls and glue thin white paper over this framework.

To make inner story script, create a sequence of pictures, animated filmstrip style, along entire length of acetate strip with Vis-a-Vis (or other waterproof marker pens) or paper silhouette cutouts. Bend strip around and tape ends together being sure completed acetate circle is slightly smaller than lantern wall. Insert inside lantern.

Place candle in center (**caution:** candle is for outdoor use only) and rotate story strip by hand. If you wish, attach an extended tab or rod control to top edge of story script to move it along more easily while light of candle shows silhouette designs. For indoor use, a flashlight may be utilized and shone inside lantern or up a central hole cut in bottom, center of plate.

A mini-version, can be made by young children. Cut down white paper bags (obtained at bakery shops) for simple lantern constructions. A modified story script, either drawn on acetate, or cut out paper silhouettes of characters can be glued to inside bag's surface. Place sand inside bag for weight (to sit on ground) and a lit candle for outdoor use. Or, puncture a hole in bottom of bag to poke a flashlight up for indoor play.

COVER PLATE WITH FOIL

1″×5″ CARDBOARD STRIPS

1×30″ CARDBOARD STRIP

BEND STRIPS UP →

4″×28″ ACETATE STRIP

TAB

PUT ACETATE INSIDE LANTERN

CUT HOLE FOR LIGHT →

BLACK SILHOUETTE CUT OUT DESIGNS

...OR CUT DESIGNS OUT OF BAG AND ADD ACETATE WITH DETAILS

BIBLIOGRAPHY & RESOURCES

ORGANIZATIONS

AMERICAN ALLIANCE FOR THEATER AND EDUCATION—A newly formed organization (1987) for perpetuating theater arts (drama, puppetry, etc.) into education offering various programs and conventions. Write to: Theater Arts Department, Virginia Tech, Blacksburg, VA 24061.

NATIONAL COMMITTEE • ARTS FOR THE HANDICAPPED—This superb organization has made widespread impact across the nation in accelerating the arts amongst the disabled population. They feature a regular newsletter with updates on grants and special arts festival held in various locations. Write John F. Kennedy Center for the Performing Arts, Education Office, Washington DC 20566.

NATIONAL STORYTELLING RESOURCE CENTER—An organization specializing in exploring and upgrading the quality of storytelling techniques. Annual storytelling convention as well as a comprehensive resource center. National Storytelling Resource Center, P.O. Box 112, Jonesborbough TN 37659.

PUPPETEERS OF AMERICA—National organization for the betterment of puppetry, with membership from many parts of the world. Offers an annual Puppet Festival; a Puppetry Store for purchasing books and puppet items; a bi-monthly magazine; consultant services and affiliated guilds located around the country. A small membership fee is required. Write for information about your local puppet guild. Puppeteers of America, Gayle C. Schluter, Treasurer, #15 Cricklewood Path, Pasadena CA 91107.

ONTARIO PUPPETRY ASSOCIATION—A Canadian puppetry organization offering various activities and services. Kenneth McKay, Executive Secretary, 10 Skyview Crescent, Willowdale, Ontario M2J 1B8, Canada.

UNIMA—An international organization that features a regular journal plus many international puppet festivals. Write to: Allelu Karten, UNIMA Browning Road, Hyde Park NY 12538.

MISCELLANEOUS SOURCES

Audio-Visuals

Children's Recordings, a fine source for all kinds of song and music recordings for children, including a holiday selection. Write: P.O. Box 1343, Eugene OR 97440.

Listening Library, a complete and excellent line of fine quality filmstrips and cassettes by popular authors, including a holiday selection. Write: P.O. Box L, Old Greenwich CT. 06870.

Tot Line, an excellent newsletter for early childhood teachers showing many, lively activities for the classroom, often including Holiday projects. Write: Warren Publishing House, Inc. P.O. Box 2255, Everett, WA 98203.

Craft Supplies

ZIMS—This mail order craft supply company sells retail all types of items, plastic eyes, glue trims, pipe cleaners, etc. There is a four dollar charge (refundable upon first order of $20 or more) for a comprehensive book on all their items of excellent value to the ardent puppetmaker. Write to Zim's P.O. Box 7620, Salt Lake City, UT 84107.

Stages

PUPPET HARDWARE—Others excellent stages to libraries, puppeteers and schools. Features probable and collapsible types as well as custom to individual needs. Constructed from steel piping. 205 Donaldson Dr., Monroe Falls, OH 44262.

BOOKS ABOUT GENERAL HOLIDAYS

Customs and Crafts

Bauer, Caroline Feller. *Celebrations*. New York: H.W. Wilson Co., 1985. A compilation of read-aloud prose and poetry and book themed program suggestions.

Black, Naomi. Celebration, *The Book of Jewish Festivals*. NY: Dutton, 1987. Richly illustrated, large format book detailing the holidays' key elements, songs, recipes and accompanying literature, with text and full color lavish photographs.

Chapman, Jean. *Pancakes and Painted Eggs*. Chicago: Children's Press, 1983. A collection of stories, verses, activities, songs and facts for Easter and all the days of the year.

Chase, William D. and Helen M. *Chase's Annual Events*. Chicago: Contemporary Books, Inc. 1986. An incredibly comprehensive collection of special days, weeks and months. This book is updated and published annually.

Cole, Ann. *A Pumpkin in a Pear Tree: Creative Ideas for Twelve Months of Holiday Fun*. Boston: Little, Brown and Co., 1976. Activities and craft ideas presented in this book are suitable for preschoolers through grade three. The ideas are as fun as the title.

Epstein, Morris. *All About Jewish Holidays and Customs*. N.Y.: Ktav Publishing House, Inc., 1959. Fact-filled, indexed compandium of facts and stories, with good explanations of words and customs.

Greif, Martin *The Holiday Book, America's Festivals and Celebrations*. NY Universe Books, 1978. A superb guide book for brushing up on origins and informative data on holidays.

Grigoli, Valorie. *Patriotic Holidays and Celebrations*. New York: Watts, 1985. This book describes patriotic holidays in America, those associated with public figures, military holidays and regions ethnic celebrations. Suggested activities conclude each description.

Jones, Elizabeth G. *Ranger Rick's Holiday Book*. Vienna, Virginia: National Wildlife Federation, 1980. Many outdoor projects are featured in this book which has a wildlife focus with a primary focus on winter, seasonal activities.

Polette, Nancy and Hamlin, Marjorie. *Celebrating with Books*. Metuchen, New Jersey: Scarecrow Press, 1977.

Purdy, Susan *Festivals for You to Celebrate*. Philadelphia: J.B. Lippencott and Co., 1969. This book covers international holidays as well as traditional American ones. It is arranged by season, with an explanation and craft/decoration suggestion given for each holiday. Instructions for several dolls and puppets are included.

Purdy, Sausuan Gold. *Jewish Holidays: Facts, Activities and Crafts*. Philadelphia: Lippincott, 1969.

Quackenbush, Robert. *The Holiday Song Book*. New York: Lothrop, 1977. Included in this book are one hundred songs for twenty-seven holidays with music arranged for easy piano and guitar accompaniment.

NEW YEAR

Customs and Crafts

Brandenberg, Aliki. New Year's Day. N.Y. Crowell, 1967. Describes how New Year's Eve is celebrated in countries throughout the world.

Shapp, Martha and Charles. *Let's Find Out About New Years Day*. N.Y: F. Waits, 1968. Brief description of New Years Eve celebration customs in many countries of the world.

Storybooks

Modell, Frank. Goodbye Old Year. Hello New Year. New York: Greenwillow Books, 1984. Marvin and Milton love celebrations so they decide to set their alarm clocks for midnight. When they sleep through the alarm, they have to celebrate a new way. Presentation: Use pots and pans, bowls and other kitchen utensils to make puppets by adding on paper features with tape. When the teacher announces it is midnight have the puppets "bang" together to make a noise.

MARTIN LUTHER KING, JR.

Storybooks

Davidson, *I Have A Dream*. New York: Scholastic, Inc., 1986. This biography contains excerpts from King's speeches and photographs from his life. The short chapters would make this a good read-aloud book for the classroom. Presentation: The teacher can ask each student to finish the sentence "I have a dream:" with one thought. Combine all those thoughts and have one student act as King reading the speech. The rest of the class should act as his followers in this dramatization.

Bains, Rae. *Martin Luther King*. Mah Wah, New Jersey: Troll Associates, 1985. This brief biography describes King's philosophical background, his good works and his death. Presentation: Ask children if there are things that they would like to change in the world. Write these down. Children can then create super heros puppets using the s/he pattern to fantacize solutions.

ARBOR DAY

Customs and Crafts

Fisher, Aileen. *Arbor Day*. New York: Crowell, 1965. A simple factual history of the trees of North America, including why & how J. Sterling Morton created Arbor Day.

Rockwell, Robert, et al. *Hug a Tree and Other Things to do Outdoors with Young Children*. Mt. Ranier, Maryland: Gryphon House, 1983. A marvelous book of simple, but appealing projects for children to do with trees and nature. What makes it so unique is its emphasis on aesthetic and affective experiences.

Storybooks

Coats, Laura Jane. *The Oak Tree*. New York Macmillian, 1987. The sun and moon rise and set, men and animals come and go, but the oak tree remains still and solid. Presentation: Make a large standing oak tree out of a large cardboard box. Using rod puppets of sun, moon, and animals, act out the various hours of the day.

Ramanova, Natalia. *Once There Was A Tree*. New York: Dial, 1985. A tree is split by lightning then felled by woodsmen so that only the stump remains. Eventually a new tree grows in its place. Who reallly owns the stump and tree? The insects and animals who depend upon it or the man who believes he owns the forest? Presentation: Use a large paper bag turned over as a stump. Have children make puppets depicting characters in story who can argue over who owns the tree.

Sabin, Louis. *Johnny Appleseed*. Mahwah, New Jersey: Troll Associates, 1985. An easy-to-read biography of Johnny Chapman who travelled the countryside spreading seedlings and the message that the bounty of nature is the gift of God.

Silverstein, Shel. *The Giving Tree*. New York: Harper & Row, 1965. The story of the relationship between a tree and a boy throughout the various stages of the boy's life from childhood to old age. Presentation: Use a sectioned Giving Tree cardboard prop as a key focus for the story that can be dismantled piece by piece (by means of double-stick tape or flannel board).

Udry, Janice May. (illus. by Marc Simmont). *A Tree is Nice*. NY: Harper & Row, 1956. Seasonal depiction of how a tree is used by many people and animals throughout a year. Presentation: Make a tree puppet out of a milk carton using the four sides to depict each season. Let the children make finger puppets and improvise a scene around the tree.

GROUNDHOGS

Storybooks

Bond, Felicia. *Wake Up, Vladimir*. New York: Crowell, 1937. Vladimir the groundhog runs away from home, digs a hole in the ground and falls asleep. When he wakes up he sees a big monster (his shadow) and runs home. Presentation: Have children take turns laying on the floor and tracing each other's body prints. These can be decorated to look like monsters after reading the story.

Hader. Berta and Elmer. *The Big Snow*. New York: Macmillan, 1948. Though the woodland animals and birds had made their preparations for winter, it would have been a hungry time if the people who lived in the little stone house had not helped the animals during the big snow. The groundhog sees his shadow and goes back to sleep. Presentation: At the end of the story, the teacher can use a paper cup with stick puppet inside to simulate the groundhog popping out of his hole. Use a strong light to create a shadow from the puppetonto a wall.

VALENTINE'S DAY

Customs and Crafts

Barth, Edna. *Hearts, Cupids, and Red Roses: The Story of the Valentine Symbols*. New York: Seabury Press, 1974. A lovely book explaining the origins of Valentine's traditions. Good for elementary students.

dePaola, Tomi. *Things to Make and Do for Valentine's Day* New York: Scholastic Book Services, 1976. Crafts projects, games, and party foods. Lower elementary grades.

Gibbons, Gail. *Valentine's Day*. New York: Holiday House, 1986. An easy to understand explanation of the origins and customs of the holiday.

Glorach, Linda. *The Little Witches Valentine Book*. Englewood Cliffs, NJ. Prentise-Hall, 1984. The Little Witch has a unique view of Halloween and many craft ideas to share.

Prelutsky, Jack. *It's Valentine's Day*. NY: Scholastic, 1983. Original humorous poems about Valentine's Day.

Storybooks

Arels, Rosemary. *Benjamin & Tulip*. N.Y: Dial Press, 1973. A story about friendship. Two raccoons, a bully and her favorite victim eventually become friends after a funny adventure with a watermelon. Presentation: Tell the story using a bib panel of a tree or tree box prop and two raccoon paper bag puppets. The leader plays the role of the mother.

Balian, Lorna. *A Sweetheart for Valentine*. Nashville: Abingden, 1979. In the village of St. Valentine a large baby is left who grows up to be a "giant". When she is of marrying age, by chance, a large young man visits the village & all ends happily! Presentation: Teacher can decorate walking finger puppets so that there are many similar pairs of puppets. Pass out the puppets to the children. Have the children find their similar puppet mate by comparing size, color, shape, etc.

Bond, Felicia. *Four Valentines in a Rainstorm*. N.Y: Crowell, 1983. One day it rains hearts so a little girl catches some and makes cards for her animal friends. Presentation: Have half the gruop make detachable hearts on string puppets so that they can make it "rain hearts." Then ask the remaining children to make animal pupepts of their choosing to receive Valentines. Set ;out the story using the children's characters.

Brown, Marc. *Arthur's Valentine*. Boston Little, Brown & Co., 1980. Arthur's secret admirer sends him many Valentines and much to his dismay he discovers who that admirer is. Presentation: The teacher can use an Arthur puppet. (A paper bag puppet with pipe cleaners to make his glasses.) Have children create "mystery puppets" and recite their own original rhymes. Let Arthur guess who wrote the rhyme.

Bunting, Eve. *The Valentine Bears*. N.Y: Clarion Books, 1983. Mrs. Bear plans a surprise Valentines Day celebration for Mr. Bear despite their usual hibernating habits at that time of year. Presentation: Using a lap board, winter bib panel, and two bear hand puppets, act out the story. Ask the children to make Valentine Hearts for you to use as you tell the story.

Carle, Eric. *Do You Want to Be My Friend?* New York: Crowell, 1971. In vain, a little Mouse asks a number of animals to be his friends (horse, crocodile, lion, hippo, seal, monkey, peacock, fox, kangaroo, giraffe) until he finally meets another mouse who says, "Yes!" Presentation: Feature the book as a stage by setting it on a desk. Make two Mice Finger Puppets and a Sock Boa. Move the Little Mouse along the front of the book. As he asks each animal to be his friend, have each child (pretending to be animals) respond in turn, negatively. At the end of the story, introduce the other mouse. A child can operate the Sock Boa Puppet as it pops up to surprise and scare the mice.

Kraus, Robert. *How Spider Saved Valentine's Day*. New York: Scholastic Books, 1985. Spider transforms into a living valentine to give to two caterpillar classmates. Presentation: During the story, children can transform an oval paper spider into a heart by means of a pinched crease in the oval booy.

The following books have good story dialogue to recreate into more formal puppet shows:

Kunhardt, Edith. *Danny's Mystery Valentine*. NY: Greenwillow, 1987. Danny the alligator receives a mystery valentine. As he and his mother visit their friends to determine the sender, the friends are busy making valentines.

Murphy, Shirley Rosseau. *Valentine for a Dragon*. NY: Ahtneium. A tiny demon loves a dragon but both are despised by the people of the town. Through loving perserverance they save the day for the town Valentine's Day party and express their love in a rainbow.

Williams, Barbara: *A Valentine for Cousin Archie*. Delightful confusion leads to several forest friends delivering valentines to the wrong person.

PRESIDENTS

Storybooks

Bulla, Clyde Robert. *Lincoln's Birthday*. New York: Thomas Y. CRowell Co. Lincoln's life story is given, as well as explanations for the beginnings of the holiday's observance and the ways we have of paying tribute to him.

D'Aulaire, Ingri and Edgar. *Abraham Lincoln*. Garden City, New York: Doubleday Co., 1987. A Caldecott Award winner which depicts Lincoln's life.

D'Audaire, Ingri and Edgar. *George Washington*. Garden City, New York: Doubleday and Co., 1936. This biography emphasizes the growth of a little boy to become the father of his country.

Fritz, Jean. *George Washington's Breakfast*. New York: Coward-McCann, 1969. A boy with the same name and birthday as George Washington wanted to know everything he could about his namesake. Not satisfied until he came across firsthand documentation. The boy finally eats his namesakes breakfast of hoecakes and tea, and wonders what to have for lunch.

Gross, Ruth Belov. If You Grew Up with *George Washington*. New York: Scholastic, 1982. The author asked second and third graders what they wanted to know about life in Washington's time and has given us, the reader, the answers.

Smith, Kathie Billingslea. *Abraham Lincoln*. New York: Simon and Schuster, Inc., 1987. This simple short biography is illustrated with drawings and reproductions of documents and photographs.

McGovern, Ann. *If You Grew Up With Abraham Lincoln*. New York: Scholastic, 1966. This book helps children understand the times in which Lincoln lived and answers questions such as, "What kind of clothes did people wear?" and "What would you do for fun?"

Smith, Kathie Billingslea. *George Washington*. New York: Simon & Schuster. This simple and short biography is illustrated with drawings and reproductions of documents and photographs.

Value Tale Series. Communications corporation publisher, La Jolla CA. A fine line of storybooks about various famous people—Ben Franklin, Thomas Jefferson, Jane Addams, Jackie Robinson, Helen Keller, Eleanor Roosevelt, Albert Schweitzer. Cochise (Native American)—all focus in on a specific moral/value lesson. (friendship, honesty, sharing, etc.)

ST. PATRICK'S DAY

Customs and Crafts

Barth, Edna. *Shamrocks, Harps, and Shillelaghs,* New York: The Seabury Press, 1977. The story of the origin of St. Patrick's Day symbols and customs, told for uper elementary grades.

Cantwell, Mary. *St. Patrick's Day.* N.Y: Crowell, 1967. Describes the customs associated with St. Patrick's Day and relates the exciting life of Ireland's famous saint.

Kessel, Joce. *St. Patrick's Day.* Minneapolis, Minn: Carolrhoda Books, 1982. Describes the customs associated with St. Patrick's Day and relates the exciting life of Ireland's famous saint.

Storybooks

Balian, Lorna. *Leprechauns Never Lie.* Nashville: Abingdon, 1980. A leprechaun is caught by two women who try to get him to tell where he hid his treasure. Presentation: Ask each child to make a leprechaun Finger Puppet. Act out the story letting the children take turns playing the leprechaun. Different areas of the classrooz »an represent the places where the leprechaun says he hid the gold.

Burstlein, Janice. *Little Bear Marches In The St. Patrick's Day Parade.* New York: Lathrop, Lee & Shepard, 1967. Little Bear and his friend Squeaky the Mouse discover that they have a magic green umbrella which makes the rain stop whenever they open it. The Mayor calls upon Little Bear to save the St. Patrick's Day parade by leading the parade with his open umbrella. Presentation: Act out the story using puppets for the Bear, Mouse and Mayor. Have the children make something green to wear in the parade and let Little Bear lead everyone around the room with an umbrella (if the umbrella is not green, attach some green ribbons to it).

DePaola, Tomie. *Fin M'Cool.* New York: Holiday, 1981. This popular Irish giant finally gets the best of the feared giant, Cocullin. Presentation: In retelling this story, children can use mens' boots and work gloves to show the relative size of giants to the narrator's normal size puppet. Have children fantasize and use as props items giants might use for everyday objects (Trees for toothbrushes, a fence for a comb, a shovel for a spoon.) They may wish to construct cardboard images to represent these objects.

Schertle, Alice and Shute, Linda *Jeremy Bean's St. Patrick's Day.* New York: Lothrop, Lee & Shepard Books. 1987. Jeremy Bean's class plans a party for St. Patrick's Day, but he forgets to wear green. An unlikely friend (the principal) lends him a green bowtie to save the day. Presentation: After the story green bowties can be made for every classroom puppet (or child)—and even your principal!

MARDI GRAS

Customs and Crafts

Supraner, Robyn. *Great Masks to Make.* Mahweh, New Jersey: Troll, 1981. This book includes instructions for easy to make masks using paper plates, paper bags and boxes.

Storybooks

Lionni, Leo. *The Greentail Mouse.* New York: Pantheon, 1973. The mice become so involved in their Mardis Gras masquerade they forget that their masks are pretend. Presentation: Have children make and wear animal masks. Have children make

animal sounds and move like the animals they represent.

APRIL FOOLS' DAY

Customs and Crafts

Cole, Joanna and Colineson, Stephanie. *The Laugh Book,* New York: Doubleday, 1986. This coilection of jokes, riddles, tongue twisters, games and stories is an excellent resource for April Fool's day.

Kelley, Emily. *April Fools Day.* Minneapolis: Carolrhoda, 1983. Explains the customs and traditions connected with the merry pranks of April Fooling, and provides several versions of how April Fools' Day came about.

Amery, Heather and Adair, Ian. *The Knowltow Book of Jokes and Tricks.* London, England: Osborne Publishing Ltd., 1985. A book for everyone who likes fooling people with tricks, majic, surprises and jokes. At the end of the book are special pages with directions to children for putting on a show. It also includes instructions for making a puppet-like jumping "Jack-in-the-Tube."

Storybooks

Allard, Harry and James Marshall. *The Stupids Have a Ball.* Boston: Houghton Mufflin Co., 1978. The stupids are a family different from yours and mine and are they ever silly! But, they always have a wonderful time, this time at a costume party.

Brown, Marc. *Arthur's April Fool.* Boston: Little, Brown, 1983. When the class bully threatens to "pulverize" him, Arthur worries about forgetting his magic tricks at the school assembly. In the end he fools the bully! Presentation: Have each child make a trick puppet or puppet that performs a magic trick. Put them all together and perform a grand magic puppet show for the class.

Seeger, Pete. *Abiyoyo.* A father's tricks (and his ukelele playing) cause them to be banished from the village until the father's magic wand makes the terrible giant, Abiyoyo, disappear. Presentation: Have children make paper bag monster puppets. Have them dance to the boy's ukelele music then disappear as the leader waves a majic wand.

Galdone, *The Three Billy Goats Gruff.* New York: Clarion Books, 1973. The three billy goats must fool the troll if they want to go over the bridge to get to the meadow where they could eat and get fat. Presentation: Using two children to make a physical bridge, dramatize the events in this story. Encourage the children to think of creative reasons why the troll should eat the *next* billy goat.

Brenner, Barbara. *Walt Disney's Three Little Pigs.* New York: Random House, 1972. The wolf tries to fool the pigs but is fooled by the pigs in the end and the three little pigs laugh and play and sing all day long.

Songs

Beall, Pam and Nipp Susan *Wee Sing Silly Songs.* Price/Stern Sloan.

PASSOVER

Customs and Crafts

Greenfeld, Howard, *Passover,* N.Y.: Holt, 1978. A history of the 3000 year old Jewish holiday of slavery and freedom, which also gives an explanation of the Seder ceremony and symbols.

Simon, Norma. *Passover.* New York: Thomas Y.

Crowell Co., 1965. A straightforward depiction of the Passover story, focusing on the history and meaning of Passover.

Storybooks

Groner, Judge and Madeline Wikler. *Where is the Afikomen?* Rockville, MD: Kar-Ben Copies, Inc. 1985. Cardboard book format, simply portraying the search for the Afikomen, the middle matzah of the ceremony, without which the Passover seder cannot be concluded.

Hirsh, Marilyn. *One Little Goat, A Passover Song.* N.Y.: Holiday House, 1979. The concluding song of the Passover service sung much like "I Know An Old Lady", with repetition and building upon each verse, with the progression of what happens to the little goat that father bought for two zuzim. Whimsical drawings of costumed children depicting the actions of the song, characterize this appealing book.

Rosen, Anne, Jonathan Rosen & Norma Rosen. *A Family Passover.* Phila.: The Jewish Publication Society of America, 1980. Photographs of a Philadelphian family and the children of Solomon Schechter Day School are featured in this description of how a typical family prepares and celebrates the holiday of Passover.

Hirsh, Marilyn. *I Love Passover.* N.Y.: Holiday House. 1985. A young child describes Passover preparations, story and ritual with warmth and fondness for the holiday and the people.

EASTER

Customs and Crafts

Barth, Edna. *Books Giving History, Factual, or Craft Information on Easter, Lilies, Rabbits, and Hunted Eggs: The Story of the Easter Symbols.* N.Y. Seabury Press, 1970. The history of Easter symbols such as painted eggs, white lillies, newborn chicks is presented in an easy to read manner.

Fisher, Aileen. *Easter N.Y.;* Crowell, 1968. A simple but good book explaining the history and customs of Easter.

Matthiew, Agnis. *The Easter Bunny.* New York: Dial., 1986. Many of the Easter Bunny's tricks are explained in order to make believors out of skeptics.

Newsome, Arden J. *Egg Craft.* New York: Lothrop, Lee & Shepard Co., 1973. Detailed instructions given for a wide variety of egg decorating methods. Adult level.

Wiersum, Beverly Rae. *The Story of Easter for Children.* Milwaukee, Wisconsin: Ideals Publishing Corp., 1979. Poem compares the rebirth of nature and holiday customs with the events of the first Easter.

Storybooks

Adams, Adreinne. *The Easter Egg Artists.* N.Y: Scribner, 1976. A yong rabbit named Orson develops his own style painting cars, houses, planes, bridges and eventually fancy Easter eggs. Presentation: Ask each child to design a pop-up Easter egg paper puppet which fits inside a styrofoam cup nest to use with the story.

Balian, Lorna. *Humbug Rabbit.* Nashville, Abingdon Press, 1974. Father Rabbit's reply of "Humug" to the idea that he is the Easter Bunny doesn't spoil Easter for his own children or for Granny's grandchildren. The above and below ground stories are told simultaneously with one happy ending. Presentation: Use two hands with finger puppet characters: one hand represents above ground; the other below ground cast.

Brown, Marc. *"What Do You Call a Dumb Bunny".* Boston: Little Brown; Co., 1983. This hilarious collection of Rabbit humor and puzzles contains finger puppet patterns and suggestions for their use in joke and riddle telling.

Brown, Margaret Wise. *The Golden Egg Book.* New York: Western Publishing Co., 1947. A charming story about a bunny who finds an egg and is surprised when it hatches with a little chick. Presentation: Have children use their vivid imaginations to make guesses about what might be in a L'Eggs container. Have them draw their suggestions on paper and fold the drawings to fit in the container. The teacher can use a bunny puppet to open the egg in which she has put each drawing and then hang up these drawings on a clothesline or bulletin board.

Claret, Maria. *The Chocolate Rabbit.* Woodbury, NY: Barron's Educational Series, 1985. When a clumsy rabbit falls in a bucket of chocolate, he serves as a model for the first chocolate candy Easter Bunny. Presentation: Use a mold to make chocolate rabbits and add a stick to make stick puppets to puppetize this story. If molds or ready made chocolate bunnies are not available then make substitutes from brown paper.

Curtis, Marian Foster. *Miss Flora McFlimsy's Easter Bonnet.* NY. Lothrop, Lee and Shepard, 1987. Miss Flora's bonnet is delivered by Peterkins Rabbit (with two plumes attached where bunny's ears might have been) and wins a prize at the Easter Party. Presentation: Ask children to create paper bonnets for a bunny puppet.

Friedrich, Otto. *The Easter Bunny That Overslept.* New York: Lothrop, Lee and Shepard, 1957. The Easter Bunny sleeps through Easter and then tries to deliver eggs on Mother's Day, the Fourth of July, Halloween and Christmas Eve. Presentation: Have teacher use basic pattern Easter Bunny. Have children make holiday accessories to costume the bunny as the holidays change while reading the story.

Miller, Edna. *Mousekin's Easter Basket.* New York: Prentice Hall, 1986. Mousekin searches for a new house and meets a large white rabbit. As children find Easter eggs, Easter Bunny Mousekin makes his new home in an abandoned bird's nest that looks like an Easter basket. Presentation: Have children create puppet totes of bird's nest—Easter baskets by decorating opened out paper bags.

Tresselt, Alvin R. *The World In the Candy Egg.* New York: Lothrop, Lee and Shepard, 1967. A beautifully illustrated story of what can be imagined by looking into a candy picture egg. Presentation: Have children use paper bags to create their own candy eggs. Using paper create scenic features to place *inside* bag. Decorate outside of egg/bag too.

Songs

Gag, Wanda. *ABC Bunny.* NY: Coward McCann. 1933. A song about the adventures of a bunny and his friends during a thunderstorm. Presentation: Dramatize this song with alphabet letter puppets. Attach stick to puppet to manipulate.

Sadler, Marilyn. *It's Not Easy Being a Bunny.* NY: Random House, 1983. P.J. Funny bunny tries to live with many animal friends but finds their habits not to his liking. Presentation: Using a bunny puppet with paper hats P.J. could decide that he would like to be various holiday characters: a witch, Santa Claus, leprechaun groundhog, etc. and decides it is best to be an Easter bunny.

MAY DAY
Customs and Crafts
Les Tina, Dorothy. *May Day*. N.Y: Crowell, 1967. Describes May Day celebrations & customs around the world.
Storybooks
Foste, Marian Curtis. *Miss Flora McFlimsey's May Day*. N.Y: Lathrop, Lee & Shepard, 1969. A doll named Miss McFlimsey has an adventure in the garden where she meets a bird, a squirrel, several porcupines and a rabbit, all of whom crown her Queen of the May! Presentation: Have children make puppets of the animal characters and act out the story using a doll or hand puppet as Miss Flora McFlimsey and a paper crown.

Hays, Wilma Pitchford. *May Day for Samoset*. N.Y: Coward-McCann, 1968. A look into America's past as a young girl names Susan celebrates a traditional English May Day in Maine (c. 1622) by giving her friend, The Indian Chief, a precious gift. Presentation: Divide the children into small groups and have them dramatize a scene from the book.

Bornstein, Ruth Lercher. *The Seedling Child*. New York: Harcourt Brace Jovanovich, 1987. A little girl finds a tiny child inside a flower and shares a magical day with her new friend that looks just like her! Presentation: After reading the story, have children draw small self portraits. Attach these to the end of straws. Use the cups cut out of styrofoam egg cartons to make flower petals. A hole in base of cup allows straw to slide in and out of flower.

Harper, Wilhelmina. *The Gunniwolf*. New York: Dolton, 1967. A little girl disobeys her mother to go into the jungle to gather beautiful flowers and barely escapes the Gunniwolf by lulling him to sleep with her song. Presentation: Children can pair up to dramatize this story using walking finger puppets through a woods groundscape. As no melody is given for the girl's song, each pair can make up their own tune.

Heller, Ruth. *The Reason for a Flower*. New York: Putnam, 1983. Factual information is presented in rhyme with vivid illustrations. Presentations: Use long stemmed artificial flowers with facial features added with paper, markers or paints to make puppets. Children can make up rhymes for puppets to recite copying the pattern of "Roses are red, Violets are blue..."

FLAG DAY

Customs and Crafts
Giblin, James Cross. Fireworks, Picnics, and Flags: The Story of the Fourth of July Symbols. N.Y: Clarion Books, 1983. Explains why the Declaration of Independence was written and discusses the customs and symbols for celebrating July 4th.

Les Tina, Dorothy. *Flag Day*. New York: Thomas Y. Crowell Co., 1965. Gives the general history of how flags were developed and especially how the American flag came to be.

Phelan, Mary Kay. *The Fourth of July*. N.Y: Crowell, 1966. A simple history of the birth of the United States of America told with action & adventure.

Shachtman, Tom. *America's Birthday*. New York: Macmillan, 1986. Through photographs the reader visualizes a New England Fourth of July celebration. Many of the photographs include men, women and children in colonial costume.
Storybooks
Berenstain, Stan and Jan Berenstain. *Berenstain Bears On the Moon*. New York: Random House, 1985. The Bears go to the moon and plant the Bear Country flag. Presentation: Cut out posterboard rockets for each child. Attach rubber bands to rockets for children to wear on forearms. Children can count down and blast off rockets.

Taylor, Mark. *Henry, The Castaway*. New York: Macmillan, 1972. A young boy sets out to explore and marks his path with red flags. When he gets lsot, it is the flags that lead the rescuers to him. Presentation: Make and "lose" one Henry finger puppet in the classroom. Mark the trail to Henry with small red flags. After reading the story let children make walking finger puppets (or stick puppets) and follow the trail.
Songs
Kellogg, Steven. *Yankee Doodle*. New York: Four Winds Press, 1976. An authentic and colorfully illustrated version of the well known song depicting a little boy witnessing scenes from the American Revolution. Presentation: Have children make paper hats and ride tube hobby horses while singing the chorus of this song. Refer to Christmas section for reindeer project for horse pattern.

Spier, Peter. *The Star Spangled Banner*. New York: Doubleday and Co., 1973. A pictorial description of the words of the national anthem. Presentation: Use a peek-a-boo panel while singing this song with children. On the front of the panel should be a ship. Behind the panels can be depictions of fireworks (rockets red glare) and one panel should have a Untied States flag.

JULY 4TH

Storybooks
Emberly, Barbara. (illus. by Ed Emberly). *Drummer Hoff*. Englewood Cliffs, N.J., Prentice Hall, 1967. A lively folk verse about the soldiers who build and fire off a cannon! It has the fun and feeling of July 4th. Presentation: Using two story gloves, attach characters to the finger tips. Make a felt cannon and attach it to the lower portion of the glove. As each character enters the story, hold up the appropriate finger. Or, have children create Bodi-Bag Puppets to dramatize the story.
Songs
Beall, Pamela and Susan Nipp. *Wee Sing America*, Los Angeles: CA: Price Stern Sloan, 1987. Sixty minutes of music and fingerplays to celebrate patriotic holidays.

FAMILY DAY

Customs and Crafts
Phelan, Mary Kay. *Mother's Day*. N.Y: Crowell, 1965. A discussion of Mother's Day customs around the world.
Storybooks/Mothers
Balian, Lorna. *Mother's Mother's Day*. Nashville: Ab-

ingdon, 1982. Hazel the Mouse goes to visit her Mother on Mother's Day, but finds she has gone to visit her own mother. Presentation: Tell the story with five little Mice finger puppets on a story glove. Add paper props to the puppets.

Hazel—Bouquet of flowers
Mother—An acorn
Grandmother—A strawberry
Great Grandmother—A basket of corn
Great Great Grandmother—Feathers

Use a cat hand puppet or stuffed animal to scare the mice.

Boyd, Lizi. *The Not-So-Wicked Stepmother*. New York: Viking Kestrel, 1987. Hessie practices a wicked face to use on her new stepmother but she is surprised to find the stepmother not at all mean, ugly or horrible. Presentation: Use paper plates to make turn around wicked and nice rod mask puppets. Children hold mask over face at appropriate parts of the story.

Brown, Margaret Wise. *The Runaway Bunny*. N.Y.: Harper & Row, 1970. A little bunny tries many ways to hide from his mother but she always finds him. Presentation: Have the children make bunny puppets and expand upon the book's content by thinking up new places to hide and other things to "become" in the classroom.

Eastman, D. *Are You My Mother?* New York: Random House, 1960. A baby bird falls out of his nest and looks for his mother. Finally, a "snort" delivers him home. Presentation: Use a finger puppet in L'Egg container as key focus. Children can hang up paper animal characters on a clothesline as the story is told. One child can play the "snort" using mechanical motions.

Kent. *Joey*. New York: Prentice Hall Books for Young Readers, 1984. Joey's mother is a kangaroo who encourages her son to invite his friends home (to the pocket) to play. When it becomes too crowded mother changes her mind. Presentation: Children take turns acting. Have one child act as the mother with paper bag pouch tied to waist. Make paper stick puppet friends to visit Joey in the pocket.

Polushkin, Maria. *Mother, Mother, I Want Another*. Crown, 1978. A little mouse's mother misunderstands that all her baby wants is another kiss. Instead she brings him more mothers. Presentation: React the story with children playing the various animal mother roles. At the end all the mothers can give the baby mouse a kiss. The leader plays the baby mouse with a puppet.

Mayer, Mercer. *Just for You*. NY: Golden Press, 1975. A young child (personified as an animal) tries to help Mother in many different ways. Presentation: Have each child use the mitt pattern in the Family Fun Section to create a child and mother image to talk about something the child likes to do with his or her mother.

Storybooks/Fathers

Aliki. *Hush Little Baby*. Englewood Ceypo, NY: Prentice Hall, 1968. In this folk lullaby, papa buys a series of presents which even when gone are for the sweetest little baby in town. Presentation: Use overhead shadow to portray the ideas in this story.

Asch, Frank. *Just Like Daddy*. New York: Prentice Hall Books for Young Readers, 1981. Child Bear tries to imitate his Father's actions, but catches a fish, just like his Mother. Presentation: Divide children into pairs. Designate one in each pair to be the father. Play a mirror game with the father child pantomining various activities mentioned in the story.

Burgess, Gelett. *The Little Father*. New York: Farrar Straus Giroux. A fantastical story in which the father shrinks (from drinking ink) to microscopic size. Presentation: Fashion a pleated paper body on a father puppet that expands and contracts during the story.

Carle, Eric. *Papa, Please Get the Moon for Me*. Boston: Picture Book Studio, 1986. Waiting until the moon grows small, a father retrieves the moon for his daughter. Presentation: While reading the story use a panel to show the moon's growth larger and smaller. Use black circle to cover the moon to make it small and uncover to make it grow large.

Mayer, Mercer. *Just Me and My Dad*. N.Y: Golden Books, 1977. A story of a young boy and his father (personified as animals) who go on a camping trip together. Presentation: Have children use the mitt puppet pattern in the Family Fun section to create a father and child image and illustrate something special they like to do together.

Parker, Kristy. *My Dad the Magnificent*. NY: Dalton, 1987. Buddy brags to his friend that his father is a cowboy, pro basketball player, deep sea diver and explorer but it turns out that being a plain old father is the most magnificent thing to be. Presentation: Use the basic s/he puppet pattern in Section one for children to create costumes to tell the story. They may wish to add new careers to the father's wardrobe.

Storybooks/Grandparents

Cazet, Denys. *Christmas Moon*. Scarsdale, NY: Bradbury Press, 1984. Patrick misses Grandpa, especially at Christmas, but his mother helps him to remember happy times with Grandpa. Presentation: Have the children make puppets of-themselves and their Grandpa orGrandma. Improvise scenes depicting something they like to do or used to do with their grandparents.

Flournoy, Valerie. *The Patchwork Quilt*. New York: Dial, 1985. Using scraps cut from the family's old clothing, Tonya helps her grandmother make a quilt that tells the story of her family's life. Presentation: Ask children to bring scraps of old clothing from home to make glued together hand puppets. Each puppet can tell the story of his/her origin.

Similar Story:

Roth, Susan L. *Patchwork Tales*. New York: Atheneum, 1984. A grandmother tells her grandaughter the family stories behind the various blocks on a patchwork quilt.

Gomi, Taro. *Coco Can't Wait*. New York: Viking, 1979. Coco and her grandmother are dying to see each other, so they cycle to each other's house, miss each other, then turn around, and collide. Presentation: Use a cardboard box theater, scenic background and rod puppets to replay story.

Heller, Rebecca. *Little Red Riding Hood*. Racine, Wisconsin: Western Publishing Co., 1985. A lively retelling, faithful to the Grimm's Brothers version of a little girl's visit to her grandmother's. Presentation: Create a groundscape of a woods scene with drain paths and rivers and three-dimensional tube trees and other woodsy suggestions. Use paper walking finger puppets of characters.

Stevenson, James. *"Could Be Worse"*. New York:

William Morrow Co., 1977. To Grandpa life is pretty boring, no matter what happens he always says the same thing. Presentation: Have children recite their own fantastical catastrophies for the teaching grandfather puppet to repeat the refrain "Could Be Worse!"

Wood, Audrey. *The Napping House*. New York: Harcourt Brace Jahanovich, 1984. Everyone piles on top of grandmother's bed to take a quiet nap. When all awake it is bedtime. Presentation: Using hand puppets have children sing lullabies and let their puppets fall asleep one on top of one another. When the last puppet (bee) is placed on by the teacher, all awake in make-believe hysteria.

LABOR DAY

Storybooks

Blos, Joan. *Martin's Hats*. NY: Mulberry Books, 1984. Martin pretends to be many exciting people by wearing various hats. Presentation: Use the basic s/he puppet pattern in chapter one for children to create worker costumes and hats.

Keats, Ezra Jack. *John Henry*. New York: Kraft, 1965. The American legend of a railroad builder who was born and died with a hammer in his hand. Presentation: Have each child make a John Henry stick puppet with an arm and hammer that swings. (Link with a brad).

Lenski, Lois. *Los Lenski's Big Book of Mr. Small*. New York: Henry Z. Walck, Inc., 1985. This book contains stories about Mr. Small as a policeman, cowboy, farmer and other community helper roles. Presentation: Have children use the s/he pattern and dress puppet in a community helper role.

Scarry, Richard. *Richard Scarry's Busiest People Ever*. New York: Random House, 1976. Every work situation imaginable is illustrated in this marvelous book. Presentation: Expanding on the story from the book "Mr. Frumble's Bad Day" have the teacher act as Mr. Frumble and the children take various roles as community helpers he visits.

Worthington, Joan and Phoebe. *Teddy Bear Baker*. New York: Puffin, 1979. This is the story of a baker who has a full and satisfying day. Phoebe Worthington has also written books starring Teddy Bear as a gardner, farmer, coalman and postman.

Songs

Hall, Carol. *Parents Are People* (poem/song) from *Free to Be You And Me*. N.Y: McGraw-Hill Book Company, 1974. p. 48-53. A lively song about all the jobs boys and girls can grow up and do! Presentation: Ask each child to make a turnaround paper plate or paper rod puppet; one side is a child and the other side when grown up. The child can make up a poem or song about what he or she wants to be when an adult.

NATIVE AMERICAN

Customs and Crafts

Behrens, June. *Pow Wow*. Chicago: Children's Press, 1983. A simple lively photography book about a modern day American Indian pow wow.

Blood, Charles. *American Indian Games & Crafts*. New York: Watts, 1981. A great source book for classroom learning about American Indians.

Payne, Elizabeth. *Meet the North American Indians*, New York: Random House, 1965. A survey of Indians in America at the time Columbus "discovered" it.

Showers, Paul. *Indian Festivals*. N.Y: Crowell, 1969. An enthusiastic description of the ancient celebrations still observed by many American Indian tribes.

Storybooks

Blood, Charles L. & Martha Link. *The Goat In The Rug*. N.Y: Parents' Magazine Press, 1976. Geraldine, a goat, describes each step as she and her Navajo friend make a rug: from the hair clipping and carding, to the dyeing and actual weaving. Presentation: The teacher can use a goat puppet to introduce the story. Children can use fringed burlap to paint designs to resemble Navajo rugs.

McDermott, Gerald. *Arrow to the Sun*: A Pueblo Indian Tale. New York: Viking, 1974. A young warrior has magic powers and becomes an arrow that shoots itself to the Kivas (Underground Names of the Indian people). Presentation: After reading the story, children can make arrow shaped puppets and play a version of Pin the Tail on the Donkey with a large sun.

Audio Visuals

Canyon Records, write for catalogue: 4143 North 16th Street, Phoenix, AZ 85016. A superb collection of native American recordings from many tribes.

ROSH HASHANAH

Customs and Crafts

Cone, Molly, *The Jewish New Year*. N.Y. Thomas Y. Crowell Company, 1966. Easy format, informative text and appealing graphics of the meanings and costoms of the High Holy Days.

Gellman, Ellie. *It's Rosh Hashanah!* Rockville, M.D.: Kar-Ben Copies, Inc. 1985. Simple, board book format of the basics of Rosh Hashanah, including the challah, apples, growth and shofar beast.

Greenfeld, Howard, *Rosh Hashanah and Yom Kippur.* N.Y.: Holt, Rinehart and Winston, 1979. Woodcuts and straightforward language characterize this background and description of the High Holy Days.

Storybooks

Cohen, Barbara. *Yussel's Prayer A Yom Kippur Story.* N.Y.: Lothrop, Lee & Shepard Books, 1981. Story of a sincere boy's unschooled prayers that reach God more effectively that those of learned men less sincerely uttered.

CHRISTOPHER COLUMBUS

Storybooks

Fritz, Jean. *Where Do You Think You're Going, Christopher Columbus?* New York: G.P. Putnam's Sons, 1980.

HALLOWEEN

Customs and Crafts

Adams, Adrienne. *A Woggle of Witches*. New York: Charles Scribner's Sons, 1971. The story of a group (woggle) of witches who are frightened by strange creatures on the nght of their special celebration. Presentations: Let each child make a flying Witch Rod Puppet and broom from black paper, using a traditional airplane, paper fold technique. Divide the playing space into scene areas. Use a pot prop for the skew.

Borten, Helen, *Halloween*. New York: thomas Y. Crowell Co., 1965. The history, beliefs, and customs associated withHalloween are presented for young children (Lower elementary ages).

Gibbons, Gail. *Halloween*. New York: Holiday House. A brief look at why we celebrate this holiday the way we do. Excellent for use with preschoolers.

Hoffman, Phyllis. *Happy Halloween!* New York: Charles Scribner's Sons, 1982. Imaginative ideas for children, such as instructions for making costumes, masks, jack o'lanterns, and simple party treats.

Prelutsky, Jack. *It's Halloween*. New York: Scholastic, 1977. A delightful collection of poems about Halloween. Presentation: Have children make white ghost hand puppets fromsheets. Using ten children at a time recite "Countdown" and end in a final unision "Boo!" Have children work in teams to create Overhead Shadow skits to illustrate other poems.

Storybooks

Barth, Edna. *Jack O'Lantern*. New York: Seabury, 1974. A retelling of the folktale of the origin of the jack-o-lantern.

Bunting, Eve. *Scary, Scary Halloween*. New York: Clarion/Ticknor & Fields, 1986. A poem about a band of trick or treaters who frighten a mother cat and her kittens on a very scary Halloween. Presentation: Have children wear cat's eyes' masks while the teacher reads the story. Make mask of posterboard or construction paper and tie on with string. Add whiskers with eyebrow panel.

Calhoun, Mary. *The Witch of Hissing Hill*. N.Y: W. Morrow, 1964. Witch Sizzle raised black cats for sale to other witches until one day a yellow cat named Gold was born and changed everything. Presentation: Have each child make a two sided cat paper plate stick puppet. Read the story to the children and at the end have the children hold up the black side then turn the puppet around to reveal the yellow side.

Carlson, Nancy. *Harriet's Halloween Candy*. Minneapolis: Carolrhoda Books, Inc. 1982. Harriet does not plan to share her Halloween candy until she tries to eat it all up herself and finds that she cannot! Presentation: Children can act this wonderful moral story with a variety of mouth puppets—paper plate, paper bag or swallowing type puppet.

Galdone, Paul. *The Teeny-Tiny Woman*. New York: Clarion Books, Tickney & Fields, 1984. Retells the story of the teeny-tiny woman who puts away a teeny tiny bone in her cupboard before she goes to sleep. Presentation: Use finger puppets to emphasize the smallness of this story. Shoe boxes or other small boxes can be used to make a cupboard and a bed. (Cut hole in box to stick hand through bottom and make teeny tiny woman appear to be in bed.) Don't forget a blanket (handkerchief or napkin) as a prop. An alternate idea is to use a Peek-A-Boo Theater presentation for scenic delivery.

Johnston, Tony. *The Vanishing Pumpkin*. N.Y: Putnam, 1983. An old man and woman in search of their lost pumpkin meet an assortment of characters including a ghoul, a rapscallion, a varmint and a lizard. Presentation: Have each child create a mask for a fantasy character who might have stolen the pumpkin. Have the old man perform a trick of turning the mask into a child and back again to mask when the masked child denies knowledge of the lost pumpkin. Teacher can use hand puppets for the old man and old woman and by wearing a tall pointed hat dramatize the role of the wizard.

Kellogg, Steven. *The Mystery of the Flying Orange Pumpkin*. New York: Dial, 1980. When a new neighbor won't allow the children to have their pumpkin they use Halloween tricks and treats to solve their problem. Presentation: Use helium filled orange balloons as basis for jack o' lanterns. Add faces with marker pens. Using Halloween masks attached to dowels have children act out this story. The leader can act as the mean new neighbor.

Mayer, Mercer. *There's a Nightmare In My Closet*. N.Y: The Dial Press, 1968. A young boy is surprised one night when his nightmare comes out of the closet. The nightmare is so frightened that the little boy tucks him in bed so they can sleep together. Presentation: Have each child imagine what their Nightmare would look like and then make a puppet in a cup theater.

Miller, Edna. *Mousekin's Golden House*. Englewood Cliffs, N.J: Prentice Hall, 1964. A little Mouse finds a safe home in a large discarded Jack-O-Lantern where he makes a nest and falls asleep during the cold snowy winter. Presentation: Make an apron bib of a large jack-o-lantern cutout or use a plastic or real pumpkin. Tell the story using a mouse finger puppet and stick puppets of the animal characters.

Tudor, Tasha. *Pumpkin Moonshine*. N.Y: A young girl finds the biggest pumpkin in the patch. On the way home the pumpkin rolls away and causes all knds of havoc. Presentation: Ask each child to make a big pumpkin paper plate mask. Tell the story letting children take turns playing the pumpkin.

THANKSGIVING

Customs and Crafts

Adler, David A. *The Purple Turkey and Other Thanksgiving Riddles*. New York: Holiday House, 1986 An illustrated collection of humorous riddles.

Anderson, Joan. *The First Thanksgiving Feast*. N.Y: Clarion Books, 1984. Recreates, through photographs, the first harvest feast celebrated by the Pilgrims in 1621 using the Pilgrim and Indian actors and the seventeenth century setting of Plymouth Plantation, a living history museum in Plymouth, Massachusetts.

Barth, Edna. *Turkeys, Pilgrims and Indian Corn: The Story of Thanksgiving Symbols*. N.Y: Clarion Books, 1975. Excellent resource book on the history and symbols of Thanksgiving.

Storybooks

Balian, Lorna. *Sometimes It's Turkey—Sometimes It's Feathers*. Nashville, Abingdon Press, 1973. Mrs. Gunn decides to hatch a found turkey egg and feed it all year for a Thanksgiving meal. When that meal is served, the turkey enjoys eating the meal rather than being eaten. Presentation: A paper bag with a feathered tail attached to the back side can make an ideal turkey puppet. Use the flap mouth with a slit cut into the paper under the flap to make the turkey eat everything. Use the puppet to tell the story or discuss food groups or table manners.

Cohen, Miriam. *Don't Eat Too Much Turkey*. New York Greenwillow Books, 1987. First graders learn the history of Thanksgiving and how to deal with a bossy friend. Presentation: Following the descrip-

203

tion in the text, make a turkey costume. Use this same costume for dramatizing the following two stories.

Brown, Marc. *Arthur's Thanksgiving*. Boston: Little Brown and Co., 1983. Arthur plays the turkey in the school play and discovers what Thanksgiving is really about.

Kroll, Steven. *One Tough Turkey*. New York: Holiday House, 1982. The Pilgrims are outwitted by such a tough turkey that they settle for squash for their dinner.

Janice (illus. Marian) *Little Bear's Thanksgiving*. N.Y: Lathrop, Lee & Shepard Co., Inc., 1967. Little Bear is invited by Goldie to Thanksgiving dinner but has to be awakened by his animal friends so he won't forget to go! Presentation: Tell the story using a hand puppet for Little Bear and a story glove with finger puppets of Owl, Sparrow, Squeaky and Squirrel. Let one child wear a paper plate clock and another child play Goldie (Wearing a fringed yellow paper wig).

The following stories have Thanksgiving good dialogue lending themselves well to more formal puppet shows:

Shurmut, Marjorie Weinman. *One Terrific Thanksgiving*. New York: Holiday House, 1985. At Thanksgiving time, Irving Morris Bear, who loves to eat, learns that it is friends, not food, for which he is thankful.

Williams, Barbara. *Chester Chipmunk's Thanksgiving*. New York: Dutton, 1978. Chester tries to share his pecan pies for Thanksgiving supper. His friends, too busy with their own families, are not interested at first, but in the end all gather for a grand shared feast.

Zion, Gene. *The Meanest Squirrel I Ever Met*. New York: Athenum, 1962. Mr. M.O. Squirrel cheats Nibble Squirrel's family out o their Thanksgiving dinner by playing nut games, but Nibble Squirrel gets them back in time for Christmas dinner. Presentation: Use nuts to make small squirrel puppets, adding features with paint, bits of paper and fuzzy pipe cleaner tails.

HANUKKAH

Customs and Crafts

Becker, Joyce. *Hanukkah Crafts*, NY: Bonim Books, 1978. A wealth of Hanukkah craft ideas that are simple, accessible and appropriate for elementary school students, all illustrated with black and white line drawings.

Drucker, Malka. *Hanukkah, Eight Nights, Eight Lights*. NY, Holiday House, 1980. Introduces the history rituals, customs, etc. associated with Hanukkah.

Fisher, Aileen. *My First Hanukkah Book*. Chicago: Chldrens Press, 1985. A simple, colorfully illustrated depiction of Hanukkah and symbols.

Greenfield, Howard. *Hanukah*. NY Holt, 1976. In large print format, but very adult text this short woodcut illustrated book describes Hanukah's history.

Storybooks

Aleichem, Sholom *Hanukah Money*. illus. by Uri Shulevitz. NY Greenwillow Books 1978. A vignette of an Eastern European Hanukah, told through the perspective of two brothers who anxiously await the gifts of Hanukah gelt.

Burstein, Chaya. *Hanukkah Cat*. Rockville, MD: Kar-Ben Copies, Inc. 1985.

Chaiken, Miriam. *Light Another Candle, The Story and Meaning of Hanukkah*. NY Clarion Books, 1981. Retells the story of Hanukah and explains its symbols by describing high points in jewish history, worship and culture.

Fox, Terry. *A Little Miracle, A Hanukah Story*, Narberth, PA: Tenderfoot Press, 1985. A touching, beautiful, simple tale of a young boy's efforts to create the best menorah ever for the candle lighting ceremony and how he feels when some bullies destroy his masterpiece.

Garvey, Robert. *The Hanukah Play*. USA: Ktav Publishing House, Inc., 1979. Rachel and David are annoyed that they've been assigned baby parts (again) in the Hanukah Play and they find a way—not quite what they expected—to get BIG parts in next year's holiday production.

Goffstein, M.B. *Laughing Latkes*. NY: Farrar Straws Giroux, 1980.

Greene, Jacqueline. *Nathan's Hanukkah Bargain*. Nathan enlists his grandfather's help in finding a special Hannukkah gift and learns about bargaining in the process.

Harrow, Betty. *A Great Miracle, The Story of Hanukah*. Irvington on Hudson: Harvey House, 1968. Depicts in great detail, the events of the Hannukkah story, focussing on both the heroic deeds and background.

Hirsh, Marilyn. *I Love Hanukkah*. NY. Holiday House 1984. A young boy describes his family celebration of Hanukkah and all the things he likes about it.

Hirsh, Marilyn. *The Hanukah Story* N.Y. Bonim Books, 1977. A well illustrated depiction of the historical basis of Hanukah.

Shulevitz, Vri. *The Magician*, an adaptation of the Yiddish of I.L. Perete. New York. MacMillan, 1973. Light hearted pen and ink drawings illustrate this idea story about a magician who visits and brings joy to the home of a poor man and woman.

CHRISTMAS

Customs and Crafts

Barth, Edna. *Holly, Reindeer and Colored Lights: The Story of Christmas Symbols*. New York: Seabury Press, 1981. The history of Christmas symbols is presented in an easy to read manner.

Gibbons, Gail. *Christmas Time*. New York: Holiday House, 1982. A brief look at why we celebrate this holiday the ways we do. Excellent for use with pre-schoolers.

Mendoza, George. *The Christmas Tree Alphabet Book*. New York: World Pub., Co., 1971. A beautifully illustrated book which uses the alphabet for the first letter of children's names from around the world. Introduces Christmas customs.

Prelutsky, Jack. *It's Christmas*. New York: Greenwillow, 1981. A collection of humorous poems concerning Christmas.

Spier, Peter. *Peter Spier's Christmas!* Garden City, New York: Doubleday and Co., 1983. A wordless picture book telling more than one thousand words about Christmas customs in America.

Weil, Lisl. *Santa Claus Around the World*. New York: Holiday House, 1987. This book tells the history of Santa Claus and describes many countries' stories and ways of celebrating Santa's arrival.

Storybooks

Aoki, Hisako and Invan Gantschev. *Santa's Favorite*

Story. Boston, Neugebauer Press U.S.A.: 1982. All the forest animals are worried that there won't be a Christmas anymore if Santa is too tired to deliver the presents. But Santa tells the animals the true meaning of Christmas and they all go to Santa's house to get the presents ready for delivery. Presentation: Have children take the part of the forest animals while the teacher uses a puppet to tell the nativity story.

Climo, Shirley, (Illus. Joe Lasker). *The Cobweb Christmas*. New York: Crowell, 1982. Tante lives in a forest in Germany and receives an unexpected bit of magic on Christmas morning when she awakes to see her tree covered with gold and silver cobwebs. Presentation: Talk about the special family traditions the children celebrate in their own homes at Christmas. Ask what kind of decorations they enjoy hanging on their trees. Have each child make a paper Spider Finger Puppet and glittered web habitat (on a small paper bag) with a looped string attached to web for hanging on tree.

dePaola, Tomie. *The Cat on the Dovrefell*. New York: Putnam, 1979. A man catches a great white bear. When the Trolls arrive on Christmas eve the bear scares them away forever. Presentation: Ask each child to make a Troll puppet. To dramatize the story, seat the children in a big circle with their Troll puppets hidden behind them. Pretend the center is a large table filled with food. The leader uses a man and bear puppet (converted stuffed animal) to create the dialogue. Trolls can be scared by the bear!

dePaola, Tomie. *The Christmas Pageant*. Minneapolis, Minnesota: Winston Press, 1978. This is a paperback edition of a popular book about a children's production of the Gospel nativity story. It includes twenty three cut out characters with instructions for puppet making and performance.

dePaola, Tomie. (illus). *The Friendly Beasts*. New York: Putnam, 1981. Based on an old English Christmas carol, the donkey, cow, sheep and dove tell how they helped Mary and the baby Jesus in Bethlehem. Presentation: Have each child select one of the animals to make as a talking mouth paper plate or envelope puppet. Grouped in a large circle, sing the song, with the puppet singing the verse associated with the character.

Fontenot, Mary Alice. *The Star Seed*. Gretna Louisiana: Pelican Publishing Co., 1985. On the night of the first Christmas, some seed from a star is accidentally scattered onto the earth, spreading light and magic all over the world. Presentation: with a creche or manger scene, retell the story using a star stick puppet with crepe paper streamers for a tail.

Haywood, Carolyn. *How The Reindeer Saved Santa*. New York: William Morrow, 1986. Deciding that his sleigh and reindeer is too old to use for delivering presents, Santa Claus gets a helicopter. After several mishaps, Santa finds his reindeer are still the most reliable transportation. Presentation: Children can make reindeer puppets from tubes as described in the Christmas section. The teacher can use cardboard sleigh and helicopter props with a Santa Claus puppet to tell the story. Pretend to hitch the sleigh/helicopter to reindeer and fly around the room.

Hill, Eric. *Spot's First Christmas*. New York: G.P. Putnam's Sons, 1983. It's Christmas eve and Spot has a lot to do before he falls asleep. Presentation: Use a peek-a-boo board to tell the story.

BIRTHDAYS

Customs and Crafts

Gibbons, Gail. *Happy Birthday!* New York: Holiday House, 1986. A bright book explaining historical beliefs, traditions, and celebrations associated with everyone's own special day—their birthday.

Hazen, Barbara Shook. *The Golden Happy Birthday Book*. Racine, Wisconsin: Golden Press, 1976. A collection of poetry and prose with suggestions for crafts and games.

Storybooks

Barrett, Judi. *Benjamin's 365 Birthdays*. New York: Athenium, 1974. Benjamin so enjoys unwrapping his birthday presents that he wraps up all his favorite possessions and celebrates his birthday for a whole year. Presentation: Have children use wrapping paper and ribbons to create presents to present to Benjamin.

Cazet, Denys. *December 24th*. New York: Bradbury Press, 1986. Emily and Louie make their Grandpa guess their reason for giving him a present on December 24th. After pretending to celebrate each major holiday, Grandpa is told it is his birthday. Presentation: Have two children act as Emily and Louie. The teacher can use a "buddy puppet" or basic s/he puppets (refer to section one) with various holiday costumes to act as Grandpa to tell this story.

Carle, Eric. *The Secret Birthday Message* N.Y. Crowell, 1972. A young man named Tim finds a secret message using a code of geometric shapes to lead him to his birthday present. Presentation: Have each child create a map on a Peek-a-Boo theater to use with finger puppet character (refer to activity in Groundhog Day section).

Flack, Marjorie. *Ask Mr. Bear*. NY: MacMillan, 1960. A child asks all the farm animals what he should give his mother for a birthday present. Finally, they tell him to ask Mr. Bear. Mr. Bear appropriately suggests, "a great big bear hug" as the perfect gift. Presentation: At the end of the story surprise everyone by popping up a Mr. Bear (stuffed doll or puppet), letting each child come up, one by one, to receive a special individual bear hug.

Hill, Eric. *Spot's Birthday Party*. New York: G.P. Putnam's Sons, 1982. At his birthday party, Spot plays hide and seek with his friends. Presentation: Convert a stuffed animal into a Spot puppet. Children can make animal friend puppets to hide behind various props for "Spot" to find hide n' seek fashion.

Kellogg, Steven. *The Mysterious Tadpole*. New York: Dial, 1977. Louis' birthday present is not an ordinary tadpole because it turns into a friendly sea monster What will the present of an unusual stone turn into? Presentation: Use a L'Egg container and hatch a paper ancient pteradactyl puppet. Let children fantasize as to what will happen to this pet. Afterwards, children can make their own versions to bring home.

Morris, Ann and Falconer, Elizabeth. *Happy Birthday!* New York: Simon and Schuster, 1986. A simple recounting of birthday activities with suggestions for thoughtful activities. Presentation: Use children's faces from old photographs on hand or stick puppets. Have these puppets count and blow out the correct number of candles on a birthday cake. (refer to "Sleeping Candles" activities in Birthday section for cake idea)

Peek, Merle. *Mary Wore Her Red Dress*. NY: Clarion Books, 1985. On Katy Bear's birthday each animal friend comes dressed in a different color to celebrate her party. Presentation: To customize this Texas folk song, have each child make a different animal stick puppet in colored dress. The birthday lead puppet should wear a party hat.

Robart, Rose. *The Cake That Mack Ate*. Boston: Atlantic Monthly Press, 1986. Written in a familiar nursery rhyme style, this story describes the origins and end of a beautiful birthday cake. Presentation: Use a glove and finger puppet to assist the reciting of this rhyme. Make paper finger puppet images of a cake; hen/egg; corn farmer/seed bag; wife and Mack (place Mack on palm area).

Zolotow, Charlotte. *Mr. Rabbit and the Lovely Present*. New York: Harper, 1962. A little girl asks for suggestions for her mother's birthday present and receives color related answers. Presentation: Children can use magazines and catalogs to cut out presents for mother. Use these cutouts mounted on colored paper or stick puppets for props in retelling this story.

BOOKS ABOUT INTERNATIONAL HOLIDAYS

Araki, Nancy K and Jane M. Horil. *Matsuri: Festival Japanese American Celebrations and Activities*. South San Francisco: Heian International Publishing Company, 1978.

Behrens. June. *Gung Hay Fat Chov—Happy New Year*. Regensteiner Publishing Enterprises, 1982. A photo essay showing activities centered around Chinese New Year's parades, family customs, dragons,

Behrens, June. *Fiesta! Ethnic Traditional Holidays*. Chicago: Children's Press, 1978.

Burnett, Bernice 1974 (rev. ed.) *The First Book of Holidays*. New York: Franklin Watts. Particularly good for holidays of American ethnic groups and European holidays.

Dobler, Lavinia G. *Customs and Holidays Around the World*. New York: Fleet Pub. Corp., 1963.

Dobler, Lavinia G. *National Holidays Around the World*. New York: Fleet Press Corp., 1968.

Epstein, Sam and Beryl Epstein 1974 *A Year of Japanese Festivals*. Champaign, Ill.: Garrard Publishing Co. Explains about different kinds of Japanese festivals for honoring the gods, people, the seasons. Includes a helpful pronouncing Guide.

Greene, Carol. *Holidays Around the World*, Chicago: Children's Press, 1982. This is an easy-to-read book illustrated with photographs which describes briefly various holidays celebrated throughout the world.

Hideo Haga 1970 *Japanese Folk Festivals Illustrated*. Tokyo: Miura Printing Co. Translated by Fanny Hagin Mayer. The color photographs provide an interesting documentation of the calendar year of Japanese festivals.

Johnson, Lois S. 1963 *Happy Birthdays Round the World*. Chicago: Rand McNally & Co. Birthday customs and how they grew as well as how birthdays are celebrated in 24 countries. Appropriate foar elementary level.

Marcus Rebecca B. and Judith Marcus. *Fiesta Time in Mexico*. Champaign, Ill.: Garrard Pub. Co., 1974.

Milne, Jean. *Fiesta Time in Latin America*, Los Angeles: The Ward Ritchie Press, 1965.

Polon, Linda and Cartwell, Aileen. *The Whole Earth Holiday Book*. Sidney, Ohio: Scott, Foresman and Co., 1983.

Sawyer, Gene, *Celebrations: Asia and the Pacific*. Honolulu: Friends of the East-West Center, 1978.

Showers, Paul, *Indian Festivals*. New York: Crowell, 1969.

Watson, Jane Weiner. India *Celebrates*. Champaign, Illinois: Gabrard Publishing Co., 1974.

Wyndham, Lee. *Holidays in Scandinavia*. Champaign, Ill.: Garrard Pub. Co., 1975.

BOOKS ABOUT CREATIVE DRAMA

Concannon, Tom. *Using Media for Creative Teaching*. Plays, Inc. 1979. An unusual book dealing with various media—overhead shadow projector, filmstrip, and video. Highly recommended for those wishing to explore mixed media.

Cottrell, June. *Teaching with Creative Dramatics*. National Textbook Co. 1975. An excellent introduction to creative dramatics for anyone working with children. Bibliographies of stories to dramatize with various age groups are included. Storytellers will find the ideas for involving children in stories through sensory and pantomine experiences very useful.

Cranston, Jernéral. *Dramatic Imagination*. Eureka, California: Interface California Corporation. 1975. Presents ideas and lesson plans for stimulating movement, including the use of props, music, and percussion instruments.

Cullum, Albert. *Push Back the Desks*. Citation Press. 1967. How Mr. Cullum integrated creative drama principles into his classroom teaching is the subject of this title. Of particular interest to librarians are the chapters dealing with, "Book Blabs," "Poetry Pot," and "Hallway Hoofbeats." Also by the same author, *Aesop in the Afternoon* and *Shake Hands with Shakespeare*.

Goodrich, Janet. *Creative Drama and Improvised Movement for Children*. Boston: Plays, Inc. 1970. A handbook providing suggestions for selecting and developing appropriate material for playmaking and improvised movement.

Goodwillie, Barbara. *Breaking Through*. Plays, Inc. Drama strategies written for children age 10 to 15. "Building the Group," "Hearing Each Other" and "Awakening Sensitivities" are focal points for challenging the energies of this age group.

Heinig, Ruth and Lydia Stillwell. *Creative Dramatics and the Classroom Teacher*. Prentice Hall. 1974. A very detailed explanation of creative dramatics techniques. Especially valuable because of the extensive annotated bibliographies of materials suitable for pantomime, dialogue scenes, and story dramatization.

Lewis, Mary Kane. *Acting for Children: A Primer*. John Day Co. 1969.

McCaslin, Nellie. *Act Now! Plays and Ways to Make Them*. New York: S. G. Phillips. 1975. Includes valuable hints on giving both rehearsed and spontaneous performances.

Nobleman, Roberta. *50 Projects for Creative Drama*.

Plays, Inc. 1971. A lightweight book of simple, but fun improvisational activities. Imagining is an important part of the drama lessons and that appeal well to children's subjects.

Olfson, Lewy. *You Can Act!* New York: Sterling Publishing Co. Drawings by Shizu. 1971.

Way, Brian. *Development Through Drama.* Humanities Press. 1967. A thorough discussion of drama in education. Way stresses the use of drama in the development of the whole child. Of special interest to storytellers are: Chapter 3, "Begin from where you are" which describes how to involve children in sound stories using an arrow for control; and Chapter 4, "Imagination" which discusses how to use stories and sounds to stimulate children's use of their imagination. A must for anyone interested in the educational use of drama.

Yerian, Cameron and Margaret Yewrian (eds.). *Fun Time Actor's Workshop.* Chicago: Children's Press. 1974. A colorful and well-illustrated book with good ideas for acting out situations that will stimulate creativity and enthusiasm for acting.

BOOKS ABOUT PUPPETRY

The following books are taken from an annotatetd list compiled by the *Puppeteer's of America Bookstore.* Also write for additional listings (specify interest area: religion, education, history, construction, etc.): Books can be ordered: P.O. Box 3128 Santa Ana, CA 92703.

Alphabet Puppets, Jill M. Coudron. This book makes learning the alphabet fun and interesting, by using the letter a week approach. The children are involved with the puppet and its story, song, and activities. You'll find patterns for each puppet, as well as songs, stories—even cooking projects.

Antique French Jumping Jacks, the Imagerie Pellerin. Contains 11 full color Jumping Jacks on heavy stock, ready to cut out and string.

The Art of the Puppet, Bil Baird. Richly illustrated with over 115 full color photographs, 138 black and white photos, and 45 drawings, this incredible volume sweeps the reader back in time.

Asian Puppets—Wall of the World, This is the catalog of an exhibition at the UCLA Museum of Cultural History. Stunning photographs illustrate puppets from China, Sri-Lanka, Vietnam, Japan, India, Thailand, Cambodia, and Korea.

Books, Puppets and the Mentally Retarded Student, John and Connie Champlin. This book explains how to best use puppetry when dealing with moderately or severly handicapped people. Puppets are helpful in introducing literature, creative dramatics, art and music to this very special population.

Buenos Dias, Pajarito!, (Good Morning, Little Bird!), Betty Polus. A bilingual experience in puppetry. The script is written in both English and Spanish. Also included are ideas for making the puppets, staging, props, etc.

China's Puppets, Roberta Stalberg. For anyone who has ever been entralled by the magic of puppetry, and for all enthusiasts of the theatrical arts, this book is a must.

Create Your Own Stage Faces, Douglas Young. Here, one of Europe's foremost makeup designers details everything a performer must know to design a successful stage face.

Creative Puppetry for Jewish Kids, Gale Solotar Warshawsky. Children from preschool through grade 7 will have a ball learning about Judaism through the use of puppetry.

Easy to Make Puppets and How to Use Them: Early Childhood, Fran Rottman. This book contains wonderful ideas on using puppets in activities such as story-hour and welcoming children.

Favorite Songs from Jim Henson's Muppets, by various song-writers. This super new book contains the music and lyrics from our favorite Muppet songs: The Muppet Show Theme, Rubber Duckie, Movin' Right Along, Fraggle Rock, and 11 others. Contains full scores for piano, voice and guitar.

Finger Puppets, Fingerplays and Holidays, Betty Keefe. Librarians and teachers of preschool through grade 3 need look no further for ideas on correlating holidays with education goals.

Finger Puppets Help Teach, Meredith Goodrich. This wonderfully clever kit comes packed in its own plastic case and contains cards with colorful finger puppets to cut out and use to tell 18 Bible stories from the Old and New Testaments.

Folding Paper Puppets, Shari Lewis and Lillian Oppenheimer. Learn to make puppets by using origami, the Japanese art of paper-folding.

Jumping Jacks, Loretta Holz. With scissors, string, and some brass paper fasteners you can make 16 toys that jump, move or dance when you pull their string. These brightly colored, cardboard figures are fun for decorations, party favors, or small gifts. You'll make a harlequin, ballerina, Humpty Dumpty, Martian, and many others.

Magic Window, The Shadow Puppet Workbook, Judy Sierra. Most projects may easily be related to the curriculum and development of language art skills. It will also provide enjoyable art and drama projects for anyone who works with children 5-12 years old. The book includes full instructions and patterns for those who just love shadow puppetry.

Making Puppets Come Alive, Larry Engler and Carol Fijan. This book, illustrated throughout with unusually helpful demonstration photographs, was conceived specifically to teach beginners how to bring a hand puppet to life.

Me and My Shadows, A Teacher's Handbook of Simplified Shadow Puppet Plays using the Overhead Projector adapted by Hope Joyce. Just the book for everyone who has wanted to use shadow puppets in the classroom, and didn't know where to begin.

Mitt Magic, by Lynda Roberts. a fun new book with new and old finger-plays and puppets for curriculum areas, holidays and special days.

Monster Make-Up, Dick Smith. How to create exciting and scarey monsters—mummy, martian, ghoul, witch, even a Weird-O. The author has had a 40-year career in motion pictures, TV, and the stage.

Music Education Through Puppetry, Mary S. Mazzacane. The Puppetry Journal calls this book "a significant contribution to educators wishing to use puppetry as a tool for teaching music."

Music for the Puppet Theatre, Lewis Mahlmann and Leonard Suib. In this pamphlet you'll find an extensive list of many musical works and their composers. The music is grouped by categories such as: love, humor, animals, and mystery.

Organic Puppet Theatre, Terry Schultz and Lind Sorenson. What a novel book! Plastic sandwich bags and crayons become lungs, kidneys and bladders come from paper cups! This book helps children learn about their bodies by using simple puppets that show the functions of body organs. Recommended!

Paper-Bag Puppets, DeAtna M. Williams, Even very young children can assemble and manipulate these charming puppets. There are patterns on how to make 48 different characters, including farm animals, Halloween, Thanksgiving, and fairytale characters.

More Paper-Bag Puppets, This additional book contains 48 more paper-bag puppet patterns, including Community Helpers, the Seasons, and characters from children's stories.

Preschool Storytime with Puppets and Drama, Carol J. Taylor. A booklet of simple activities centered around the major holidays including poems, short story ideas and language arts challenges.

Puppet Dialogues, Charles E. Magnet. 24 Old Testament and New Testament stories told with puppets.

Puppeteer, Kathryn Lasky. Paul Vincent Davis is a man with a problem. Across a 3½ by 2½ foot stage, he must move forty slaves, forty camels, and forty elephants. For Paul Davis is a hand puppeteer preparing a production of Alladin and his Wonderful Lamp for the Puppet Show Place in Boston. You'll discover just how a puppet show comes together—from the research and script writing.

The Puppeteers Library Guide, J. Frances Crothers. VOL 1: The Historical Background—Puppetry and Its Related Fields. The first two volumes of a projected six-volume set. The first volume includes bibliographies of puppetry literature and materials on organizations and publications devoted to puppetry.

VOL 2: The Puppet as an Educator. This volume, developed especially for educators, lists the many fields within education where the puppet has been found to be useful. As wonderful resource for all educators.

Puppets, Methods and Materials, Cedric Flower and Alan Fortney. This wonderful new book is sure to become a puppetry classic. It is an exciting, comprehensive guide to creating and using puppets. Combining clear, concise text with outstanding line drawings and photographs, the authors explain how to use traditional as well as contemporary materials.

Two Christmas Puppet Plays, Phil McPharlin. The plays are Little Lost Angel, and The Christmas Stowaway. Suitable for hand or shadow puppets, or marionettes.

Wit and Wisdom of Polyfoam Construction, Donald Devet and Drew Allison. This super new book is a real delight. You'll have many chuckles as you learn to use polyfoam and a glue gun to construct durable, lightweight puppets.

Try On My Shoe—Step Into Another Culture, Camy Condon, illustrated by Lynne Jennings. This very delightful and large book contains folktales from North America, East Africa, Mexico, and Vietnam. Each play features cultural notes (which are excellent for classroom use), and patterns for making many types of puppets.

Writing Your Own Plays, Carol Korty, Do you want to put on a play but have no script or ideas yet? This practical handbook teaches how to choose a story, write a play, develop ideas and rehearse your play.

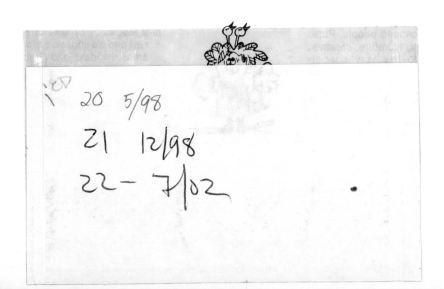